The
Spiritual Journey
of
Alejandro Jodorowsky

The Spiritual Journey of Alejandro Jodorowsky

THE CREATOR OF *EL TOPO*

Alejandro Jodorowsky

Translated by Joseph Rowe

Park Street Press

Rochester, Vermont

Park Street Press
One Park Street
Rochester, Vermont 05767
www.ParkStPress.com

Park Street Press is a division of Inner Traditions International

Originally published in French under the title *Mu: Le maître et les magiciennes* by
    Editions Albin Michel and in Spanish under the title *El maestro y las magas* by
    Ediciones Siruela, S.A., Madrid
First U.S. edition published in 2008 by Park Street Press

The Library of Congress Cataloging-in-Publication Data
Jodorowsky, Alejandro.
    [Maestro y las magas. English]
    The spiritual journey of Alejandro Jodorowsky : the creator of El topo / Alejandro
Jodorowsky ; translated by Joseph Rowe.
        p. cm.
    Summary: "Jodorowsky's memoirs of his experiences with Master Takata and the group
of wisewomen magiciennes who influenced his spiritual growth"—Provided by publisher.
    Includes index.
    ISBN 978-1-59477-173-6
    1. Jodorowsky, Alejandro. 2. Authors, Mexican—20th century—Biography. 3. Authors,
Mexican—20th century—Biography. 4. Authors, Chilean—20th century—Biography.
5. Theatrical producers and directors—Mexico—Biography. 6. Theatrical producers
and directors—Chile—Biography. 7. Actors—Chile—Biography. I. Title.
    PQ7298.2.O3Z46 2008
    868'.6409—dc22
    [B]

                                                                            2008008149

Printed and bound in the United States

10 9 8 7 6 5 4

Text design by Virginia Scott Bowman and layout by Priscilla Baker
This book was typeset in Garamond Premier Pro, with Helvetica Neue and Serif Gothic
used as display typefaces

To Marianne Costa
Magician of magicians

Contents

Mu, mu, mu, mu, mu,
Mu, mu, mu, mu, mu,
Mu, mu, mu, mu, mu,
Mu, mu, mu, mu, mu.
WU-MEN HUIKAI, 1183–1260

The ox has spoken and he has said "moo."
A SPANISH PROVERB APPLIED
TO SOMEONE WHO RARELY SPEAKS
BUT UTTERS NONSENSE WHEN HE DOES

Prologue

Though I have written these memoirs in novelistic style, all the people, places, events, books, and quotations by sages are real.

I was raised by a merchant father. All the wisdom he had to offer me could be summed up in two proverbs: "Buy low and sell high" and "Don't believe in anything." I had no teacher from whom I could learn to love myself, others, and life. From adolescence on, driven by the thirst of an explorer lost in the desert, I sought a master who could show me that there was some meaning in my useless existence. A voracious reader of literature, I found only self-absorbed and pretentious meanderings there. A very cynical phrase by Marcel Duchamp led me to flee that sterile world: "There is no finality; we construct from tautology and arrive at nothing."

I sought consolation in books of Eastern philosophy, holding for dear life onto the notion of *enlightenment* or *awakening*. I learned that Shakyamuni Buddha awoke while meditating under a tree. According to his disciples, the holy man perceived the deepest truth by ceasing to preoccupy himself with the question of his survival after death. Twenty-eight generations later, in China, Bodhidharma sat in silence for nine years in front of a stone wall until he discovered in his consciousness that fathomless emptiness, like a pure blue sky, in which neither truth nor illusion can be distinguished. . . . The longing to free myself from the terror of dying, of being nothing, of knowing nothing, had dragged me implacably into a quest for this mythic awakening. Striving for silence, I ceased to be so attached to my ideas. To further this goal, I wrote all of my beliefs in a notebook, then burned it. After this, requiring calm in my intimate relationships, I shunned the vulnerability of any sort of self-abandon, always setting up aloof relationships with women, thereby protecting my individualism behind panes of ice. When I met Ejo Takata, my first true master, I wanted him to guide me to enlightenment by purifying my mind of the last illusions I had not yet succeeded in uprooting. I saw myself as conqueror of both mind and heart.

"Feelings no longer dominate me. Empty mind, empty heart." When I solemnly proclaimed these words before my Japanese teacher, he burst into laughter, which was quite disconcerting.

Then he answered: "Empty mind, empty heart—intellectual raving! Empty mind, *full* heart: That is how it should be."

This book is a story of two practices. The first, with the master, was that of taming the intellect. The second, with the magical women, was that of breaking down emotional armor so that I would finally come to see that the emptiness I longed for was a flower rooted in the ground of love.

In this book I tell the stories of four magical women, but there are three others whose portraits are absent. One is the healer (*curandera*) Pachita, whom I have previously described at length in *Le Théâtre de la Guérison* and *La Danse de la Réalité*. In these books, I tell of the life-changing experiences I had with her. Yet there is one event that I omitted from those books (perhaps out of a sense of caution). It happened when I was participating in a séance featuring one of her magical operations. The *hermanito* ("little brother," Pachita's trance-controlled personality) was about to use a hunting knife to cut into the chest of a sick man and remove his heart. The replacement heart was waiting in a large jar. (Where on earth had the sorceress found that organ? And why did we, the entranced onlookers, find it perfectly natural that she should propose curing a sick, living heart by replacing it with a dead one? A mystery.)

Suddenly, in the very midst of the dramatic operation (moving shadows, blood everywhere, a horrible stench in the air, the screams of the patient), Pachita seized the ring finger of my left hand and, with a single, swift movement, slipped a gold ring onto it. It fit perfectly, as if it was made for my finger. Without pausing to observe my reaction, she continued with the operation: she pulled a palpitating mass of bloody flesh from the man's chest (which her son hurriedly wrapped in black paper and took away to be burned in the toilets), she placed the dead heart in the bloody wound, and she closed the wound by pressing her palms upon it. Then we rubbed the man's chest with alcohol, noticing that there was no scar at all, just a small, triangular bruise.

I returned home, totally overwhelmed, and slept deeply. When I awoke, the ring was no longer on my finger. I spent hours searching for it in vain. What was the meaning of Pachita's gesture? Was it some sort of spiritual marriage? Perhaps. Thanks to my relationship with her, years later, in Paris, I was able to create what I call *psychomagie* (psycho-magic) and *psychochamanisme* (psychoshamanism). Did the curandera foresee that this would happen? Or was she doing something to make it happen, because she intended it to? A mystery.

Maria Sabina, the mushroom priestess, is also absent from this book's account. How old was she when we began our dream relationship? A hundred years? Possibly more . . .

I never met her in the flesh. In order to do that, I would have had to undertake a ten-hour drive into the Mazatec Sierra and then a climb through a narrow pass surrounded by dizzying precipices in order to reach Huautla.

The truth is that I had never harbored any intention of seeking out the *abuelita* (little grandmother), as she was known. It was she who sought me out. As I was preparing for the shooting of my movie

The Holy Mountain, I had also created a marionette show, *Haut les mains* (Hands Up), which depicted visions produced by the seeds of a plant known colloquially as "seeds of the Virgin" (*ololiuhqui*—"round thing"—in Nahuatl), a sort of natural, LSD-type hallucinogen that Toltecs and Aztecs regarded as a divinity worthy of worship.

One day, I was chewing a handful of these seeds while perched on a ladder to adjust some spotlights for the stage in the Casa de la Paz (House of Peace), and I had a vision: I saw the totality of the universe as a compact mass of light having the form of a round body in perpetual expansion, and in full consciousness. This was so powerful that I emitted a guttural cry, lost my balance, and fell from the ladder. I landed hard on my feet, dislocating both ankles. In a few hours they were very swollen, causing me great pain. After taking several sedatives, I fell asleep and dreamed I was a crippled wolf dragging two wounded hind legs. Maria Sabina appeared to me. She showed me a very large, white book surrounded by light.

"My poor animal! This book is the perfect word, the language of God. Don't worry about knowing how to read it. Just enter its pages and merge with them."

I moved toward the light. My whole body except for the paws of my hind legs entered it. The old woman then caressed me with such tremendous love that I woke up in tears. I saw with astonishment that my ankles were no longer swollen, and I felt not the slightest pain.

In those days I certainly did not believe that it was the Mazatec curandera herself who had literally come to heal me. I attributed her image to a construction of my unconscious, and I was gratified by my ability to heal myself alone, thanks to a therapeutic dream.

Some time previously, Maria Sabina had apparently initiated contact with me through the intermediary of a painter friend, Francisco Fierro. Returning from Huautla, where he went to eat mushrooms with the curandera, Francisco had brought me a jar of honey in which were embedded six pairs of the *niñitos santos,* or the "sacred little children."

"These are a gift to you from Maria Sabina. She saw you in a dream. It seems you are going to accomplish a work that will help the world realize the true values of our culture. Nowadays, the hippies are destroying the ancient traditions. Huautla is overrun by tourists, drug dealers, journalists, doctors, soldiers, and police agents. The niñitos santos have lost their purity. But these twelve apostles are special, because they have been blessed by abuelita. Eat all of them."

I have already recounted my experience with these magic mushrooms in *La Danse de la Réalité,* but I must confess that at first I had doubts about my painter friend. Perhaps the old woman had not really dreamed of me; perhaps, with all the best intentions, Francisco had concocted the story himself. I found it difficult to believe that someone could influence reality through dreams, yet Francisco insisted that these mushrooms contained all the wisdom of ancient Mexico. He ate them often, and he did not hesitate to feed them to his young daughters—two strange creatures who were five and six years old, with large, adult eyes.

Hence my utter astonishment when, on the same morning that I woke up with my ankles healed, I received a phone call from Francisco Fierro: "Tonight, abuelita visited me in my sleep and told me that she was going to heal you. How were you feeling when you woke up this morning?"

Coincidence? Telepathy? Could Maria Sabina really enter into my dreams and heal my body in that dimension? My intuition said yes, my reason said no. This is why I have not included Maria Sabina as one of the characters in this book: I cannot exclude the possibility that she is a sort of illusion personal to me. In any case, whether illusion or reality, Maria Sabina continued to appear in my dreams until the time of her death—always in difficult moments, and always in a way that was very helpful to me.

The third person absent in this account is the Chilean singer Violeta Parra. Her fame is so great—she is praised by poets such as Pablo Neruda ("a saint of the finest clay"), Nicanor Parra ("a bird of earthly paradise"), Pablo de Rokha ("subterranean simplicity"), and so many others—that what I could add would be superfluous. I met her in Paris, where she resided during two periods: first in 1954 for two years, then in 1961 for three years. During the first period she was not yet famous, and she earned her living singing in a small cabaret in the Latin Quarter called *L'Escale*. Her miserable wages were just enough to pay for a room in a one-star hotel. There, she often cooked a simple Chilean meal of char-grilled meat, cornbread, and tomato and onion salad, which she would share with her six main friends, of whom I was one. She refers to this in her autobiography, written in verse:

> *As the law commands,*
> *justice must be rendered in all things;*
> *obeying this with delight,*
> *I hereby name six*
> *archangels, who, you see,*
> *protect me with their friendship,*
> *offering me affinity in this distant world;*
> *and when their hands reach out to me,*
> *my darkness lights up.*
> *I say it and repeat it:*
> *a little heart of coriander*
> *for my friend Alejandro,*
> *who comforted me in Paris*
> *with a clove-scented flower*
> *and a friendly smile.*
> *His hand was a delight*
> *down there in that absent life;*
> *yesterday, you planted some seeds;*
> *today, they flower and bear fruit.*

She says that I comforted her in Paris, but it was she who helped me, inspiring me with her tenacity and energy. Violeta would sing from ten o'clock at night until four in the morning, then get up at eight o'clock and rush off to record Chilean folk songs ("to the human and to the divine"), which she had collected and learned directly from the lips of old peasants. She recorded these for the Chant du Monde ethnomusicology library, and for the Phonothèque Nationale at the Musée de l'Homme.*

I was indignant: "But Violeta, they are not paying you a *centime* for this! You must see that they are exploiting you in the name of culture!"

"I'm not stupid. I know they're exploiting me, but I do it with pleasure. France has one of the greatest museum cultures, and I know they will always conserve these songs. I'm saving an important part of Chilean folklore. For the good of my country's music, it doesn't matter if I work for free. In fact, I'm even proud not to be paid for it! Sacred things should be protected from the power of money."

Thus Violeta taught me a lesson I never forgot. It was her example that inspired me always to offer tarot readings and psychomagic counseling free of charge.

When she returned to Paris seven years later, it was as a singer who was famous and respected in Chile not only for her art but also for her precious research in forgotten folklore. Now she recorded her own songs on the famous Barclay label (including the celebrated *Gracias a la Vida*). She also sang at the huge annual festival of popular music organized by *l'Humanité,* the French communist daily newspaper. In spite of this success, she remained a simple woman, resembling a humble peasant. Yet her delicate frame was inhabited by a soul of superhuman strength.

One day, she and I walked together along the banks of the Seine and arrived at the Louvre.

"What an incredible museum!" I exclaimed. "The weight of so many great works of art, so many great civilizations . . . we poor Chileans are crushed by it. Our traditions are mere straw huts compared to pyramids, mere clay pots compared to the Sphinx . . ."

---

*[The French national museum of anthropology. —*Trans.*]

"Be quiet!" she commanded me with an imperious tone. "The Louvre is a cemetery. But we—we are alive! Life is more powerful than death. I'm just a tiny woman, but this huge edifice doesn't impress me. Mark my words: Before long, you'll see my works exhibited here."

I didn't know whether to consider her crazy or just the victim of an extremely naive vanity. Besides, she was a singer, not a painter or sculptor!

Violeta had very little money. She bought some iron wire, some cheap rag cloth, some wool of different colors, some clay, and some tubes of oil paint. With these modest materials, she began to fashion tapestries, jugs, little sculptures, and oil paintings. They were her own works, yet they also were an expression of a Chilean folklore that had disappeared from history but was still alive in my friend's unconscious. In April 1964, Violeta Parra inaugurated her great exhibition at the Musée des Arts Décoratifs at the Marsan Pavillion attached to the Palace of the Louvre!

This incredible woman taught me that if we desire something with the totality of our being, we will finally achieve it—perhaps not always as rapidly as in this instance, yet Violeta showed me that the impossible becomes possible through patience and commitment.

I saw another example of this immense patience and perseverance in the Spanish writer Francisco Gonzalez Ledesma, who, under the pseudonym Silver Kane, wrote more than a thousand cowboy novelettes for the popular market. He began producing them in 1951, when he was twenty years old, in order to earn his living. He continued until 1975, at the rate of one book a week. After that and continuing to the present, he began to write under his real name. These were the books he really wanted to write: a type of detective novel written in high literary style. These works earned him the Planète Prize in 1984 and also the French Mystère Prize for the best foreign novel.

Under the Franco regime, writers were treated as lowly workers, receiving no royalties and only a meager salary. They were required to arrive at an office early in the morning and to work for ten hours at a stretch. When Francisco returned home, having spent the whole day writing plots for comic books and working on the publisher's accounting as well, he worked on his Silver Kane books. Very late in the night, he spent time on what he really wanted to write: books that he could sign with his real name. He was also assigned the task of researching the American West. His integrity caused him to refuse the temptation to use the same theme twice, and he always based his books on historical facts. Furthermore, he found time to study for the exam that allowed him to earn a diploma of attorney, a profession at which he succeeded brilliantly. When I asked this titan how he was able to accomplish all this (to say nothing of being married with children), he replied: "By sleeping very little—almost not at all."

The publisher's rules for his Silver Kane work were so extreme that if he did not hand in his manuscript when the office opened on Friday mornings, he could lose his job. One night, when there was an electrical failure, he sat on the roof and wrote by the light of the moon.

He wrote these cowboy adventures with total humility; he harbored no hope that they would attract educated readers, knew they held no possibility of expounding at length on the deeper aspects of thought, and understood full well that these works would be despised by literary critics. Furthermore, he knew that they would enable him only to survive and never to become rich. This attitude is strangely akin to the philosophy of certain Zen proverbs: "Act without any final goal," "Do your best at whatever holds your work," "Seek not perfection, but authenticity," "Discover the inexhaustible in the silence of the ego," "Abandon all will to power," "Practice day and night, without sleeping."

This is why I have selected phrases from Silver Kane as epigraphs at the beginning of each chapter in this book. They have the same direct language as Zen koans, a purity where rational calculation has no place. Both tragic and comic, they exude the perfume of enlightenment.

Many people know nothing of koans, and even those who do know do not accord them their essential importance. A koan is a question that a Zen master gives to a disciple who is then to meditate and reflect upon it and (sometimes immediately, sometimes years later) offer a response. A koan is an enigma that holds a fundamental absurdity, for it is impossible to reply to one by using logic. And this is precisely its purpose: to open our initial point of view to the universal so that we understand that the intellect (words, words, words, and still more words) is useless in helping us find a response. In fact, we do not really live in the world; we live in a language. We think that we are intelligent because we can manipulate ideas and that things become known and real because we are able to define them—but if we really want our life to change, we must undergo a mutation of the mind, opening the doors of intuition and creative energies so that our unconscious becomes an ally.

Some students take twenty years to find the right response to a koan. Others, instead of searching for a response that engages every aspect of their being (a response far more complex than the words of ordinary language), choose to identify with their intellect, offering a response that is actually a clever explanation. They then imagine that they have become Zen masters because of their cleverness. If our response to a koan leaves us as we were before, then we have resolved nothing. To truly resolve a koan is to undergo a mental cataclysm that causes our worldview, our psychic stance, and any sort of self-concept to crumble, precipitating us into the void—a void that engenders us, enabling us to be reborn freer than before and, for the first time, to be in the world as it is instead of as we have learned it is.

In a certain book on personal development (which I shall refrain from naming) the writer, a Zen disciple, receives a koan from a woman master: "How can you get a goose out of a bottle without breaking the bottle or hurting the goose?" Faced with the student's total perplexity, the master offers this response: "The easiest way to get the goose out without hurting it is to put the bottle on its side, and place some food outside the opening. Then the goose will simply walk out of the bottle.

After all, this koan never mentions how large the opening is, so there's no reason to assume it's too small for the goose to pass through easily." Such an answer serves to show only the student's stupidity—or cleverness . . . but the purpose of a koan is not to test a student's cleverness. This so-called master cheated by imagining a bottle without a narrow opening. If that was the case, the goose would not be trapped in the bottle in the first place and could enter and leave as it pleased. In the real Zen tradition, the student spends days or months trying to resolve this enigma. One day, he appears before the master, beaming with joy:

"I've finally solved the koan!"

"How?" asks the *roshi* (spiritual leader).

"The goose is out!" exclaims the student.

The goose is a living principle enclosed by rigid, inert limitations. This answer shows that the disciple has actually freed himself from his logical intellect, which separated him from the totality of life to which his being belongs.

But the writer of this book on personal development is convinced he understands it all. He poses to his readers (in rather awkward terms) one of the most classic koans: A monk says to his student, "Observe, my dear student, the sound of a clap," and the old master claps his hands. Then, watching his student attentively, he says: "Now, dear student, can you demonstrate for me the sound of only one hand clapping?"

Again, the author proposes an extremely naive solution: "We begin with the assumption that it is impossible to clap without using two hands. Yet the sound of a clap can in fact be produced by only one hand whipping the fingers quickly against a part of the palm. . . . I suggest that the reader practice this movement as if he was playing castanets. He will observe that this can produce the sound of a clap made by only one hand."

Is this supposed initiate trying to tell us that in order to solve one of the most famous of all Zen koans, it helps to be a good castanet player? We cannot resist conjuring up the image of a severe, ancient Zen master whipping out a sword, cutting off both this initiate's hands with a single blow, and then asking: "Now what is the sound of no hands clapping?"

I have written this book in an attempt to give an accurate explanation of the nature of the struggle that allows us to understand koans and the beneficial change that occurs when we truly resolve a koan. It is also a summary of the first five years I spent in meditations guided by the most honest human being I have ever known.

1
"Intellectual, Learn to Die!"

"But what hells, what roasted vultures, what sizzled coyotes does this imply?"

SILVER KANE, *CARA DURA CITY*

The last time I saw Master Ejo Takata was in a modest house in one of the overpopulated suburbs of Mexico City. There was a room and a kitchen, no more. I had come there seeking consolation, my heart broken by the death of my son. My pain was so great that I did not even notice that half the room was filled with cardboard boxes. The monk was busy frying a couple of fish. I was expecting some sort of wise discourse on the nature of death: "We are not born, we do not die. . . . Life is an illusion. . . . The Lord giveth and the Lord taketh away, blessed be the name of the Lord. . . . Do not think of his absence; be grateful for the twenty-four years when he filled your life with joy. . . . The divine droplet has returned to the original ocean. . . . His consciousness is dissolved into blessed eternity. . . ." I had already been telling myself such things, but the consolation I sought in these phrases had given my heart no peace.

1

Ejo said only one word in Spanish: *Duele,* "it hurts." Then, bowing, he served the fish. We ate in silence. I began to understand that life goes on, that I must accept the pain instead of struggling against it or searching for consolation. When you eat, you eat. When you sleep, you sleep. When it hurts, it hurts. Beyond all that, there is the unity of the impersonal life. Our ashes must merge with the ashes of the world.

Then it occurred to me to ask him what was in the boxes.

"My belongings," he answered. "They've loaned me this house. They might ask me to move out any day. Here, I'm feeling good. So why shouldn't I feel just as good somewhere else?"

"But Ejo, this space is so small. Where do you meditate?"

He shrugged indifferently and casually gestured toward a corner. He needed no special place to meditate. It was not the space that made meditation sacred; it was his meditation that made the space sacred. In any case, for this man who had cut through the mirage of opposites, the division between sacred and profane had no significance.

In the United States, in France, and in Japan I have had the good fortune of meeting a number of other roshis. I even met my master's master, Mumon Yamada,* a very small man with the energy of a lion and hands as delicate and groomed as those of a lady (the nails on his little finger were more than an inch long). Yet no one could ever take the place that Ejo had conquered in my heart.

I know little of his life. Born in Kobe in 1928, he began to practice Zen at the age of nine in the monastery of Horyuji, under the direction of Roshi Heikisoken, the head authority of the Rinzai school. Later, at Kamakura, he entered the Shofukuji Monastery founded in 1195 by Yosai,† the first monk to bring Chinese Zen Buddhism to Japan. There,

---

*Mumon Yamada (1900–1988), a man of great compassion and knowledge with a Ph.D. in philosophy from a Buddhist university in Japan, was a disciple of Kawaguchi Ekai. In 1953, he joined the Shofukuji Monastery as master.

†Also known as Eisai (circa 1140–1215 CE). In his youth he made several voyages to China, where he learned the teachings of Ch'an (Chinese Buddhism, the ancestor of Zen) and of the Rinzai school, which he used to revive Zen in the Tendai school, founded in 805 CE. This aroused opposition from Tendai monks.

he became a disciple of Mumon Yamada of the Soto school. The life of these monks aspiring to enlightenment was very hard. Always living in groups, deprived of intimacy or privacy, they ate little and poorly, worked hard, and meditated constantly. Every act of daily life—from how they slept to how they defecated—adhered to a strict ritual: "A monk must sit with his back straight, keeping his legs covered by the corners of his robe, looking neither to the right nor to the left, never speaking with his neighbors, never scratching his intimate parts, making as little noise as possible when excreting and accomplishing the act quickly, because others are waiting their turn. . . . The monks of the Soto Monastery must sleep on their right side; no other position is permitted. The monks of the Rinzai school sleep on their back; no other position is permitted."

After living in this way for thirty years, in 1967 Ejo Takata decided that the times were changing. It was useless to preserve a tradition by remaining closed up in a monastery. He decided to leave Shofukuji and encounter the world. His determination led him to embark for the United States, for he desired to know why so many hippies were interested in Zen. He was received with great honor in a modern monastery in California. A few days later, he fled this place with only his monk's robes and twenty dollars in his pocket. He reached a major highway and began to hitchhike, communicating mostly with gestures, because he spoke little English. A truck carrying oranges picked him up. Ejo began to meditate on the odor of the fruit, with no idea where he was going. He fell asleep. When he woke up, he found himself in the immense city that is the capital of Mexico.

By a coincidence that I would qualify as a miracle, he was seen wandering in the streets of this city of more than twenty million people by a man who was a disciple of Eric Fromm, the famous psychiatrist who had recently collaborated with D. T. Suzuki to publish a book called *Psychoanalysis and Zen Buddhism*. This man was so astounded that he could not believe his eyes: a real Japanese monk, robes and all! He stopped his car, invited the monk to get in, and ferried him off as a treasure to be presented to his students in Mexico City.

Maintaining a jealous secrecy regarding Ejo's presence, the group set him up in a small house in the suburbs, which was transformed into a temple. Some months later, Ejo learned that before meditating, these psychiatrists took pills to help them endure with a beatific smile the hours of rigorous immobility. He thereupon bid them farewell and never returned.

By a series of coincidences (which I have described in *La Danse de la Réalité*), I had the chance to meet this master. Seeing that he was homeless, I offered him my house, inviting him to transform it into a zendo. There, the monk found his first honest students: actors, painters, university students, martial arts practitioners, poets, and so forth. They were all convinced that through meditation they would find enlightenment: the secret of eternal life that transcends that of the ephemeral flesh.

It was not long before we realized that Zen meditation was no game. To sit very still for hours, striving to empty our mind, enduring pains in our legs and back, and overwhelmed by boredom was a heroic undertaking.

One day, when we had all but lost hope in ever attaining mythic enlightenment, we heard the rumbling of a powerful motorcycle, which came to a screeching halt in front of the house. Then we heard the vigorous steps of someone walking up to our little meditation room. There entered a large young man with broad shoulders, muscular arms, and blond hair. He was dressed in red leather, and stopped in front of the master and addressed him insolently, with a thick American accent:

"You deserted our monastery because you think you're so superior, with your slanted eyes! You think that truth needs a Japanese passport? Yet I, a 'despicable Westerner,' have solved all the koans, and I'm here to prove it. Question me!"

We disciples were frozen in place, as if we were in a cowboy film in which one gunslinger challenges another to see who has the fastest draw.

Ejo, however, was unperturbed: "I accept!" he said.

And then a scene began to unfold that had us gaping in wonder.

For me, as for the others, koans were unsolvable mysteries. Whenever we read them in books, we understood absolutely nothing. We knew that in Japan, monks sometimes meditated on these riddles for years or decades—questions such as "What is Buddha nature?" and answers such as "the cypress tree in the garden" had led us to despair ever understanding them. Zen does not seek philosophical explanations, but rather demands immediate understanding beyond words. "The cypress tree in the garden" left us disconcerted, revealing that we understood nothing, because we were not enlightened.

On one occasion, when I confessed my perplexity to Ejo, he replied brusquely: "Intellectual, learn to die!" This is why it was such a deep shock to see this aggressive, disrespectful, arrogant young man reply rapidly, with no hesitation, to the master's questions.

Ejo clapped his hands. "That is the sound of two hands clapping. What is the sound of one hand clapping?"

The young man sat down with crossed legs, straightened his back, and raised his right arm wordlessly with his palm open.

"Good," Ejo said. "Now, if you can hear the sound of one hand, prove it."

Still silent, the youth repeated the gesture.

"Good," Ejo said again.

My heart was pounding like a drum. I realized that I was witnessing something extraordinary. Only once before had I felt this peculiar kind of intensity: when I saw the great bullfighter El Cordobés decide to provoke the bull by freezing like a statue. The animal charged several times, his horns passing within a fraction of an inch of the man's body, yet he was never gored. A strange vortex of energy seemed to envelop both man and beast, plunging them into an enchanted space-time, a "place" where error was impossible.

Confidently and with perfect style, this invader responded to every challenge presented by my master. There was such an intensity between the two men that we disciples began to dissolve little by little into the shadows.

Ejo asked him: "When you have turned into ashes, how will you hear yourself?" Again, the youth stretched out his hand.

Then Ejo said: "Is it possible that this one hand could be cut off by the sword of Suimo, which is the sharpest of all swords?"

With a smug expression, the visitor answered: "If it is possible, show me that you can do it."

Ejo insisted: "Why can't the Suimo sword cut off this hand?"

The youth smiled: "Because this hand reaches through the whole universe."

Ejo arose, came close to the visitor's face, and said loudly: "What is this one hand?"

The man answered, shouting even louder: "It is the sky, the earth, man, woman, you, me, the grass, the trees, motorcycles, and roast chickens! All things are this one hand!"

Ejo now murmured very softly: "If you hear the sound of one hand, make me hear it too."

The young man arose, slapped Ejo in the face, and sat down.

The sound this made was like a rifle shot to us. We were on the verge of jumping this insolent youth and giving him a sound thrashing, but the master restrained us with a smile.

He asked the young man: "Now that you have heard the sound of one hand clapping, what are you going to do?"

The visitor answered: "Ride my motorcycle, smoke a joint, take a piss."

In an urgent voice, the master commanded him: "Imitate this sublime sound of one hand clapping!"

The youth imitated the sound of a truck that happened to be passing in the street at that moment: "Vroooom . . ."

The monk let out a deep sigh. Then he asked him: "This one hand—how far can it travel?"

The youth leaned over and pressed his hand on the floor. "It can go no farther than this."

Ejo Takata burst into laughter, and in an astounding gesture that left no room for ambiguity, he offered his place to the visitor. The latter, assuming the air of a proud winner, sat down in the master's place.

"You have done very well in resolving this koan. It was first posed by Hakuin Ekaku."*

Here the youth interrupted the master, demonstrating his erudition, "Yes, Hakuin, the great Japanese Zen monk, born in 1686 and died in 1769."

Ejo bowed respectfully. Then he continued. "Now that you have demonstrated the perfection of your enlightenment, I request that you explain the significance of your gestures and words to my disciples, who are most intrigued by them. Can you do this?"

"Of course I can," Master Peter (for this was how he now wished us to address him) replied proudly.

"When this monk asked me to prove that I had heard the sound of one hand clapping, I swept away any rationalization with a gesture meaning, 'It is what it is.' When he asked me if I was going to be a Buddha—to become enlightened—I did not fall into the dualistic trap of enlightenment–nonenlightenment. What nonsense! My outstretched hand says, 'Unity, here and now!' As for when I have become ashes, I did not fall into the trap of existence–nonexistence. If I am, I am here and now—that's all! The concept of 'after death' exists only when we are alive. As for the Suimo sword that cuts everything, I replied that there is nothing to be cut. Why can this one hand not be cut? Because it fills the universe, eliminating all distinction. When he asked that I make him hear the sound of one hand clapping, I slapped him to show that he should not underestimate his own understanding of the koan. And I knew he was setting a trap for me when he asked me to imitate

---

*Also known as Hakuin Zenji (1686–1769 CE), he was born to a samurai family and was one of the masters who shaped the Rinzai school and systematized the koan way of teaching. In his childhood, he had been traumatized by a sermon on the torments of hell, causing him to question many things about his tradition, which led to his having to endure harsh treatment by his master. He was a man of great kindness, a gifted teacher, and a major scholar.

the 'sublime' sound of one hand clapping. Expecting some extraordinary experience is an obstacle on the path to enlightenment. By imitating an ordinary sound that occurred at the moment, I was showing him that there is no difference between ordinary and extraordinary. As for the question of what I am going to do now that I am enlightened, I simply gave some details of my everyday actions. There is no need for future plans regarding enlightenment! We must understand that we have always been enlightened without realizing it. He also tried to trip me up with the question, 'How far can this hand go?' Enlightenment, however, is not located in space."

Well-satisfied with his own words, Master Peter now tapped his own belly, exclaiming with a proud, authoritative tone: "Here! Only here, and nowhere else but here!"

Faced with such obvious arrogance and vanity, we were hoping that Ejo would now expel this American from his place. We were appalled at the prospect of having to accept this character as a teacher. But Ejo did nothing. He simply sat there as if he had now become a disciple.

Smiling, he said to Master Peter: "In Hakuin's teaching there are two koans that are more important than all the others. You have resolved the first of these with perfection. Now I would like to see if you can resolve the second . . ."

"Of course!" the American interrupted with a smug expression. "You mean the question about the nature of a dog."

"Yes. The question to which Joshu gave the answer . . ."

Again, Peter interrupted, reciting with speed and precision: "Joshu, the central figure of Chinese Zen, born in 778 CE. While still very young, he began to study with Master Nansen.* When Nansen died, Joshu was fifty-seven years old. He remained in the monastery for three more years, honoring the memory of his master. Then he left in a quest for truth. He traveled for twenty years. At the age of eighty, he settled

*Zhaoshu Congshen (778–897 CE), whose Japanese name is Joshu Jushin, was eighteen when he met his Chinese master, Naquan Puyan (748–855 CE), known in Japan as Nansen Fugan.

in his native village in the province of Jo. There he taught until his death at the age of one hundred."

"What amazing erudition!" Ejo exclaimed.

Then, looking in our direction, he ordered us: "Applaud!" I joined my companions, but I was applauding with a feeling of jealousy. Master Peter stood up and bowed to us in return with several ostentatious flourishes.

"Now let us see," Ejo continued. "A monk asked Master Joshu: 'Does a dog have Buddha nature?' Joshu answered: 'Mu.' What do you say?"

Peter began to stand up, muttering, *"Mu* in Chinese means 'no'; it means nonexistence, emptiness—it might as well be a tree, a barking dog, whatever . . ." Now standing and facing Ejo Takata, he yelled so loudly that the windows shook: "MU!"

Then began another round of the duel of questions and answers.

"Give me the proof of this Mu."

"MU!"

"If that is so, then how will you awaken?"

"MU!"

"Very well. Now when you have been cremated, what will become of this Mu?"

"MU!"

The gringo's yells were growing louder. Yet Takata, by contrast, was questioning him in a tone that was more and more gentle and respectful. Little by little, he seemed to abase himself utterly before this exalted being who always found the right answer instantly. I was afraid that the dialogue might continue on this way for hours, but now a subtle change took place. The responses were becoming longer.

"On another occasion, when Joshu was asked if a dog had Buddha nature, he answered yes. What do you think of that?"

"Even if Joshu said that a dog has Buddha nature, I would simply yell 'MU!' with all my strength."

"Very good. Now tell me: How does your enlightenment act with Mu?"

Peter stood up and walked a few paces, saying: "When I walk, I walk." Then, sitting down again, he said: "When I sit, I sit."

"Excellent! Now explain the difference between the state of Mu and the state of ignorance."

"I got on my motorcycle and rode to Reforma Boulevard. Then I walked to the government palace. Then I walked back to Reforma, got on my motorcycle, and rode it here."

This response baffled us all. The gringo looked at us with a disdainful air. "Your Japanese monk has just asked me to explain the difference between enlightenment and nonenlightenment. In my description of a walk that began in one place and returned to that same place, I was refuting the distinction between the sacred and the profane." Grudgingly, we felt compelled to admire the cleverness of this response.

"Very good indeed!" Ejo said, beaming, with a smile that seemed full of admiration. "Now what is the origin of Mu?"

"There is neither sky nor earth nor mountains nor rivers nor trees nor plants nor apples nor pears! There is nothing, neither myself nor anyone else. Even these words are nothing. MU!"

This last Mu was so loud that some dogs in the neighborhood began barking. From this moment on, the pace of the dialogue began to accelerate.

"So—give me your Mu!"

"Take it!" Peter said, handing Takata a marijuana cigarette.

"How tall is your Mu?"

"I am five feet nine inches tall."

"Tell me your Mu in way that is so simple that a baby could understand it and put it into practice."

"Mmm, mmm, mmm. . . ." Peter hummed, as if lulling an infant to sleep.

"What is the difference between Mu and all?"

"If you are all, I am Mu. If you are Mu, I am all."

"Show me different Mus."

"When I eat, when I drink, when I smoke, when I have sex, when I sleep, when I dance, when I'm cold, when I'm warm, when I shit, when a bird sings, when a dog barks, MU! MU! MU! MU! MU! MU!"

His shouts went on and on, becoming deafening. Now he had lost control and was really causing a scene! He seemed like a man possessed, as if he would go on with this mad yelling indefinitely.

With a single bound, Ejo leaped up, seized his flat Zen stick (*kyosaku*), and hurling an impressive cry of "Kwatzu!" he began to strike Peter. Outraged at this, Peter attacked Ejo. Resorting deftly to some judo technique (an attainment he had never mentioned to us), the master immediately caught Peter in a hold and flipped him expertly to the floor. When Peter was gasping on his back with his four limbs flailing in the air, Ejo Takata placed a foot on his neck, immobilizing him.

"Now let us see if your enlightenment is stronger than fire!"

Dragging the bewildered gringo outside forcefully, he snatched a kerosene lamp on the way. There were two of these lamps always handy, as well as a number of candles, because we often had electrical failures in that neighborhood.

Outside, before the eyes of the terrified visitor lying on the ground, Ejo emptied the lamp kerosene all over his motorcycle. Then he held up a lighter with the flame burning. The gringo cried out, "Oh no, no no!" But when he tried to get up, Ejo knocked him down with an expert kick to the chest, landing him on his back.

"Calm yourself! Here is a koan especially for you: 'Enlightenment or motorcycle?' If you reply 'Enlightenment,' I'll set the motorcycle on fire. If you reply 'motorcycle,' I'll allow you to leave on it—but before you do, you must give me that book, which I know you have memorized."

Master Peter seemed but a crumpled heap now. He whined softly: "Motorcycle." Then he arose slowly and opened the storage compartment at the back of his machine. He pulled out a book with a red cover and handed it over silently to the man who had reassumed his role as our true master.

Ejo read the title aloud: *"The Sound of One Hand Clapping: 281 Koans and Their Solutions."** Then he sternly admonished the defeated one: "You trickster! Learn to be what you are!"

The visitor's face was now the same color as the book and his leather clothes. He kneeled before the monk, prostrated himself with his hands outstretched upon the ground, and implored him humbly: "I beg you, Master . . ."

With his flat stick, Master Ejo struck him three times on the left shoulder blade and three times on the right. The six slaps on the leather were as loud as gunshots. Then Ejo stretched out an open hand in a gesture.

The American stood up. He seemed to have learned an essential lesson. He sighed: "Thank you, Sensei."

Then he cranked up his powerful motorcycle and rode away forever, the sound vanishing in the distance.

---

*Hau Hoo, *The Sound of One Hand Clapping: 281 Zen Koans and Their Solutions,* translated by Yoel Hoffmann (New York: Basic Books, 1975). Originally published as *Gendai Sejizen Hyoron* [A Critique of Current Pseudo-Zen] (Japan: n.p., 1916).

2
The Secret of Koans

"If there are any tracks, I'll find them—even at the bottom of a well."

SILVER KANE, *EL GUARDAESPALDAS* (THE BODYGUARD)

When Ejo Takata first visited my house in order to choose the right space for his teaching, I showed him my large library proudly. I had been surrounded by books since childhood, and I loved them as much as I loved my cats. I had a sizeable collection of books on Zen—in English, Italian, French, and Spanish—but the monk glanced at them only briefly. Opening his fan, he moved it rapidly to cool himself. Then he left the room without a word. My face darkened with embarrassment. With this gesture, he was showing me that my erudition was nothing but a disguise for my lack of true knowledge. Words may show the way to truth, but they are not the truth. "When you've caught the fish, you don't need the net anymore."

In spite of this lesson, however, I could not resist sneaking out at nightfall to the garbage can where Ejo had consigned the mysterious book he had taken from the American. Digging among the trash there,

13

I found it and pulled it out. I felt like a thief, but not like a traitor. Covering it in black paper, I placed it inconspicuously among the many volumes of my library without opening it.

Time passed. Thanks to the support of the Japanese embassy, Ejo was able to set up a small zendo in the university quarter of Mexico City. For five years, I arose each morning at six o'clock to drive for at least an hour through heavy traffic in order to arrive at the zendo for two meditation sessions of forty minutes each. Yet it became clear to me that my path in life was not that of a monk.

My ambitions were becoming centered on the theater. Nevertheless, Ejo Takata's teachings—to be instead of to seem, to live simply, to practice the teaching instead of merely reciting it, and knowing that the words we use to describe the world are not the world—had profoundly changed my vision of what theater should be. In my upcoming production, a theatrical version of Nietzsche's *Zarathustra,* I had stripped the stage of its usual décor, including even curtains and ropes, and had the walls painted white. Defying censorship, the actors and actresses undressed completely on stage after reciting lines from the Gospel of Thomas: "The disciples asked him: 'When will you be revealed, and when will we be able to see you?' And Jesus said: 'When you shed your clothing without shame, and when you take your jewels and cast them under your feet and trample them like little children, then will you be able to contemplate the Son of the Living One and have no more fear.'"*

The production was a success, with full houses from Tuesday through Sunday. I then proposed to Ejo (without much hope) that he meditate before the public during the performance. To my astonishment, the master accepted. He arrived punctually, took his seat on the side of the stage, and meditated without moving for two hours. The contrast between the actors speaking their lines and the silent monk

---

*[These passages do not constitute an accurate quotation of any logion of the Gospel of Thomas. Instead, they are a kind of montage of passages from that gospel, drawn from different logia and edited for theatrical purposes. —*Trans.*]

dressed in his ritual robes had a staggering effect. *Zarathustra* continued to run for a full year and a half. After the last performance, Ejo said to me: "By having me participate in your work, you have introduced many thousands of Mexicans to Zen meditation. How can I thank you?"

I bowed to him to hide my shame, then I confessed: "I took that American guy's Zen book and hid it. I've never opened it, but I'm dying of curiosity to see what is in it. If I read it, will I be betraying you?"

He burst out laughing. "We'll read it together and write commentaries about it!" Then he told me the story of this mysterious book.

"This text is *Gendai Sojizen Hyoron* and actually amounts to a critique of pseudo-Zen. Appearing in 1916 and written by a mysterious provocateur, it set off a huge scandal among Zen monks. In the Rinzai school, koans and their answers had been transmitted secretly for generations, supposedly in a notebook written by Hakuin himself, the founder of the technique. A number of masters were furious at having these secrets published. They went to great lengths to confiscate and destroy all copies of it. But someone managed to keep one. It passed from hand to hand, and finally, in the 1960s, photocopies of it began to circulate with an English translation and commentary by the learned scholar Yoel Hoffmann.

"When I first visited that monastery in California, I realized that a number of monks were repeating phrases from it like parrots and imitating actions from it like monkeys. That is why I fled that place. Knowing the answer to a question is not the same as mastering it."

Thus began a new phase of my life. Ejo proposed that we meet once a week at midnight—he chose this dark hour because it is symbolically the beginning of the new day's conception. We engaged in conversations that literally began in the darkness and ended with the light of dawn. Every one of the koans was an immense challenge for me. I had to solve not only the riddles the masters offered but also the incomprehensible replies of their disciples. My reason was made to endure agony.

I had to concentrate all my energy only to open a door in the wall of an absurd blind alley. To act or not to act? To follow reason or to follow intuition? Choose this one or that one? Trust others or myself?

Seeing how uncertain I was, Ejo quoted these words from Hakuin: "If you constantly explore a koan with total concentration, your self-image will be destroyed. An abyss will open beneath you, with no place to gain a foothold. You will confront death. You will feel a great fire burning in your chest. Then, suddenly, far away from body or mind, you and the koan will be one. You will go far and enter unmistakably into your own nature." Ejo paused, and fanned himself for a while. Then, with a huge grin, he added: "Master Rinzai* said: 'All the sacred scriptures are nothing but toilet paper.' Words won't solve a koan."

Yet as a person who has spent much of his life reading, finding an indescribable joy in books, I protested: "Wait just a moment, Ejo. You say that you can't solve koans with words, but I'm sure that there are words that can dissolve them. Just as cobra venom can serve as an anti-dote to the poison of a bite, I believe that the poetic mind is capable of providing a kind of cleaning service: One luminous, poetic phrase could nullify the question that has no possible answer."

Ejo laughed. "If you believe that, then you must think you can do it. You confuse poetry with reality, but I accept the challenge. Now give me a poetic response to the koan in the book that comes after the 'sound of one hand' and 'Mu': 'What was your original face before your birth?'"

I concentrated intently and was about to say: "The same as my face after my death," but I felt this would be falling into the trap of accept-

---

*Rinzai Gigen, whose Chinese name was Linji Yixuan, was born in an unknown year in Nanhua and died in 866 CE. As a child, he entered the monastery and taught there during the era of the widespread persecution of Buddhists (842–845 CE). Besides founding the Soto school, he founded one of the great Ch'an schools that bears his name (Linji, or Rinzai in Japanese). His school, which had a reputation of especially severe discipline, emphasized the transcendence of dualistic thought, and the use of koans in the search for an awakening that was believed to be sudden and unexpected.

ing the concept of birth and death by asserting that there is some face or individual form that we possess beyond this reality. So instead I exclaimed: "I don't know! I didn't have a mirror then!"

Ejo laughed again. "Quite ingenious. It is true that you have nullified the question with this exclamation—but what is the use of that? You remain a prisoner of having or not having. You accept that there is an original self, but you do not see it. Despite the fact that you managed to escape the duality of seer–seen, your words are still based on what you believe rather than on what you experience. In the traditional response given in the book, the disciple stands up and wordlessly places his two hands upon his chest. What do you think of that?"

"It seems to me that with this gesture he is saying: 'There is no before, no after; I am here and now, that's all I know. The question you ask has no answer.'"

"You are not going deeply enough. The disciple is not saying anything. He has withdrawn into himself, free from his hopes and illusions; his intellect is silenced. He feels this 'here' reach out to the whole universe; this 'now' include the totality of time, becoming eternal; and this individual 'me' dissolve into the cosmos. He has ceased to define, to believe himself master of his body, to judge, or to identify himself with his concepts as if they were real. He no longer allows himself to be carried away by the whirl of emotions and desires, for he understands that reality is not what he thinks or expects.

"As a response, the disciple stands up. In this way, he shows that he has accepted his own emptiness so that meditation is no longer necessary. Meditation is not the end, but the means. It is a mistake to confuse *zazen* (meditation) and awakening."

I stood up, placed my hands upon my chest, and bowed. Ejo smiled and went into the kitchen, returning with two cups of green tea.

Now smiling myself, I said: "Ejo, this is not a Mexican drink. Enough of this Japanese culture!"

He answered immediately: "I have coffee too!" And he hurried to the kitchen again, returning quickly with two cups of steaming coffee.

As we drank it in the light of dawn, whose rosy hue was staining the dying blue of the night, Ejo lit a cigarette and inhaled the smoke with sensual delight. Noticing my disapproving air, he quoted a text from the Advaita Vedanta tradition, attributed to the poet Dattatraya: "Do not worry about the master's defects. If you are wise, you will know how to make use of the good in him. When you cross a river, it may be in a boat painted in ugly colors, but you are thankful to it for helping you cross to the other side."

For two or three days after that, I was in a state of euphoria. I walked the streets of the city and saw it all with new eyes. Everything seemed luminous to me. With every step I took, I rose up on my toes. I must confess, I felt I was enlightened. "Why do I need to keep seeing Ejo? When you resolve one koan, you resolve them all. Koans are not different truths; they are only different roads that lead us to the one and only light." But then two humiliating events occurred in rapid succession and cut me down to size.

A young man named Julio Castillo came to see me. "Master, I want you to teach me about light," he said.

My mind was flooded with an uncontrollable vanity, which I dissimulated by adopting a saintly expression. So this intelligent-looking youth was somehow able to perceive the degree of my spiritual attainment! I gave my best explanation of the nature of empty mind, detachment from desire and ego, and unity with the cosmos, the here and now. I read quotes to him from Hui-Neng* and showed him photos of monks in meditation. Then I sat down in the zazen position and invited him to do likewise—but Julio Castillo only stood with a pained and embarrassed expression.

"Excuse me, master, but I fear there is a misunderstanding," he murmured. "I am a theater student. I have come to ask you not to save

---

*Hui-Neng, or Ejo in Japanese (638–713 CE), was the sixth patriarch in direct succession from Bodhidharma. Hui-Neng is considered to be the founder of Zen. (See the note in chapter 10 defining the Bodhidharma.)

my soul, but to teach me about light—how you place your projectors to get your effects on stage."

I felt so ridiculous that I started coughing to hide my embarrassment.

The evening of that same day, I went to a party given by a surrealist painter, Leonora Carrington. Her dazzling personality contrasted sharply with that of her husband, a man with a grave expression who rarely said anything and, when he did, uttered only a few syllables. In spite of the heat, he was wrapped in a thick, black overcoat, and a beret was pulled down to his ears. Like an observer from another planet, from a corner he watched the noisy party, where drink flowed copiously.

"Please don't think he is some sort of ogre," Leonora said to me. "Go talk with Chiki (as she called her husband)—you'll see that he knows many interesting things. He reads five books a day. Right now he is studying Tibetan religion."

It so happened that I had learned a very complicated Tibetan *mudra* (sacred hand gesture), which I had copied from a manuscript I had seen. With each thumb, I pulled the ring finger of the opposite hand toward my chest, and pressing the ring fingers against each palm, I brought together the two ring fingers like a symbolic mountain. I then used each of my index fingers to grasp the ring finger of the opposite hand and bring it down parallel to the little finger.

Approaching Chiki, I performed this complex operation and proudly displayed the mudra to him, asking him at the same time (with the hope of impressing him and starting an interesting conversation): "What is this?"

He shrugged. "Ten fingers."

With this one stroke, like a violent wind sweeping away all garbage, he banished all metaphor from my mind. No matter how much I entangled my fingers, I would never arrive at truth, only at a symbol that was as useless as the mutterings of an idiot. Ten fingers are still ten fingers. Awkwardly, I excused myself and hurried away to drown my humiliation in a glass of tequila. There and then, I decided to continue my meditations with Ejo.

———※———

"How can you walk in a straight line through the forty-nine hairpin turns of a mountain path?"

I reflected for a minute, which seemed like an eternity. An answer came to my lips: "A labyrinth is only the illusory complication of a straight line," I said.

Ejo clapped his hands loudly, though I didn't know whether it meant applause or, on the contrary, that I was asleep and must wake up.

"Explain, poet!" he commanded.

"I mean that the very act of asking us how to attain a goal makes us see a straight path as full of curves," I answered.

Ejo smiled. "Let's see what our secret book has to say about it." He read aloud: "The disciple, leaning and turning to the side, twisted around the room as if he was climbing a narrow mountain path." Then he told me, "Without a word, imitate the disciple. Then tell me what you have understood."

After I had done so, I said: "Ejo, the monk is showing us how illusion—symbolized by the twisting and turning—complicates our lives. If we free ourselves from illusion, we see that the path that seemed complicated is actually straight and simple."

"Well, your poetic answers certainly have power, but the only thing they can accomplish is to do away with the question without reaching its essence. When you use words to conquer words, you find yourself ultimately on a battlefield full of corpses. By giving an intellectual explanation to a mute gesture offered by Hakuin's teaching, you become lost in the labyrinth. The disciple is not trying to demonstrate anything. Silently, he stands up, leans over, moves in curving paths, climbs an imaginary mountain. But he does not change; he remains empty. He is who he is, without wondering who he is. He abides in the unity at the center of the ten thousand things. If you understand that, you will have no difficulty answering the next koan: How do you take a stone from the bottom of the ocean without wetting your sleeves?"

Using the skills I had learned as a mime, I plunged into an imaginary ocean, swam to the bottom, lifted a large stone in my arms, came to the surface, and emerged from the water. Confident of the rightness of this gesture, I placed the stone before Ejo and awaited his enthusiastic response. But instead, he asked me abruptly: "What is this stone called?"

I was silent for a moment. "It . . . is called 'stone,'" I stammered. "It is called 'awakening' . . . it is called 'Buddha' . . . it is called 'truth.'" I could have gone on like this, but Ejo silenced me with a blow of his flat kyosaku.

"Intellectual, learn to die!"

I was offended. This was the first time he had said this to me. Then he struck me again.

"Awakening is not a thing. It is not a goal, not a concept. It is not something to be attained. It is a metamorphosis. If the caterpillar thinks about the butterfly it is to become, saying 'And then I shall have wings and antennae,' there will never be a butterfly. The caterpillar must accept its own disappearance in its transformation. When the marvelous butterfly takes wing, nothing of the caterpillar remains. . . . Now come on, let's play a game!" he said. "You be me, and I'll be you. Ask me a question."

Imitating his Japanese accent, I said: "What is the name of this stone?"

Imitating my Chilean accent, he said: "Alejandro."

Now I understood: This stone was me, identified by my name, my imagined limits, my language, my memory. To remove the stone from the bottom of the ocean—the world as it is, an inexplicable dream—meant removing my identity in order to realize that it is illusory, seeing that there is no difference between master and disciple, for one is the other and all apparent multiplicity is eternal unity.

I took his stick and gave him a blow on each shoulder. He bowed to me as if he were my disciple. Then he went to the kitchen and returned with a large bottle of sake.

"Now, master, we are going to celebrate this!" he exclaimed, pouring me a glass of the delicious beverage. We finished our glasses and continued drinking. Ejo was frolicsome but very conscious. I also felt that my mind had been set free. Only my body, with all its muscles relaxed, seemed still to be living its own life, far from me.

"Alejandro, poetry—at least the way you use it—is a game that I do not know. It amuses me to see how you use it to nullify koans. It is also a sacrilege, but that is good: Without sacrilege, a disciple cannot realize himself. 'If you meet the Buddha on the road, cut off his head.' Now let us see how you will nullify the two major koans of the Rinzai school!"

"Oh, Ejo," I protested, "I have had too much to drink to be able to do that."

Ignoring this, he clapped his hands. "That is the sound of two hands clapping." He then raised his right hand. "What is the sound of one hand clapping?"

I lifted my hand and placed it directly opposite his hand. "The sound of my one hand is the same as the sound of your one hand."

The monk laughed uproariously and continued: "Does a dog have Buddha nature?"

"The Buddha has dog nature."

Staggering as a man staggers on a boat in choppy water, he went to the kitchen and returned with another bottle. Filling our glasses, he said: "Let's continue. This is an excellent game."

We drank until the dark sky began to fill with light. He challenged me with a great many koans. I do not remember all my responses, but what I cannot forget is the immense joy I felt in being one with the master. By the end of our session, I no longer knew who was asking the questions and who was answering them. In the zendo, there were no longer two people, only one—or none.

"It never begins and it never ends. What is it?"

"I am what I am!"

"How does the intellectual learn to die?"

"He changes all his words into a black dog that follows him around!"

"Do the shadows of the pines depend on the moonlight?"

"Pine roots have no shadow!"

"Is the Buddha old?"

"As old as I am!"

"What do you do when it cannot be done?"

"I let it be done!"

"Where will you go after death?"

"The stones of the road neither come nor go!"

"If a woman advances on the path, is she your older or younger sister?"

"She is a woman walking!"

"When the path is covered with snow, is it white?"

"When it is white, it is white. When it is not white, it is not white!"

"How do you escape when you are imprisoned in a block of granite?"

"I leap and dance!"

"Who can remove the collar from the ferocious tiger?"

"I will take it off myself!"

"Can you say that without opening your mouth?"

"Whatever I say or do not say, keep your mouth closed!"

"How many hairs are on the back of your head?"

"Show me the back of yours, and I'll count them!"

"All the Buddhas of the past, the present, and the future: What do they foretell right now?"

"Now I yawn, because I'm drunk!"

Holding each other steady in order not to stumble against the walls, we walked out into the street. We mimicked pissing against a post. Ejo lifted a leg, imitating a dog. "The Buddha has dog nature!" I imitated him. Then we were both seized by a long fit of joyous laughter. When we calmed down finally, he bowed good-bye to me. Then he said: "Art is your path. Accept my friend Leonora Carrington as your teacher. She doesn't know any koans, but she has resolved them all."

3
A Surrealist Master

Everything consisted of a murky, infinite call which, little
by little, was stifled by the shadows of the night.

SILVER KANE, *VERDUGO A PLAZOS*
(HIT MAN ON CREDIT)

When I woke up after a ten-hour sleep, I called the master.

"Ejo, do you remember the last thing you told me yesterday? I was
wondering if perhaps too much sake was . . ."

He interrupted me. "A great Japanese poet wrote: 'To remain silent
in order to appear wise is despicable. Better to get drunk on sake and
sing.' A poet from your own country, Pablo Neruda, once exclaimed:
'May God preserve me from fabricating things when I sing!' What I
told you yesterday, I repeat today. Go see my friend Leonora."

"But Ejo, it is you I want to study with!"

"Do not be deceived, Alejandro. Empty mind does not mean empty
heart. Perfection is empty mind and full heart. You can rid yourself
of concepts but not of feelings. Little by little, you must empty your
head and go into your heart, gathering and refining, until you arrive

at that sublime state which you call happiness. According to what you have told me, you have not yet finished with the bitterness you harbor toward your mother. Feeling deprived of this essential tenderness, you are still an angry child who rejects women in every domain except that of sex. You think that you can learn only from men. The archetype of the cosmic father dominates your actions. The Great Mother is still surrounded with shadows. . . . Before continuing to unravel koans, go and lay down your sword before the flower; bow down to her. Without knowing it, you have always been waiting for this. You are an artist, as is Leonora. She is the being appropriate for you. Let her give you the inner woman who is so lacking in you."

The little I knew about Leonora Carrington was gleaned from what I had read in André Breton's *Anthologie de l'humour noir*. He described her in these terms: "Those respectable people who, for a dozen years, had invited her to dine in a prestigious restaurant have still not recovered from the embarrassment when they noticed that, while continuing to take part in the conversation, she had taken off her shoes and meticulously covered her feet in mustard."

I also knew she had been the mistress of Max Ernst. When the painter was imprisoned in Spain by the Franco regime, she underwent a crisis of madness. After recovering from this, she described it in her book *Mémoires d'en bas*. From that time on, she had abolished definitively the walls that separate reason from the realm of dreams. She had a mythic reputation among Mexican painters; she was an incarnation of the most extreme surrealism. During a party, Luis Buñuel, seduced by Carrington's beauty and emboldened by the notion that she had transcended all bourgeois morality, proposed (with his characteristic bluntness) that she become his mistress. Without even waiting for her answer, he gave her the key to the secret studio that he used as a love nest and told her to meet him at three o'clock the next afternoon. Early the next morning, Leonora went to visit the place alone. She found it tasteless: it looked exactly like a motel room. Taking advantage of the fact that she was in her menstrual period, she covered her hands with blood and used them to make bloody handprints all over the walls in order to provide a bit of decoration for that anonymous, impersonal room. Buñuel never spoke to her again.

When I arrived at her place, a house with no facade, just a bare stone wall with a high window and a narrow door on Chihuahua Street, I was surprised to notice that I was trembling from head to toe. An absurd, uncontrollable shyness made me unable even to ring the bell. I remained standing, petrified, for at least a half hour. I knew she was waiting for me, but I felt incapable of taking action before this prisonlike dwelling. There arrived a small woman with a strong and youthful body, pulling a little cart full of vegetables, fruits, and cigarette cartons.

"Are you the mime that the Japanese sent to us? I'm Kati Horna, Hungarian photographer, and I'm Leonora's oldest friend."

She lit a cigarette and began speaking rapidly, without waiting for any response from me. She paused in her talk only to take quick drags from her cigarette. Her Spanish was poor, and she punctuated her verbiage with many large gestures.

"Last night I dreamed of three phrases. When I woke up, it was as if I had brought them into the light. They were already in my life, like a sort of cyst. Everything I know, I receive in dreams. Sentences come to me fully composed. When I wake up, my behavior changes—I leave a country, sometimes I try to kill someone. 'Live like a star!' 'Eliminate the superfluous!' 'Concrete manifestation!' What do you think about that? The stars shine without worrying about the darkness of the planets. The sun and the moon use no ornaments. Matter contains everything. . . . By the way, I have some of my photographs in this envelope. Would you like to see them?"

Without waiting for my answer, she brought them out and displayed them one by one with great rapidity. They were portraits of beggars, survivors of concentration camps, the mentally ill, women of the Spanish Civil War, and children in misery. All of them seemed to have the face of Christ, all of them seemed to be waiting, certain of not being disappointed.

"Good dreams always come true in the end."

Then she rang the doorbell herself, murmuring: "To want . . . to dare . . . to be able . . . to obey . . ." Her skirt, made of ordinary cloth, was blown up by the wind, but she paid no attention.

With a creaking of rusty hinges, the door opened slowly. I walked into a cold, dark, hostile room. From the floor above, someone had been pulling on a cord that lifted the bolt. With a dry mouth, I climbed the stairs. I had just turned thirty. According to what Breton had said, Leonora was born in 1907, which meant I would be meeting a woman of fifty-two. I feared that I would be received by an old miser whose shadow had the form of a tarantula. In those days, age was associated with ugliness in my mind.

I was pleasantly surprised. I beheld a being rather than a woman standing at the top of the stairs. I perceived, rather than a body, a kind of silhouette, like a concrete shadow, and two eyes shining with an impulsive yet crystal-clear spirit. Her very look seemed to be made of soul stuff. Confronted with this intensity, any formalities, any masks I might have worn, fell from me like dead leaves. To enter into the mind of such a woman was as if I was being immersed and baptized. My voice changed, my gestures seemed to rediscover a forgotten delicacy, my consciousness lit up like a flame. I knew that I would never be the same after this encounter. . . . Much later, she wrote me a letter about what she had felt at this moment:

You knew Leonora was home. You came to have tea—with a suspicion that it would be a terrifying experience. You washed your hands three times more than you normally do, you wondered why you were going to see this starchy, powerful woman who made you afraid. You could not decide which was more courageous: to go there or to leave without saying anything. As for me, I had already made my preparations to petrify you with respect. I savored your discomfort, which radiated an enchanting stench that would be able to make me into a goddess for a certain time. You entered into a room perfectly designed to make you feel claustrophobic so that you moved with difficulty among my traps. You realized that there was an egg stain on your coat that began to shine like the setting sun before my eyes. In despair, you wondered if your fly was open. You did not want to, but I insisted you sit on the couch, between the two Anubises in the tapestry covering it. You barely allowed yourself to cross your legs, for any other movement would have seemed an outrage. With panic, you looked at the tea and dry biscuits, for you felt you were being observed while you committed the pornographic act of drinking—and worse, eating—in my presence. At that moment an owl came down the chimney and disappeared in my bust. Your heart beat with an infinite compassion, for you suddenly understood my lamentable condition. In my own way, I asked you to deliver me, a deliverance that you alone can give me. Is it you, then, who will set chance in motion?

Although expressed in surrealist language, this description corresponds perfectly to what I was feeling at that time. If the outside of the house was like a prison, the inside was the magical extension of her mind. The painter and artist was in every piece of furniture, every object, in each of the many plants that flourished in every corner. Sitting here and there were large, delicate dolls, some of them hanging from the ceiling, swinging slowly like pendulums. The armchairs were covered with tapestries that glittered with strange symbols. The one covering the couch featured two godlike young men with dogs' heads squatting and looking toward each other.

With an imperious gesture of her white-gloved hand, Leonora bade me sit between these two men. Then she spoke with a strong English accent. "Ejo told me that, among other things, you are a mime teacher. I want you to show me how you move. This will help me to know you better."

At that very instant, I realized that this artist wore absolutely no jewelry—no necklace, rings, earrings, or watch. She wore no makeup, and her dress was a simple black tunic. Before such a presence that was shorn of any ornament, to engage in pantomime seemed vain, infantile, and vulgar. The idea of demonstrating some stereotypical mime technique such as carrying a weight, pulling a rope, walking against the wind, creating imaginary objects or spaces with my hands, or simply walking like a robot made me ill at ease. I had the impression of being dressed in an old, useless overcoat. Thanks to my work with koans, I was able to purify my mind by emptying it of abstractions; but I knew that I must also empty my gestures of any sort of imitation in order to arrive at a purity of movement. I undressed, and in that otherworldly space where silence nestled in the very air, I began to move with no goal. One with my body, a union of flesh and spirit inspired by Leonora's eyes, I allowed myself to be possessed by movement. I have no idea how long it lasted—a minute, an hour? I had found *the place,* and I knew the ecstasy of freedom from the domination of time.

Suddenly, I fell upon the couch. Drowsily, as if waking from a deep sleep, I began to dress.

Smiling, she whispered, "Silence. Let us not disturb the mystery." Then, walking on tiptoe in order to avoid making noise, she left and returned with two glasses of tea and some biscuits. She sipped the drink, which was sweetened with honey, then she lifted her tunic, which covered her down to her ankles, and showed me a small wound on her calf. With the teaspoon, wearing the childlike expression of a sorceress, she scraped the scab away from the wound and let the spoon fill with blood. She brought it carefully over to me without spilling a drop, emptied the red liquid into my glass, and bade me drink it. I sipped it with the same slowness and attention I had learned in the Japanese tea ceremony. Then, rummaging in an oval box, she pulled out a small pair of scissors and cut my fingernails as well as a lock of my hair. She put them all in a tiny sack that she hung around her neck.

"You will return!" she said.

For a long time, we sat in silence. It was broken by the footsteps of her two children, Gaby and Pablo. Actually, it would be more accurate to say that the silence was *completed*. These two children belonged fully to the strange world of this artist. There was nothing abnormal about them, but they were different—as beautiful and incomprehensible as their mother's paintings. They each sat on one side of me, directly upon the Anubises. They showed no surprise at my presence and acted as though they had always known me. The thought occurred to me that I was their brother, for the same blood now circulated in my veins and theirs. While the children devoured the biscuits, Leonora gave me a key to the house.

As I walked down the stairs, she said from above me, as a sort of good-bye: "I am nine doors. I shall open the one on which you knock."

That night I could not sleep. It was three o'clock in the morning, and my eyes were wide open. I was possessed. I could feel this woman in my blood, like a boat moving upstream. "Come, come," she was saying with a voice that seemed to emerge from a distant past. I got dressed, went outside, ran though the streets until I was out of breath, and arrived at her house, opening the door silently with my key and making no noise on the stairs. From the room that served as her painting studio, I saw the flickering light of a candle and heard her voice reciting a litany. Eldra, the watchdog, wagged her tail and let me pass without growling. I saw Leonora seated on a wooden throne whose back was carved with the bust of an angel. Naked except for a Jewish prayer shawl, her gaze fixed, unblinking, and focused on infinity, she seemed like a figure on the prow of a ship from an ancient civilization. She had left the world of the rational. She continued to recite in English, taking no notice of my presence. I sat on the floor, facing her. There was little left of any individuality in her. She seemed possessed simultaneously by all women who had ever existed. The words poured out of her mouth like an endless river of invisible insects. I remember a few of her verses:

> *I, the eye that sees nine different worlds and tells the*
> *tale of each.*
> *I, Anuba who saw the guts of pharaoh, embalmer,*
> *outcast.*
> *I, the lion goddess who ate the ancestors and churned*
> *them into gold in her belly.*
> *I, the lunatic and fool, meat for worse fools than I.*
> *I, the bitch of Sirius, landed here from the terrible*
> *hyperbole to howl at the moon.*
> *I, the bamboo in the hand of Huang Po.*
> *I, the queen bee in the entrails of Samson's dead lion.*
> *I, the tears of the archangel that melted it again.*
> *I, the solitary joke made by the snow queen in higher*
> *mathematics.*
> *I, the gypsy who brought the first greasy tarot from*
> *Venus.*
> *I, the tree of wisdom whose thirteen branches lead*
> *eternally back again.*
> *I, the eleventh commandment: Thou shalt despise no*
> *being.*

I barely noticed Chiki's arrival. He wore the same Spanish beret that was on his head day and night, and he was dressed in pajamas with vertical stripes, like a concentration camp uniform, and house shoes shaped like rabbits' heads. I noticed that he had broad shoulders and looked Jewish (Hungarian, Russian, Lithuanian, Polish?). With the air of a well-trained dog and never acknowledging my presence, he placed his large hands on Leonora's fragile shoulders and, with infinite tenderness, lifted her slowly and led her, step by step, into the bedroom. I could see him making her lie down on a wooden bed that was higher at the foot than at the head. Then Chiki went to lie down in another bed. Stretched out on her back, Leonora continued to murmur her interminable incantation until she drifted off to sleep.

I wandered around the dark house like a disembodied shadow. Leonora, her husband, her two children, and the dog were all sound asleep. No one was disturbed by my presence, which seemed utterly natural to them. Either I did not exist for them or I had become a ghost—or perhaps just one more of the dolls. I glided from room to room, living a long-held fantasy of mine: to become an invisible man and observe others in their intimacy without any interaction between us. In the master bedroom, lit by a lunar light, I saw a large oil painting: a portrait of Leonora by Max Ernst. Very young and beautiful, she wore a dark green dress blown by the wind and seemed to be on the lookout in the midst of a forest of black trees.

Young Gaby was sleeping next to a pyramidal pile of poetry collections, arms wrapped around a wooden princess who wore a crown shaped like a half moon. Upon young Pablo's desk was a candy box, and pinned on it was the cadaver of a large toad, its belly sliced open so that its entrails were exposed. Several scalpels and other surgical instruments were lying on his bookshelves along with some instruction books on the techniques of taxidermy. Eldra, half awake and drowsy, lay on the couch between the two Anubises, gnawing contentedly on a small statue of the Virgin of Guadalupe.

Down on the humid ground floor I discovered a photography lab. Its walls were covered with photos of baptisms, First Communions, birthdays, marriages, and funerals. This was how the antisocial Chiki earned his living: taking photographs of groups of people who all seemed to have the same face. When looked at together, these photographs gave the impression of an anthill.

As the darkness gave way to daylight, I ceased to be a shadow. Ill at ease in my dense body, I returned home.

Three days passed, during which I could do nothing. I spent hours lying in a hammock, allowing my mind to ruminate cowlike upon my experiences in this household, where people lived by laws that were not those of reason.

Then I was awakened at five o'clock in the morning by a phone call from Leonora. She spoke very fast in a low, conspiratorial, almost whispering voice.

"Your name is no longer Alejandro. It is now Sebastian. Beware! They are watching us. To seal our union, we must commit a sacred misdeed. Get up now and rent a room at the Hotel Reforma. [Some years later, this building would be destroyed by an earthquake.] Do not accept any room but number 22. Don't worry, for according to the laws of St. Random, this room will be free. Come dressed in black, as if in mourning."

Then she hung up abruptly without waiting for any response from me.

I took a bath, washed my hair, and put on some scent, clean underwear, and a black suit that had recently been returned from the cleaners. On the way to the hotel, I bought a dozen red roses. Overcoming an attack of timidity but clearing my throat like a guilty person, I demanded room 22. I had no hope of getting it, for the hotel was packed with people attending a horsemanship convention. To my great surprise, room 22 was the only vacancy. I settled in, strewing the roses along a counterpane with multicolored stripes. I closed the curtains to hide the ugliness of the room, lighting only the small bedside lamp, which I covered with a pillowcase in such a way as to cast a discreet, rosy aura in the room. Every five minutes I washed my hands, which were sweating profusely. My genitals were filled with a deathly cold. Any erection seemed totally impossible. I felt castrated by ancestral fears of maternal incest. I thought of Ejo. I took up a position of meditation, intoning "om" constantly, emptying my mind of every other word.

At exactly nine o'clock, seven soft knocks on the door announced Leonora's arrival. I tried to hurry over to open the door, but my legs had gone to sleep. I dragged myself as best I could, stumbling and shaking my feet to restore circulation, and with a dry mouth, I opened the door.

It was a new Leonora who stood facing me. She was dressed completely in black, like me, except for green leather shoes. Her head was covered with a veil. She glided into the room with the grace of a fifteen-year-old girl. Her voice had also changed: she spoke no longer in the low tones of a priestess, but instead assumed a musical voice full of enchanting shyness. She bore two cubical boxes, one wrapped in silver paper, the other in gold. After I closed the door, she made sure it was properly bolted as well. Then, in a murmur, she asked me to remove her veil. Slowly, with trembling hands, I did. For the first time, I saw makeup on her face—discreet, but sensual. In her carefully coiffed hair there were five authentic green scarab jewels.

We sat on the edge of the bed. I soon realized that any suspicions I harbored of sexual intentions on her part were totally unfounded. The misdeed she spoke of had nothing to do with adultery. I breathed a sigh of relief. What I felt for her had nothing to do with sexual or romantic desire. My soul wanted to unite itself with hers. My rational conscious-ness wanted to drown in her limitless spirit. What I truly desired was to taste the soma of holy madness.

Leonora opened her boxes. From the golden one she took a skull made of sugar—the kind Mexicans use on the first day of November, Día de los Muertes. It had ALEJANDRO engraved on its forehead. From the silver box she took another skull engraved with LEONORA. She gave me hers and kept the one with my name.

"Now we shall devour each other," she said, and bit into the skull with my name. I did the same with hers. Our eyes were fixed on each other, and we seemed to forget everything—the world and even ourselves—as we ate the skulls slowly. For an instant her face disappeared, and I saw my own in its place. At this moment, as if sharing the same hallucination, she said, "From now on, your face is my mirror."

When we had finished this strange breakfast, she put a finger on her lips as a sign for me to be silent, donned her veil, placed one of the scarab jewels on my hand, and with no further ado, opened the door and left.

The next day, Kati Horna brought me a letter, saying: "This is from

Leonora. If you open the door to her house, I implore you not to let in any bees, because they come from Venus. They can transform her into a woman. If, by misfortune, you make her cry, you must realize that her tears are not liquid; they are of hard, frozen ice armed with geometrical points that can make her go blind."

Along with the violet envelope, she gave me a small wooden doll: a bearded goddess with horns. Reaching into a deep pocket of her large skirt, she gave me a fish of the variety known as *huachinango* in Mexico. Then she took a photograph of me and backed away, disappearing.

With trembling hands I read:

Long ago your naked footprints already sketched out the labyrinth in front of you, which is your path. Listen: By absolute necessity, I rediscovered my mother, the Spider. She offered her multiple hairy arms to my tongue. On each hair, a drop of honey glistened. "Lick!" she commanded. I obeyed. Then she gave me her web to dress my shadow and yours. Come!

I ran all the way to her house. I was utterly fascinated by Leonora's mind. In her universe, thought was so concentrated that it was transformed into a dark stone submerged in the phosphorescent ocean of an unconscious with no barriers. A multitude of feelings and strange beings inhabited its depths: joys such as earthquakes, anguishes and terrors disguised as beautiful husks, angels as delicate as endless threads, repulsive yet comic.

Hidden in the folds of the envelope, I found an additional detail:

I have discovered the marvelous qualities of my shadow. Lately it has been detaching itself from me by virtue of its powers of flight. Sometimes it leaves wet footprints. But I confess: I constantly sleep wrapped in it, and the moments when I am able to awaken are rare.

I found her in her studio, working on a large canvas. When she saw me, she exclaimed: "Sebastian, don't move! I want you to come into my painting!"

I saw myself already depicted there: My body was elongated; a large, black chrysanthemum was pictured in place of a head and two enormous eyes were figured on my chest. I was pale, and on my shoulders, I bore a pale blue dwarf with a round, flat head like a soup bowl. With a gesture of frenetic uncertainty, this little being was pointing toward three paths that led to other spaces.

After two hours of immobility, I dared to move slightly to look at the other paintings that leaned against the walls. On one of them, in the middle of a kabbalistic sketch, there floated the head of Maria Félix so realistically painted that it almost could have been a photograph. When I let out a small exclamation of surprise, Leonora understood immediately.

"Do not suppose that I am capable of mastering a style that I detest. That famous actress insisted on paying a very high price for a portrait signed by me. She demanded that the likeness of her features be exact to the fraction of an inch. She didn't care about the rest and left that to my imagination. You see that hole in the wall there? While the diva was posing, Jose Horna, Kati's husband, was watching and painting her from the other room. He has no imagination, but he does have an incredible talent and technique for reproduction. As you see, the only thing Maria's head is missing is the ability to speak in that black scarab voice of hers. I am thinking about painting her with three transparent, superimposed bodies in the middle of a magic forest. The contrast between my style, with its hazy borders, and that face will give birth to an angelic demon. Its soul will be satisfied by my painting and its narcissism will be satisfied by that of my friend.

"But don't think I have disdain for Jose. He is an extraordinary being, a Spanish gypsy with emerald eyes. I've known him for many years. When he was still a humble carpenter, he came to see me because he had had a dream about me. He was inside a cathedral, standing before a very high pillar. Looking up, he saw the eyes of a serpent. Its body was white, heavy, smooth, and covered with prophetic messages. It slithered down the pillar and passed by him like a sigh. It then changed into me. Turning around and smiling, I said: 'I am going. Follow me always.' Jose obeyed and followed his dream serpent. He came to Mexico with Kati in order to find me. For years now, they have been my neighbors. He takes care of my plants, he sculpts my dolls, he makes my furniture and the frames for my paintings. I know that his emerald eyes belong to the hidden unicorn in the tarot."

She had to finish the painting of Maria within a week. The actress was going to Europe and wanted to hang it in her luxurious house there. For the next few days, I arrived at six o'clock each morning and assisted Leonora during this period of feverish activity. My task was to stand by as she worked, paint flowing uncontrolled over the canvas from the brush she held in each hand, which created two forms simultaneously around the famous face. As she did this, she asked me strange questions that I took as surrealistic koans.

"Every thing lives because of my vital fluid. I wake up when you sleep. If I stand up, they bury you. Who am I? . . . We shall transform ourselves suddenly into two dark, dashing Venezuelan men drinking tea in an aquarium. Why? . . . A red owl looks at me. In my belly, a drop of mercury forms. What does it mean? . . . A transparent egg that emits rays like the great constellations is a body, but it is also a box. Of what? . . . Only bitter laments will enable us to cry a tear. Is this tear an ant?"

How could I answer? To each of her questions I rose up on tiptoe and let my body dance.

On the ground floor there was a rectangular courtyard full of flowering plants and trees that rose up to the second story. Kati watered them and at the same time photographed every flower, leaf, and insect. Suddenly, we heard her calling us with loud screams. Thinking that some accident had befallen her, we all ran tumultuously down the stairs—Leonora, Chiki, Gaby, Pablo, Jose, the dog, and me.

Kati was standing there, safe and sound, photographing a chrysalis.

"Look, look! This is a divine moment! The caterpillar is dying and the butterfly is being born. The coffin of one is the cradle of the other. But at this moment, though the caterpillar has died, the butterfly is not yet born—so there is nothing. I am photographing nothingness."

As a fiery-colored insect arose to flutter among the flowers, Kati murmured: "Nothingness has densified, and a new illusion is born."

Leonora added, "We, too, should open ourselves as the chrysalis opens, to emerge completely new—our hair prickling like rays of light, unimaginably other."

The portrait was completed on time. The disconcerting realism of Maria Félix's head floated like a deaf and blind planet in a threefold, magical body. The world Leonora had painted vibrated with ecstasy. In it, the classic head, satisfied with its limits, seemed like a prison.

"I will give it to her today, this evening at nine o'clock. I want to prepare a dinner for her and a few friends, and I'd like you to help me in the kitchen."

Wearing a dress covered with tiny stars, and with me in the kitchen as the only onlooker, she commenced the preparations for the feast. In five chamber pots (brand new, of course), she planned to serve thirty-three pounds of caviar, about six pounds in each pot. I was appalled at the fortune this must have cost. With a mischievous smile, Leonora revealed her trickery: in fact, she had drenched cooked tapioca grains with black squid's ink. Using this simple technique, she managed to obtain a delicious pseudocaviar.

Then she explained how the soup was to be made: "With an unbroken stream of incantations spoken in the voice of a lion, I make my soup on wild rocks while looking at certain stars. The ingredients are simple: half a pink onion, a bit of perfumed wood, some grains of myrrh, a large branch of green mint, three belladonna pills covered with white Swiss chocolate, and a huge compass rose, which I plunge into the soup for one minute before removing it. Just before serving the soup, I add a Chinese 'cloud' mushroom, which has snail-like antennae and grows on owl dung."

At exactly nine o'clock, the great lady arrived. Only male guests had been invited so that the actress would have no feeling of competition. They all stared at her, tongue-tied. There were four painters, two writers, a film director, a banker, three important lawyers, and me—a theater director whom the others seemed to regard as a visitor from another planet. Chiki, who detested this sort of event, had taken refuge with his children and the Hornas in the red shadows of the photography lab. The resplendent painting, covered with a veil, was set on an easel in the middle of the room.

In person, Maria Félix was far more impressive than on the screen. Her luxurious, jet-black hair; her fine features; her queenly bearing; her potent, castrating regard; her intoxicating Mexican beauty; her baroque jewelry; her splendid evening gown; and especially the imperious flash in her eyes were breathtaking. A palpable testosterone silence hung in the room like a pall. Leonora broke it by whipping away the veil from the canvas dramatically and tossing it into the air so that it flew like a bird over our heads and struck a window before falling out of sight.

With a gasp of admiration, Señora Félix stood in front of the painting, her naked back toward us. Then she turned slowly around to face us, as if gazing upon her audience from a high throne. An invisible flame seemed to shoot out from her pupils as she looked at each of us fully in the eyes, one by one, with the clear intention of arousing us. Finally, her gaze strayed to the dog, Eldra. With great satisfaction, the señora pronounced these sultry words, which slithered through the air like a snake:

"Even the dog desires me!"

When I heard this, I felt a ripping sensation deep inside me. I remembered the terrible words my mother, Sara Felicidad, had said to me when I was seven years old: "After giving me a black eye because he imagined I had flirted with a customer in the shop, your father raped me and got me pregnant. I have hated him ever since, and I cannot love you. After you were born, I had my tubes tied."

It is a cruel blow to know that your birth was not desired. This is why I had always lived with the feeling that nothing really belonged to me; in order for the world to belong to us, we must believe that the world desires us. Only that which desires us can be ours. By feeling that she was desired even by the dog, Maria Félix was a queen who possessed everything.

From that moment on, I began to work on myself: to affirm the conviction that the world desires my existence. This world includes all of humanity, past, present, and future. My father and mother identified themselves with their acquired personalities, their families, and social and cultural influences. Their insane ideas (inherited from their parents and ancestors) gave rise to negative emotions, unhealthy desires, and false needs. They believed that they had not desired me, had not loved me. They saw me more as a tumor in my mother's stomach than as an embryo. I was protected by the placenta from the attacks of antibodies that wanted to destroy me. The life that had been granted me was able to resist these assaults. Something mysterious, immense, and profound had already decided, since the beginning of time, that I would exist. Because they desired my presence in this world, all the forces of the universe cooperated so that I could be born. Thus every living being represents a victory of cosmic desire.

I had come to Leonora wanting to be loved, seeking the perfect mother, which arose from the same need as my infant cries and weeping in the cradle. I was demanding and needy. Yet how could I give, for nothing was really mine? If the world did not desire me, how could it receive my love? I had only learned to desire myself, which split me in two—or more.

I escaped to the kitchen. The frivolous aspect of Leonora's world had become cloying to me. A few minutes later she entered wearing a doe's head as a hat.

"Don't lie to me, Sebastian. I have heard the temple veil tearing. A force now inhabits you that is foreign to me. Please excuse me, but I must withdraw. I'm afraid you will let loose a bee in my secret spaces."

I understood: our relationship had arrived at an end. Without a word, without looking back, I walked down the stairs, out of the house, and into the street. In those days, the sky of Mexico City was still clear, and the stars lit up the sky almost like a full moon. I was stopped in my tracks by a cry like the wailing of a bird being slain. It was Leonora.

"Stop, Sebastian!" she called, running to catch up with me, her clothes falling from her little by little as she approached me. Her body, bathed in the starlight, was silver. With a voice so soft it seemed to emerge from a beehive deeper than the earth, she spoke:

"Before you go, I want you to know that your appearance has been absolutely essential for me. It goes beyond personal limits, beyond the celestial bodies that shine in the caverns of animal gods, beyond the murmurings of the praying mantis in my hair. It goes beyond that, and yet perhaps, even more, it is still under threat by the human body. I speak as one submerged in time. This umbilical cord exists only if we allow it to exist. You can always cut it, but as long as you want it, it will be there. For you, I am exactly what you desire, but never believe that you can lose me, because my role changes relative to you. That could happen—I could also become your bearded, toothless grandmother or your ghost or even an undefined place. If I withdraw someday, for human or nonhuman reasons, you should never fear to look for me, because you must know always that you will find me when you wish it. Later, we will communicate in such a perfect way that all our terrors and weaknesses will become bridges. Meanwhile, the ways remain warm and open. If by chance you sever ordinary communication for a period, I will be here each time you wish to find me, because the subterranean elements do not depend in the slightest on our personal will."

Worried about her public nudity, I said, "Cover yourself, Leonora; someone might come by." She bent double, as if I had struck her in the stomach.

"You do not yet understand," she groaned. "I am the moon!"

Chiki arrived, carrying an astrakhan cloak. Without deigning to look at me, he covered her, lifted her delicately in his arms as if she were an amphora full of precious liquid, and bore her away.

Dawn was breaking. Ejo Takata would be arising right now to prepare for his morning meditation. I took a bus full of schoolchildren. With little toy bows they shot small paper arrows at me. Suddenly an idea formed in my mind: "I am like St. Sebastian being shot through by koans."

Furious, I returned to the zendo.

4
A Step in the Void

"This is a sacred place," moaned the shepherd.
   "So much the better. The silence will make the bullet even louder."

SILVER KANE, *¡NO HABRÁ TIROS!*
(THERE WILL BE NO GUNSHOTS!)

Ejo received me with a small bow. "Leonora has put you on the very top of the highest mast. What will you do to go farther?"

I was so angry that I could feel the blood rising to my face. I replied: "With lowered head, I will descend until I reach the ground."

In Japanese style, he hesitated between approval and disapproval. "Your answer would be correct if you had the impression that your climb up the mast was an illusory quest. You would be thinking: 'There is no beyond; all that is must be here.' But what is the true nature of this *here?* Is not the world an illusion? On the other hand, at the extreme pinnacle of the mast, where the thinkable dissolves into the unthinkable, if you were afraid of the darkness of the soul and therefore came back down, then you deserve several blows from my stick."

"Ejo, stop playing cat and mouse with me and tell me right now how your own teachers would reply!"

"They would say: 'In order to advance, I take one more step, into the void.' They dare to climb farther, they risk entering the unknown, where there is no measure or signpost, where the *I* is erased, where consciousness raises itself over the world without trying to change it in order to perceive that which is beyond words. There, you have no more definitions; you have nothing. You are only what you are without asking what you are, without comparing yourself to anything, without judging yourself, without any need for honor. Do you understand?"

Sarcastically, I answered, "Yes, I understand, Ejo! My true, eternal, infinite being knows everything! My numberless pockets are full. I need nothing!"

To calm me, the monk had me kneel and gave me three blows on each shoulder blade. Then, in a gesture of false modesty, I joined my hands and bowed. He groaned.

"Well, because that's the way it is, resolve this koan: What will you do to extinguish a lamp that is six hundred miles away?"

After anxious concentration, this response came to me: "I will reach out with an arm that's six hundred miles long!"

I could not tell whether it was with pity or with contempt that he looked at me. "You think you understand. You are clever, but you are blinded by ambition. With that response, you imply that your mind has no limits, that it can attain the infinite—but you do not see that you have put the lamp outside yourself. You think it, but you are not it!"

I now saw my error and was ashamed. "What does the book say?"

"'Without a word, the disciple raised one hand, twirling his thumb and fingers to imitate a flame. Then he blew on it and put out the flame.' There is no distance. The lamp is his thought. When he extinguishes it, he awakens."

"There is still something I don't understand: Why should I extinguish a lamp that for me is the symbol of knowledge and tradition?"

"Symbols have no fixed meaning; they change according to the level of consciousness of whoever contemplates them and the cultural context in which they appear. The lamp we are speaking of here is not carried by a Buddha. It is burning away in a faraway room where there is no one to put it out. It is a waste of fuel. The wisdom that you call 'tradition' is far from your essence. It shines without illuminating anything in you. If you *are* the fathomless night, you need no theories to illuminate you. These so-called teachings only corrupt your darkness. In your cultivation of erudition, you stretch your arm six hundred miles, which takes you farther away from your center. The intellect that burns with a useless flame and does not know how to extinguish itself is constructed of definitions born of the fear of the unthinkable. This is precisely what the following koan refers to: 'A prostitute saved a spirit from the world of suffering by filling a vessel of water and then removing her necklaces and bracelets and plunging them in the water.' And you—how would you save this spirit? Answer!"

"The answer seems obvious, Ejo. I would save it by removing my own ornaments: ambitious thoughts, vain emotions, useless luxuries, self-indulgent definitions, display of my medals and diplomas . . ."

"Enough! Once again, you stir up the surface, thinking you are reaching the depths. Now listen to the traditional answer: The disciple took on the anguished expression of the spirit, and joining his hands, he begged: 'Please save me!' The spirit that the prostitute sees is her own. Because she is all decked out to conquer her clients, she rids herself of her jewelry and throws it into the water, which reflects her own face. In separating herself from her jewels in this way, she sees that they are like the reflection. She abandons her desires and sees the uselessness of seduction, and her illusory individuality disappears. . . .

"When the Buddha saw the present as the world of suffering in which the ego is trapped by its desires, he proclaimed its emptiness. Abhorring sickness, old age, and death, he decided to escape the wheel of reincarnations and never be born again. Yet might it not be that this illusion we call 'ego' is an element essential to perfect realization? Why not consider birth a celebration? Cannot life be happiness when we accept that this ephemeral existence is a degree in eternal existence? If the unthinkable God is in everything, then suffering is nothing more than a concept and consciousness is a treasure accorded us for all eternity. You cannot suffer the loss of something that is not yourself. You are what you are, forever. As bodies grow old, the spirit appears little by little. Time is our friend, for it brings us wisdom. Old age teaches us not to be attached to matter. The banks of a river do not try to keep the water from flowing. Why fear illnesses? They are our allies. Bodily ills reveal problems that we dare not face and heal the illnesses of the spirit. Why be afraid to lose our identity? The summation of all identities is our identity. Why be afraid of abandonment? When we are with ourselves, we always have company. And why be afraid of not being loved? Freedom is to love without asking to be loved in return. As for the fear of being trapped, where is the trap when the universe is our body? Fear of the other? The other is our mirror. Fear of losing a battle? To lose a battle is not to lose ourselves. Fear of humiliation? If we conquer our pride, no one can humiliate us. Fear of the night? Night is inseparable from day. Fear of being sterile? The soul is our supreme daughter."

Ejo Takata now stopped and gave a loud laugh. Then he began to fan himself.

"I have fallen into the trap. I've been vomiting words. My tongue is soiled and your ears are as well. Come into the kitchen, I have a bottle of good sake. Let us drink and give ourselves over to the only valid response for all these questions: silence."

Ceremoniously, we heated the alcoholic rice drink, and the more we drank, the denser our silence became. Ejo seemed more Japanese than ever to me. His slanted eyes regarded me with a reptilian intensity. I do not know whether it was real or the effect of the alcohol, but suddenly, I felt that his mind was a predatory animal trying to get inside my brain. I shook my head violently. "Stop reading my mind!" I cried.

Ejo leaned over on his back, lifted his legs in the air, and emitted a fart so stupendous that the paper walls shook.

Then he took the secret book and began reading: "A long time ago, the magus Daiji traveled from India to the capital of China. He claimed to have the rare power of reading minds. The emperor Daiso commanded his old teacher, Etchu, to test the monk's claims. When Etchu stood before the foreigner, the latter bowed and took a step to the right. Etchu said to the magus, 'If you have the power to read minds, tell me where I am now.'

"Daiji replied, 'You, the master of a nation, how can you go to the Western River to watch a boat race?' 'Tell me where I am now,' Etchu said a second time. 'You, the master of a nation, how can you remain on the Tenshin bridge watching monkeys perform their antics?' A third time Etchu said: 'And now, tell me where I am.' After a long pause, the magus was unable to respond.

"Etchu cried: 'You poor fox, what has become of your ability to read minds?' Daiji gave no answer. Then Etchu returned to the emperor: 'Your Majesty, do not let yourself be fooled by foreigners.'"

Ejo closed the book. "Now *you* answer! Where was the master?"

The sake fumes dissipated quickly from my brain. I felt a wave of cold move through my body. Ejo had taken me by surprise. Myriad explanations swarmed in my mind. Deliberately exaggerating my drunkenness, I rambled haltingly, discovering what I thought as I heard my own words.

"I see a vast palace; fine silk clothes; servants; concubines; priests; lavish banquets; sublime musicians; fierce warriors; and the imposing figure of the emperor, a great statesman, the most powerful of men. Yet the great representative who is capable of making and unmaking the world is behaving as a child before his master. What can a sage teach a person who has everything? Perhaps he can teach him how to die. . . . From the west, the mysterious region where the sun goes down, a magus arrives, wearing the dress of a holy man. He is preceded by a reputation so great that he is received by the emperor. What does this man want? Clearly, he desires to impress the emperor with his gift for reading minds, thereby fascinating him and replacing the old counselor.

Thanks to the shrewdness that has brought him so much power, the emperor sees through the bold plan of the magus. His ability to read minds says nothing about his moral qualities. So he decides to have Etchu, his spiritual teacher, test him. This is the first setback for the magus: to be deprived of direct contact with his intended prey, the emperor himself. Instead, he finds himself before the wisest mind in the country.

"When the magus faces Etchu, he bows to the teacher. The gesture might be sincere, but at the same time he steps to the right, thereby showing his hypocrisy by refusing to face him fully. Like every Zen master, Etchu has meditated for most of his life. He has reduced his needs to a minimum, calmed his passions, filled his heart with peace, ceased to identify himself with his thoughts. He knows that words are not what they designate; he is free of personal mind, for the universal spirit is manifest in him. Possessing nothing, he knows how to be truly responsible and therefore a true servant to the emperor and, through the emperor, to the nation and, through the nation, to all humanity. His mission will be fulfilled only when all living beings attain supreme consciousness. In order to unmask this wily monk who thinks he is wise but whose talent consists only of capturing illusory images by conferring certainty upon them, the sage creates the image of a river with himself watching monkeys. Their antics symbolize those of human beings: The ordinary man is a mere imitator. Like a predator, he seizes others' ideas for himself constantly, without having really lived them. Thus the sage places a mirror before the magus, who expresses surprise that such an important person would amuse himself watching monkeys. In reality, however, it is Etchu who is observing the monkey-like nature of the supposedly omniscient mind of Daiji. The magus is unaware of this and feels certain he has already won with the second test. He thinks he has the old man's number, and, in his vanity, he is already anticipating the prospect of replacing him and gaining power over the emperor. But then Etchu shifts into consciousness of the real. He empties his mind of all thoughts, images, words, feelings, desires, and needs. He does not go anywhere. He is everywhere and nowhere, all and nothing. The ego is gone, the mirror has vanished. Confounded, the magus can find no reflection to seize upon, and he flails and grasps in an empty space. He is unable to read an individual mind that does not exist . . .”

Here I had to stop. “This is a trick, Ejo! In asking me where the master has gone, you underestimate me. We do not 'go' anywhere, we are not the self-image that we fabricate. There is no actor who moves with respect to a spectator. Unity excludes all duality, all change of place.”

Ejo slapped the palm of his hand with his fan. “Bravo! You remind me of a giant steamroller, demolishing the problem. But what do you say right now?” And suddenly he twisted my nose as he asked the last question. I cried out in pain and pushed him away, offended. He looked at me mockingly. “If there is no individual existence, who is it that just cried out and pushed me away?”

He must have known that I had not yet attained a level that would enable me to answer this question, for he did not wait for my reply.

“The first point is this: in your long explanation with all those details, you adopted a position of master yourself and spoke to me as to a student. There's a good illustration of vanity! The second point is that you fell into the trap of idealizing the counselor. You described him as a perfect master who was able to nullify the magus's powers. In our little book, when the disciple is asked where the master is, he exclaims: 'What a pathetic incompetent!' After this there follows a commentary that may well puzzle you: 'When Etchu was twice discovered by Daiji, he was totally overcome by hatred.' In your version, you made the mistake of supposing that the magus was able to read the thoughts that the counselor deliberately allowed him to read in order to expose him. Yet the commentary suggests that in the first two questions, Etchu was possessed by his role of mentor to the emperor. He was not truly himself and was instead identified by his official role of testing Daiji's claims. The first reply came as a surprise and a blow to his pride. He was offended, which enabled Daiji to humiliate him a second time. Only with the third reply did he perceive his error. He then let go of his identification with his role and his desire to please the emperor, abandoning all his official self-importance to become simply Etchu again. This put him in a state of no mind. But this is not some sort of total disappearance. Instead, it is a detachment from past and future to enable him to be only in the mind of the present moment. . . . If it is warm, it is warm; if it is cold, it is cold. The mind does not create any problem beyond the here and now. It responds with absolute immediacy. This does not exclude any sensation of discomfort due to heat or cold, but the mind does not linger on such sensations any longer than the sensation lasts. Do you understand? Now—twist my nose!"

Awkwardly (his nose was rather small), I obliged him. He yelped with pain and jumped back. Then he grinned without the slightest reproach.

"When I feel pain, my mind knows pain. When the pain ends, there is no more pain in my mind. Etchu was insulted by the student because he insulted the magus. In calling him a 'poor fox,' he fell back into his official role, attempting to deny Daiji's powers. Once more, he was overcome by hatred. What a pathetic incompetent! We should be grateful to those who put us in an embarrassing situation that exposes our weaknesses, for it offers us an opportunity to come closer to who we really are. Now tell me very quickly: What is the foremost weakness?"

Like all of Ejo's sudden questions that come like a gunshot just at a time when my mind, absorbed by other thoughts, was not expecting it, this one disconcerted me. I had the sensation of falling from a dream-like summit toward the hard ground of reality. Before me, I saw several levels of weaknesses: moral, physical, sexual, emotional—an avalanche of obstacles seemed to descend upon me, and I felt a weakness in my very essence. Who can claim to be strong when confronted with the inevitability of death? In a tiny voice, I answered: "My greatest weakness is being born."

I will never be able to describe the look Ejo gave me then. It lasted only a fraction of a second, but it reduced me to dust. The depth of my ignorance was revealed to me. Yet instead of acknowledging this revelation, as Etchu did, I immediately fell into anger. I felt like punching him right in his cobralike eyes.

Untroubled and speaking with great tenderness, as if to a child, he whispered: "What a pathetic incompetent!"

Suddenly, I felt I understood the koan. In my very bones I felt what Etchu had experienced. I subdued my anger, joined my palms, and bowed my head.

"Thank you, Sensei."

"Don't bow yet, we haven't gone deeply enough! Here is a koan that is capable of throwing you into the real abyss. Listen: In a temple in Kyoto, why is there a cat in the painting depicting the Buddha's entrance into nirvana?"

I answered with a long string of questions. "Is the cat in nirvana? Is the cat the Buddha's companion? Does the cat come there alone and find the Buddha there? Perhaps the cat is an answer to Joshu's koan: 'Yes, the cat has Buddha nature'? Or is it a symbol? Felines see in the dark; they hunt at night. The Buddha saw in the dark night of the soul, saw through all the mysteries, but if he is depicted as entering nirvana, it means he is not there yet. Perhaps the cat symbolizes the Buddha's animal nature, which is not yet overcome. When the cat disappears, the Buddha will dwell forever in the center of nirvana. Or perhaps the opposite is the answer: the true Buddha is the cat, the animal nature, and the Buddha is one of its dreams. Does that mean that there is no spiritual Buddha, that what really awakens is our body when we see that we are simply animals?"

Ejo gasped for air as if suffocating, fanning himself rapidly. "What a torrent of words—sake ravings! Close your mouth in silence and listen now to the good disciple's answer to the master as recorded in our secret book: 'Why is there no mouse here? And why do you not have a wife?' This disciple does not fall into the trap of drowning himself in speculations, as you do. And why is there no mouse? Why not a monk with a crane's head, a white horse being eaten by nuns, or a heart with four legs of fire, or a mountain of dung giving birth to butterflies? And why do you have no wife, no thousand-pound spider, no mother who flies against the wind? Simply: There is a cat in the painting because the painter painted a cat! How many cats, Buddhas, and nirvanas are churning in your mind?"

My mouth was dry. I felt I could never speak another word without disgust. I took a *zafu* (a black meditation cushion), went upstairs, and sat in the center of the terrace, legs crossed and palms open to the sky, waiting for the dawn to break. I wished for this clear light to cleanse my mind of everything that encumbered my memory. I had a vision of the illusory Tocopilla perched upon the rock, overcome by heat, parched with thirst, squeezed between the sea and the Chilean Cordillera, with its municipal library, about forty square yards of walls covered with bookshelves, the place where I had spent my childhood, friendless, lacking parental affection, reading anything and everything to fill my solitude—my first nirvana, which had pursued me all my life. I voyaged here and there—Santiago, Paris, Mexico City—always hauling boxes with tons of books, re-creating the nostalgic space of my childhood. And the interiors of empty theaters were another nirvana—vacant seats, empty stages, a small service lamp casting a dim light with a grave silence that could have been plundered from a temple, a total break from the miseries of the world. This was also a personal territory, a private palace, a nirvana that became filled with male and female cats when the play began. Capricious actresses, egomaniacal divas, jealous critics, thieving unions, corrupt officials: I had sought them out, seduced them, provoked them, brought them into my life because I wanted to become a famous artist—and then a seductive, revered sage. It was shadows pursuing shadows, the desire to attain the summits of renown so that they would look at me without frowning, so that they would give me prizes, so that the master would declare me a roshi, so that God himself would enter me through my navel and fertilize me, so that I would give birth someday to a perfect mind. . . . In sum, this was how I saw myself in my whole life up to this moment: a painter of Buddhas and cats entering perpetually into an inaccessible nirvana and never arriving at its center!

I tried to cry, then I tried to vomit. Impossible. My legs were tingling with loss of circulation; my eyes were burning, swollen with fatigue. I felt empty but not clean. In my life I had been actor and spectator, and both of them had been sick. The koan had come like a breath of wind, sweeping away the dark clouds that prevent the spectator from knowing the self as impersonal and unlimited. Yet the spectacle of my ignorance, vanity, and so many other miseries caused me great suffering. I felt an unbearable hollowness in my chest. I had never been able to love, because I did not know how to love myself.

Almost insensibly, perhaps because of the fatigue of insomnia, my body arose and went back downstairs into the zendo. Suddenly, I found myself standing before Ejo, sitting in meditation on his platform. I ventured to interrupt him:

"Ejo, I am leaving for good. I am filth. I do not deserve your friendship."

As if feeling my sadness in his own heart, he placed his palms together at his chest and offered me a new koan. "When Master Kyo-o abandoned his mountain monastery, he was given fire as a parting gift. How was he able to carry it?"

Without answering, I walked out of the small meditation room, sat down on the doorstep, and put on my shoes. What good would it do to answer? Whatever my words, the master would make fun of them. If the only true response to a koan is something beyond words manifesting an attitude of living fully in the present, why strive to resolve absurd questions with words? Yet I felt frustrated. I could not help thinking that the fire that Kyo-o was given was spiritual awakening, which he carried by realizing it. He did not leave the monastery in a spirit of rejection; quite the contrary. He left it as a butterfly leaves its caterpillar chrysalis, for his metamorphosis is accomplished. Kyo-o left as a victor, but I was leaving as a loser. What is enlightenment? The truth was, I still imagined it as a marvelous object of attainment, a gift, a fire that would fill my mind, consuming everything—my concepts, my self-image, the mirages that I called reality . . . but Ejo Takata had given me nothing save blows and mockery. At that moment, I thought, "I am nothing, I know nothing, I can do nothing," and I began to weep convulsively.

The next thing I knew, Ejo was beside me, caressing my head.

"Do you know what Kyo-o did when they offered him the fire? He opened the large sleeve of his kimono, and said 'Please put it here.' Sometimes, giving is knowing how to receive. Sometimes, offering is not giving. Who can give you what you already have? Is awakening a sort of currency that passes from hand to hand? How can fire be offered apart from the wood in which it burns? Life is the oil that saturates the torch, and the torch is you. It is you who burn. When you consume yourself and there is no more wood or flame, you return to ashes, scattered by the wind. And your ashes are like mine, like those of Kyo-o or the Buddha. You have put all your energy into trying to possess something. Have you ever once surrendered?"

"Ejo, the truth is that my head is full and my heart is empty. I have lost the capacity to receive without barriers. I have deprived myself of the fire that this word *enlightenment* has perverted. I want to change, but I do not ask myself why I want to change or what I want to become. I try to eliminate the symptoms rather than the cause of my suffering. Among the gamut of pains, I have chosen the least. I cannot imagine feeling good; I aspire to feel only not too bad. . . . But where is the joy of life in all this? How can each new day become a day of celebration? Will I ever resolve the primary koan of accepting to die? Will I ever be able to say, as the old beggar says: 'I am even greater than God, because I am nothing'? Sincerely, I don't believe so."

Sadly, I murmured, "*Arigato* (thank you)," and I left the zendo, deciding then never to return.

As I went back to my home along the endless Insurgentes Avenue, a dark-skinned, effeminate boy, fifteen years old at most, approached me with an uncertain smile. He wore tight pants and a sleeveless shirt.

"Give me twenty dollars, and I am yours," he said.

The frustration that had accumulated in me because of my failure in Zen washed over me like a raging sea, and I punched the poor boy in the chest. He fell down, sitting. When he got up, I ran after him for almost a block, kicking at his behind. Then, continuing on my way, I began to speak to myself aloud: "I, too, deserve to be kicked in the ass! I'm a spiritual whore, inviting the Buddha to possess me and offer me enlightenment as payment. I've had enough! Meditating, immobile as a statue, serves no purpose! I must be honest with myself. I must confess what it is I am really looking for."

That same day, the Gurza brothers contacted me, surrounded by their usual aura of marijuana smoke. They owned many animals, which they rented to the film studios at Churubusco. "The Tigress saw your photo in a magazine. She said you please her, and she wants to meet you." I was terrified. They were referring to Irma Serrano, a famous Mexican pop singer. A millionaire whose strange beauty was due to extensive cosmetic surgery, she was rumored to be the mistress of the president of Mexico. It was also said that he had lost an eye when she broke a chair over his head in a fit of jealousy. Yet in spite of my fear, I decided to visit her that very evening at her theater. Perhaps this Tigress was what I was looking for: a ferocious female who could help me to take root in this land of Mexico, which so fascinated me.

5

The Slashes of the Tigress's Claws

⟨✦⟩

Her voice was grating and harsh, like the sound of the lid
of a badly made coffin.

SILVER KANE, *LA HIJA DEL ESPECTRO*
(THE SPECTER'S DAUGHTER)

Behind the dilapidated post office, amid bars, billiard halls, huge fruit stores, and hideous apartment buildings, the Frou-Frou Theater's doors were open like an absurd flower. At the end of a long corridor whose walls were covered with photos of the Tigress, there stood a coffinlike counter and a cagelike ticket office protected with iron bars. Gloria, the cousin of the star, was counting the receipts of the performance already underway. To my great surprise (we had never been introduced), she emerged from her cage and embraced me enthusiastically.

"I heard about the reception of your film in Acapulco. The audience wanted to lynch you. Bravo! The boss will be very happy to see you—she loves scandals."

She ushered me into the theater. Proudly, she showed me the vast salon and bar decorated in "French" style with two dominant colors: crimson and gold. There were little angels, floral motifs, Louis XV armchairs, dwarf palms, satin drapes, frivolous posters—and standing right the middle of all this bric-a-brac, there was a larger-than-life statue representing the naked Tigress. It had an upright bust, stringy arms, and voluminous thighs on colossal legs. Such bad taste made me want to laugh, but all mirth died on my lips when Gloria pointed to a certain place on the floor and told me: "Under that spot three sheep lie buried. To ensure prosperity, my boss had them slaughtered in a satanic ritual. Ever since, we've had sold-out houses every night."

Then she led me into the theater, and offered me a special seat. Most of the audience seemed to be working-class males. There was an odor of mingled sweat and church incense. "This is the last act of *Nana*," she whispered. "A prostitute lives in luxury, kept by bankers and aristocrats, but everyone abandons her in the end when she catches smallpox. I'll take you backstage when it's over."

In a sordid room, Nana was lying on a bed of burlap potato sacks stuffed with cotton. A dark veil covered her pockmarked face as she sang a song of farewell to life. Suddenly, a huge drunken man in the front row started yelling: "No clothes! No clothes!" I shrank in my seat. This sort of hoi polloi came here only for sexual excitement. In some of the city's theaters, a rumba dancer would even challenge a spectator to copulate with her on stage "because you're so macho." Such men had not the slightest interest in scenes of dying singers covered from head to toe. At first the Tigress merely gave him a baleful look without halting her swan song, but now he was standing and leaning over the stage, shouting even louder and adding phrases such as, "Show your tits!" and "Show your ass!"

Suddenly, she leaped off the bed and walked off stage. She quickly returned with a large pistol, walked up to the big man, and pressed the barrel against the front of his head. "Now listen, you son of a whore of a mother who gave birth to you! I don't come harassing you in the middle of your work. So don't come here fucking around with us artists! You either shut your mouth or you'll wake up in hell with a hole in the front of your head! You understand?" By now the drunk lowered his upper body face down upon the stage and began kissing her feet. He answered in a child's voice, "Yes, my little mother." A large ovation from the audience supported her. Then the Tigress resumed her place upon the bed—still holding the pistol—and finished her song. There was a religious silence at the end; the curtain had already begun to fall when thunderous applause broke out. I could feel fascination, desire, and fear in the air. The big drunk applauded louder than anyone.

Gloria came for me and had me sit behind the curtain on a corner of the stage. "The boss is freshening up. She'll have to sign a few autographs, and then she'll receive you. She wants to see you alone. Chucho will keep you company while you're waiting." Chucho had long false eyelashes, fluorescent red lipstick, and a plaster cast on his right wrist. Uncomfortable with his arch winks, I asked him about the cast.

"Oh! During the scene when the Tigress sings and dances, fondled by her admirers, I squeezed her leg too hard. It enraged her, and right there in front of everyone, she broke my wrist. Then—though you'll find this hard to believe—she dragged me off stage by the hair of my head!"

My mouth was dry and I was feeling distinctly ill at ease. I noticed that the stagehands, seeing me talking with Chucho, were making obscene jokes about my manhood. Offended, I strode backstage and gave a sharp knock on the Tigress's door. A husky, mocking voice answered, "Enter if you dare."

It was as if I had entered the cage of a wild beast. A person never forgets even a glimpse of a woman like that. The carnivorous look in her large eyes showed no sign of any sort of pity. Her lush, black hair surrounded the face of a country girl transformed by skillful surgery into that of an Aztec princess. Her teeth had even been filed, though not pointed, in order to suggest knife blades. Two silicon-enhanced breasts strained at an almost transparent bodice. Her very large legs were resting upon the dressing table. With her back reclining against the wicker chair, she regarded me in the mirror. A carelessly painted beauty mark glistened between her eyebrows, a little off-center. I wondered if this error might be due to the length of her clawlike false nails. It was impossible to guess her age. The surgery made her look thirty, but she might have been more than forty. Her voice was impossible to describe. Every word she spoke floated upon a muffled growl. At any moment, her words could become daggers. I tried to gather my courage.

"I have very much wanted to meet you, Madame. I congratulate you for your performance!"

"If you want to have an affair with me, don't ever lie to me, you bastard. When I perform, I'm aware of everyone in the audience. When I was crying, you had to keep from laughing. Of course, this isn't your sort of avant-garde cinema. But anyway, I also wanted to meet you."

She lowered her legs. Her fine-pointed high heels scraped the floor, making a wailing sound. "I'm tired of standing up. The surgical filling in my calves weighs four pounds, but the masses get hysterical when I expose them."

From a closet filled with gaudy costumes, she took a bottle of mezcal. Its label showed a crow perched on a skull. "Now let's see if you're an *hombre*," she said, filling two water glasses full of this corrosive liquid. "Bottoms up!"

I accepted the challenge and drained the whole glass without stopping. She did likewise and filled the glasses again: "Bottoms up!" And again, we drained our glasses.

"Steady on now, don't fall by the wayside!" she said.

"I'm quite steady, thank you, Madame—more so than you."

After seven glasses, I saw a greenish aura around the empty bottle. "She is calling for her sister," said the Tigress, and set down another full bottle. I was so drunk I had to hold on to my chair, but I continued to imbibe. She began to make a halting speech, finding it difficult to get from one concept to the next.

"I am what I want to be, that is my law. . . . When I first came here from my village, I felt defenseless before men. By luck, Diego Rivera had me model for his murals. . . . One afternoon, an Indian whom the painter knew well arrived from the mountains with a package. 'Here you are, boss,' he said. 'Good fresh human meat. I guarantee that it was a Christian in good health. I killed him myself.' Diego roasted the bloody meat on a spit, cut it into small pieces accompanied with chopped onions, coriander, and chili peppers, and made tacos, which he shared with me. . . . As I chewed this delicious meat, the beast that had been sleeping in me awoke. I could eat men. . . . I could make them fall to their knees before me. . . . In order to accomplish this, all I would have to do is transform my body into the body of their ape dreams. Big breasts? I'll give them big breasts. Big buttocks? I got them with three hundred gelatin injections. Little by little, as my songs became hits, I saved up money for surgery on my cheeks, my chin, my full lips, my eyelids, hair implants, a thin waist. . . . Hell, creating your own body is just as impressive as creating a painting! I am the daughter of my own willpower. In my shadow, not even God calls the shots. . . . Besides, I've sent God to hell and chosen the devil. He's a lot more useful. He buys your soul, he gives you power—and that's everything in this world. . . . What do you think? Anyway, no matter what you say, you're risking your life with me. My master is a jealous one . . ."

In the dense alcoholic fog, struggling with my swollen tongue and my lust to possess this arrogant woman, I found myself reciting a koan: "What is the way?"

Quickly, the Tigress interrupted me, "I'm not a railroad track; don't ask me. And you—do you know what the way is?"

This contemptuous retort made me aware of my mental confusion. The crow and the skull, life and death, good and evil, truth and lies—how to choose? In my all-consuming desire to master consciousness, I had lost the way. Tears came to my eyes as I quoted Master Haryo: "Because I was an open eye, I fell into the well." The Tigress burst out laughing. She rocked so hard against the back of her chair that it fell over. Sprawled on the floor with open legs, showing me that dark mouth that all Mexicans desired to see, she said: "Good. Now, open your eyes and forget your bullshit way. Fall into my well—but I warn you, it has no bottom."

Suddenly, all my reason vaporized. Heedless of the consequences, I leaped at this wild beast on the floor, lifting her up with great effort (her body seemed to weigh a ton). Then, half undressed, I had her straddle my back. She giggled like a girl. We both arose and staggered out of the dressing room. Laughing constantly, we stumbled on, ignoring the astonished stares of the stagehands, dancers, and striptease artists. We walked out of the theater toward the street exit. Gloria ran behind us, speaking with urgency: "Beware, my boy! Get her into the car very quickly so that the caliph doesn't find out and make mincemeat out of you!"

A long, silver limousine with a chauffeur dressed like a Mexican cavalier pulled up in front of us. I got her inside and sat beside her. We began fondling and kissing each other with brutal, drunken lust. A small overhead lamp cast a dim light in the interior of the car.

"Turn it off, faggot!" she ordered the chauffeur.

"I can't, boss; my orders are to have it lit at all times."

"No one spies on me!" She smashed the lamp with her fist and wiped the blood from her knuckles on the seat of the car.

"And lower that fucking mirror—if you try to spy on us, I'll tear out your eyes!" Obediently, the chauffeur lowered the rearview mirror, relying only on the side-view mirrors as he drove. Then, with no witnesses in sight, we attempted to make love in the shadows, but we both passed out.

When I awoke, I had lost all sense of time. The Tigress snored, her head on my lap. The car was gliding through quiet streets in a wealthy neighborhood. Only high walls could be seen, hiding the houses behind them. We pulled up before a vast edifice, an imitation medieval castle built out of cement. The front gate lowered like a drawbridge.

The Tigress awoke abruptly and gave me a strange look. I thought she was going to bite me, but then she smiled and looked carefully out the window. "Get out with your head lowered, and go inside fast. Don't let them get a photograph of your face. The caliph has spies in the house across the street."

I did so and entered the anteroom of the castle. I was standing in front of the statue of an enormous devil with raised wings and a huge phallus. Offerings of flowers, marzipan fruits, and incense sticks were scattered at its feet. As in the Frou-Frou, everything was colored red and gold.

The Tigress waited for an old lady dressed in a Huichol Indian costume to turn the handle that raised the gate. She took me by the hand, saying, "The chauffeur will sleep in the limousine. When you leave, wake him up and tell him to take you to a taxi stand. Never let him take you to your house. I think he is also a spy. If they find out where you live, they could send guerillas there to castrate you. Now come with me!"

She led me through her castle. In the kitchen there was barely room for an enormous Chinese banquet table with twelve chairs decorated with monks and dragons. In the saloon I saw a magnificent 1950s phonograph and awnings decorated with photos of various Mexican presidents, especially Diaz Ordaz, with his big mouth and his tiny, fanatical iguana eyes.

We crossed a small cactus garden, arriving at her bedroom door. I drew back in surprise, seeing that a real, live tiger seemed to be lying there! She gave a cruel chuckle. "Whoever wants paradise must deserve it. Stroke his back. If he growls, it means he accepts you and you can go in. But if he doesn't like you—well, I won't say what will happen."

Though I could now see that the cat was not so big, the hair on my neck was bristling and my body was trembling. Nevertheless, my pride made me not only stroke the beast but also massage its neck. Soon, not only did it growl, it turned over on its back with lazy sensuality and offered me its stomach to scratch. The Tigress now made fun of me:

"Actually, it's a harmless ocelot. I've had its teeth and claws removed." And she pushed me into the room.

The bed was round with blood-red silk sheets and covers. At the head there was an enormous seashell ten feet high and about seven feet wide with a predictable gold color. On one side of the bed was a holster with a large revolver and extra ammunition.

"Now the tourist visit is over. Get undressed."

Lighting a violet candle, she turned out the lights. I found myself stretched out next to the naked Tigress in the middle of the red circle. I tried to excite her by caressing her smooth, cold body with my humid hands. It felt as though it was not flesh I was touching. Her breasts, her legs, and her buttocks were as hard as marble. Also, she was totally passive, which caused my erotic passion to wither. In a few seconds, my phallus became a mere penis.

Seeing this, she demanded, without an ounce of sympathy: "You must do everything. I have no reason to do anything at all."

"But . . ." I stammered, "it's impossible like this. After all that mezcal, fatigue, and danger, you won't even participate. It's too difficult . . ."

"Shut up. I don't want to hear your excuses. If you don't get it up, I'll tell the journalists and all Mexico will know that you're impotent."

It was a serious threat. She had important connections to the media. If I did not succeed, I would be humiliated by banner headlines in the newspapers.

I concentrated as never before. Rummaging in all my pornographic memories, I opened the doors to everything bestial in myself. After a short but agonizing moment, I had an erection. Fearing that it might be short-lived, I climbed immediately onto the statue and, with the aid of saliva, began to penetrate her indifferent vagina—but she stopped me. "Calm down, artist. You've proved that you can do it. Even more important, you've proved it to yourself. That's enough. I don't need your sperm. What I want is your talent. With this act, we've signed a contract. We're going to work together. I have a big project, but now I want you to let me sleep. Leave quickly. The caliph could arrive at any moment, and what belongs to him . . . never mind. Come to the theater tomorrow."

She inserted earplugs, closed her eyes, turned over on her stomach, and fell into such a deep sleep that it seemed like an implosion.

The object of lust for thousands of Mexicans, not only because of her voluptuous curves (artificial or not) but also because of her legend as the presidential whore, the Tigress had attained a status of mythic femininity rivaled only by the Virgin of Guadalupe. In spite or because of this, she now occupied the summit of my mental pyramid. She was an authentic warrior, knowing how to survive and prevail in a world dominated by corrupt politicians. If she had to give her body, she managed to do it without dishonor, distancing herself from it and transforming herself into an invulnerable and implacable creature. The people had reason to elevate her to a popularity comparable to that of the dark Virgin—for this woman was able to maintain an impenetrable purity in her mind. To seduce her, to succeed in inflaming her real desire, to become the soul of her inward castle seemed like an impossibility to me. I knew that she regarded our relationship as a game of chess in which I was a simple pawn to be moved by her—and this fascinated me. I was curious to see how she would use me, and I wondered how I would be able to transform this humiliating situation into a victory. A true koan!

As I waited on the stage for her to finish her autographs, Chucho bustled up to me, whispering with a confidential air, "Hey, you—I don't know why I should take a liking to you, but that's how it is. I'm offering you a warning. That woman is a real witch. Her chauffeur, who knows quite a few things, told me (for a bribe) that he drove her to a sordid neighborhood where sorcerers live, and that they sold her a plant that had been germinated in the sperm of a hanged man. Who did they hang to get the sperm? We'll never know. Did they also splatter the poor Christian with dog's blood? We'll never know. The Tigress paid a big wad of bills for that plant. Then she peeled the plant, sprinkled it with lemon juice, and ate it. *Ugh*—how dreadful! But that's not all. A week ago, they brought her a live badger. She called me into her dressing room and made me hold the poor animal down while she slit its throat. That's exactly what she did. Then she took a black knife and dug through the dead animal's organs, looking for something. I was so horrified I closed my eyes. When I opened them again, she was holding a small bone, and she put it into a powerful blender with I don't know what horrible liquid inside it, ground it all together, and drank the mixture. It's obvious that woman is capable of doing anything to obtain power. You be careful or you'll wind up like that little badger's bone."

Now Chucho was staring at the other side of the theater with a fearful expression. "What do you see up there, in that old disused balcony condemned by the theater authorities, to the left of the front row?"

"I think it's a mannequin dressed in old-fashioned clothes . . ."

"That's right. But that dummy is possessed by the devil. No one is ever allowed up there. It's crowded with old, useless debris. Yet every night, the dummy changes its place. Mireya, a dancer friend of mine, ridiculed our fear of it. One night, at midnight, she sneaked up onto the balcony, cleared her way to the dummy, threw it on the floor, and stomped it to pieces. The next night, it was sitting in an armchair, completely intact. From that time on, Mireya has been cursed by horrible luck. Her agent put a bullet through his head, her father was murdered, her fiancé left her for another woman, and now she has become obese and has had to quit dancing. She went on all sorts of diets but gained a hundred pounds. She finally went insane, dreaming every night of being devoured by a pack of dogs."

Noticing my skeptical look, Chucho shrugged, turned away huffily, and left, dismissing me forever from his sphere of interest.

As I continued to wait for the Tigress, sitting on the same burlap sacks where Nana sang her swan song twice a day, I dismissed the perturbations in my mind caused by the dancer's gossip and arch looks and tried to concentrate on my own reactions.

Mexico: a country where two old women organized a concentration camp for prostitutes, exploiting them and then murdering them by the dozens; a country where a schoolteacher strangled his mother, ate her entire body, bones and all—and then, in prison, having already experienced the supreme culinary delight, refused any other food and died of hunger; a country where a famous singer killed herself by swallowing a glass full of needles; a country that has an entire market specializing in sorcery materials right in the center of the capital; a country in which a male prostitute, just before servicing an aged tourist, makes the sign of the cross with his penis, waving it in the four directions and thereby transforming his sordid virility into a sacred act. Yes, I could well believe anecdotes about mandrake plants and badgers, but a lifeless mannequin animated by the devil was a bit much. Yet in Tepozotlán, in times of drought, prominent elder citizens speak to the mountain (which appears to them in a vision as a white-bearded man), offering candles, T-shirts, and house shoes to induce him to bring rain; and in the back room of an esoteric bookstore, a Huichol shaman comes once a week to cure patients by sucking out their sickness and then spitting it out in the form of pebbles; and the grandmother who eats sacred mushrooms leaves her body and enters other people's dreams; and in the mountains live sorcerers who claim to transform themselves into crows or dogs.

How much truth is there in all this? Over the real world soars an imaginary world that is far more active. If the truth is that all is illusion, then I must learn to imitate life. I thought of the Tibetan holy man Marpa,* who grieved inconsolably over his dead son. His disciples asked him: "But Master, why do you weep when you have taught us

*Marpa Lotsava (1012–1097 CE) was a Tibetan master and translator who made several voyages to India, studying and transmitting the Dharma (the Buddha's teaching). He is famous as the master of Milarepa. The end of his life was marked by the death of his son, Darme Dode.

that all is illusion?" The old man answered: "It is true, my son was an illusion—but he was the most beautiful of illusions!"

Reality is aggressive, murderous, unknown, and ugly. Only illusory beauty makes it bearable. If truth is a fathomless mystery, then we can only edify it with lies. As for myself, I seemed to be playing the role of an artist, sitting in this imitation Italian theater, watching an imitation French melodrama that's played by a diva with an imitation body of Venus who owns an imitation castle with a tame ocelot that imitates a fierce tiger and sleeping in a bed with a huge seashell at its head in imitation of Botticelli. And what if the story about her being the mistress of the president of Mexico turned out be just another lie, a rumor she cultivated? Perhaps even the fat drunk whom she threatened with a revolver was a hired plant. How did I know she had even met Diego Rivera, with whom she claimed to have eaten tacos containing cooked human flesh? Even the story about selling her soul to the devil could be seen as self-promotion. A person could easily arrange for the porter to earn a bonus by moving the mannequin each night when the theater was locked and no one could see him. Even if all this was true, however, I realized I was still interested in her. Even if she used trickery, she was still a magician capable of organizing the imaginary world and living in it.

With the exception of Ejo Takata, I had always lived among human beings who were incapable of being themselves, who always wanted to have what others had, who creating facades, copied values, schemed to obtain diplomas, danced for pay in a barbarous carnival. I'm not saying I felt superior to them, but I certainly felt like a foreigner—not in some other country, but in strangeness, the unreal zone of the unadapted: "to be in the world, but not of it." This was of no help to me, for my soul, like an exhausted bird flying over the scene of a disastrous deluge, could find no place to land. If I learned to die as an intellectual, no place in the illusion could harbor me. Reality—that which is without beginning or end—seemed impalpable, indifferent, with no relation to my life, a life that was 99 percent antisocial. At that moment, sitting upon those absurd burlap sacks, I understood that the Tigress, queen of the world of imitation, could, through her poisonous machinations, become the guide who would give me the necessary maturity to build a temple in the dimension of mirages.

When I entered her dressing room, she was wearing only panties of minuscule size and was occupied with the task of putting black dye on the long hairs on her legs. "I want them to see that I'm not another Indian but the descendant of Spaniards!"

I sensed that in her feline mind I was conquered prey. Now I was so much hers that she didn't bother to hide her tricks from me. It was not a female seductress that I saw before me, but a cold strategist.

"We're going to bring down the house and give them the scoop of the year! You are an avant-garde director whose audience never amounts to more than a thousand people, but the critics praise you because they believe that everything European is worthy of admiration. For me, they have only derision. What I do seems contemptible to them. Yet my audience is never less than five hundred. I think we must unite our forces. Using all your talent, you shall direct me in a theater piece which will please the people. We'll create a brilliant and lavish production of *Lucretia Borgia.* You'll have a percentage of the profits. You've never made a peso with your obscure, incomprehensible films. With me, you'll be rich. Is it a deal?"

The prospect of directing her fascinated me. "It's a deal!"

"I knew you'd like the idea—but we must proceed carefully. We don't want to rush our car down a slope that drops us off a cliff. If we offer this me-and-you cocktail too suddenly, it would be undrinkable, both for the pop audience and for the intellectuals. We must file and smooth the rough patches, creating a huge sense of expectation. I don't mean an artistic one—that wouldn't bring any audience at all; I mean a sexy one. Fame is nothing; notoriety is everything. Only scandal brings success. I'm going to propose something outrageous now. I'm telling you in advance not to worry, your life will be in no danger, because the caliph will know it's all fake and will agree to the plan. What we shall do is announce that we have fallen in love and are going to get married!"

"Er, I regret to say that although the idea seems excellent, we can't just do it like that. You see, I'm already married."

"Who do you think you're dealing with? I have my sources. Your wife, Valerie, wants success as an actress. You are her sun; she orbits around you. If you promise her a good role, with her name in huge letters on the marquee, she'll do anything you ask of her."

"Anything but divorce. And I don't want that either."

"Nor do I! Don't you get it? The whole thing from A to Z will be fake. When we announce that the great avant-garde theater director is divorcing his wife for the vulgar Tigress, the newspapers will eat it up. During the rehearsals, your wife will fake a suicide attempt. You and I, in our extravagant compassion, will help her out of her depression by offering her the role of a witch, the enemy of Lucretia. And we can count on people's morbid curiosity to fill the theater; they'll want to see our tormented triangle acted out on stage. We'll rake in the profits as you've never imagined!"

"When should we announce it?"

"Next week, in a big hotel on Reforma Avenue, all the journalists will be celebrating Press Day. Because the hotel offers free dinner and drinks in exchange for the publicity, all the scroungers are bound to be there—reporters, editors, photographers, critics, TV and movie stars, athletes—in short, the cream of the shit of the Mexican media. Right in the middle of the festivities, we'll drop the bomb!"

Valerie and I went over the Tigress's plan point by point. The first obstacle we had to overcome were the doormen, five guerillas who absolutely demanded a photo ID of every guest. The Tigress had obtained one for herself and one for me, because we were known artists. Valerie, however, was still unknown, and had no access to Parnassus. We decided to hide her in the trunk of the limousine. The plan was for her to lie there for an hour until the time was right. This was made even more difficult by the Tigress's insistence that Valerie wear a plaster cast on her leg to appear with a limp.

Inside, obscure reporters wandered around with a bored air. For once, they instead of "stars" were the ones being honored. Nevertheless, there was a constant clicking of hidden cameras, like a chorus of crickets. The stars were there, walking around with a false ease, aware constantly of being reduced to images.

When the Tigress and I entered together, hand in hand, they all froze for a minute then got on with their farce, trying to hide their curious glances at us behind a ridiculous air of indifference. No one seemed to notice us, but we knew we were center stage in their minds. I was dressed in a very sober black suit, but my companion wore a brazenly transparent chemise; leather spike heels eight inches long, her naked legs sporting her hairs, dyed bright silver for this occasion; and a skirt covered with green, white, and red sequins—the color of the Mexican flag. The skirt was so short that every swishing step she made revealed her crotch. In order to hide the intimacy of her real vagina, she wore a specially made shell covered with what seemed to be pubic hair. Glued to her vulva, it suggested that any possibility of penetration was forbidden. This detail inspired a cynical explosion of flashbulbs.

We took our seats in the most distant corner. This was Press Day and the tacit agreement was that no journalist was supposed to try to interview us. Nevertheless, they walked back and forth in front of us like hungry dogs. An hour passed. Only the bones of the banquet were left on the table. Cheap rum had replaced the good drinks. The guests were now beginning to weave and stagger as if on an ocean liner in heavy weather. The sound of voices, which had been clear before, thickened into a gelatinous rumble. This was the moment the Tigress had chosen for Valerie's entrance.

She duly appeared with her leg in the cast, holding two crutches. Her dress was ordinary and full of stains, her hair was greasy, her face was without makeup, and her eyes were full of artificial tears. She seemed plunged into deepest sadness. Like a wounded crow, she made her way across the room, directly toward us. In an instant, the alcoholic fog lifted. As Valerie arrived at our table, she let a crutch fall. In the deadly silence, it bounced loudly on the floor. Then she took me by the hand and began moving her lips. Her voice was so low no one could hear what she said (in reality, she was reciting multiplication tables), but everyone believed she was imploring me. I moved my lips in reply, gesturing with my hand toward the Tigress. Of course they interpreted this as my telling her that I loved the other woman. Valerie collapsed onto a chair. I gathered her crutches, helped her up, and accompanied her to the door, and she exited the scene. Then I came back to my chair next to the Tigress and pretended to break into tears. Still showing her crotch, she took my arm and left with me, practically dragging me along. Hardly had the door closed when we heard a deafening uproar of voices break out behind it.

Just as predicted by this clever scheme, the entire Mexican press, from the most abject rags to the most "serious" journals, announced the event in headlines. On that day alone, tickets sold out for the next three months of performances.

Events were now happening rapidly. In two hours of concentrated work, I managed to concoct a medley of situations that could have come from the lowest-grade novels and films, added some songs, and finally arrived at an erotico-musical tragedy that the Tigress demanded to sign as coauthor. I brought together a troupe of respectable actors, found a high-quality stage designer, a very talented musician, an excellent choreographer, and a very fashionable Argentine singer for the important role of Julius Caesar. In ten days, rehearsing twelve hours a day, I fixed the style of the actors' interpretations, the décor, the dances, costumes, and musical accompaniments. And I accomplished all of this without the presence of our Lucretia, whom we had decided would prepare her songs separately. When she finally was to appear in rehearsal, we were waiting with great enthusiasm and impatience, eager to see the creation of the complex character of the poisoner. I was confident that, with intense work, I would be able to present her to the public transformed into a great actress. Rehearsal time was set for nine in the morning, but the Tigress did not show up. Five hours passed. We left to eat some cheese crepes. When we returned, she was still not there. At six o'clock the stagehands evicted us, because they had to set up for the 7:30 performance of *Nana*. Worried, I asked Gloria if her cousin was sick. She only shrugged, dashing my hopes.

"That's the way my boss is. She doesn't like rehearsals. She's very tired when she finishes performing. She sleeps late and then has to deal with the press, her makeup, and so forth, and the day just goes by."

"But what are we going to do if she doesn't rehearse?"

"Trust her! On opening night, right in the middle of your strict scene, she'll improvise everything. And don't worry about her memorizing the text; she has these little electronic devices to wear in her ears, and a prompter will be whispering her lines to her."

I paled. I was about to protest, but Gloria changed the subject.

"How is your wife doing? Are the rehearsals going well for her? No problems?"

"None. She is a responsible individual. Her sorceress will be a true creation."

"I must warn you to beware. In my boss's mind, though these press stories are of course instigated by her, what the media say is more real than the truth. This morning, she sent me to a pet store to buy a black cat, and she also had me buy silk ribbons and beeswax. I'm sure she's preparing a curse to separate couples. With the beeswax she'll make two dolls, a man and a woman. After painting them with her menstrual blood, she'll pin photos of you and Valerie on the head of each doll. Then she'll fasten them to two boards with black, white, and red ribbons woven together, and throw the boards in two gutters, very far away from each other. . . . I repeat: Beware! Don't drink anything she offers you. She's planning to sacrifice the cat, and she'll try to get you to drink a bit of its blood, which could be mixed with anything. Also, she'll keep the severed head of the cat in her refrigerator, and in its mouth will be the names of you and Valerie, written on a bow of ribbons stolen from a cemetery. The head will remain in the refrigerator until the day you separate."

In spite of my awareness that the cousin could be lying about this, I felt a shudder through my entire body. I remembered a koan from the secret book that I hadn't understood until then: "While Master Rinzai was going toward the great hall to give a speech, a monk interrupted him: 'What if they threaten us with a sword?' Rinzai muttered: 'Disaster! Disaster!' and added the commentary: 'When waves rise up like mountains and fish become dragons, it is stupid to use a bucket to try to empty the ocean.'"

Rinzai was about to speak to his disciples—in other words, to use intellectual means to communicate knowledge to them. The monk was saying that beautiful ideas are useless in the face of an enemy who can kill us. Yet Rinzai's repetition of the word *disaster* did not refer to the impotence of the intellect when we have a sword at our throat. Nor was he saying that to be threatened with death is simply a catastrophe, in spite of all edifying teachings. The two disasters refer instead to the notion that the monk held of himself and of his master. When teachings are reduced to mere explanations, it is a disaster, because the monk is identified with his own intellect. When we identify ourselves with a system of ideas, with who we think we are, then we are paralyzed with the fear of losing ourselves in the face of death. But Rinzai has realized his awakening and surrendered to the simple happiness of being. He has ceased to identify himself with his own image and dwells in inner silence. He is not identified with his teachings, for they are not himself; they are only efforts to describe impersonally the way to peace.

Takata said of this koan: "Some come, others go. I am a stone on the road. Rinzai tells the monk: 'You see yourself and me as two minds. Disaster and disaster. That is why you think a sword could upset us. A murderer might be able to cut off my head without blinking an eye, but I can also let my head be cut off without blinking an eye.' Even when the waves and sea creatures attack you (for reality does not behave according to your expectations), your inner silence is unperturbed. To measure life with your intellect is as stupid as trying to empty the ocean with a bucket. Zen is the same, whether in the peace of a monastery or in the midst of combat. The disaster is not in the attack. Let go of the separate self and give yourself to the combat with joy, as if it were a dance with yourself."

I brought the members of the troupe together and calmly informed them of the problem. I proposed that we walk out on the Tigress and find another theater where we could stage an honest performance with a genuine actress. With the exception of the Argentine singer, everyone agreed that it was degrading for us to serve the vanity of a capricious diva, and they decided to follow me.

The newspapers were chock-full of headlines announcing the end of the romance. Finally, someone had dared to defy the Tigress . . . and her response was not long in coming. It was a low blow, something I had not expected at all. In several tabloids headlines appeared that said such things as "Avant-garde Artist Swindles the Tigress!" Others said I was in hiding, sought by the police. The diva herself was quoted as saying I had stolen a large sum of her money. In their legal consequences, these lies were harmless, but they certainly succeeded in tarnishing my image. I could have denied the libel strenuously, but in Mexico it seemed useless, because of the power of the proverb, "Where there's smoke, there's fire." So now I was a crook.

This insult created a breach in my intellect, like a koan. My feeling of shame became a good lesson. Until this point, my disputes with the Tigress had been a kind of game, a sort of artistic bargaining. By accusing her of laziness, it's true that I was making fun of her, but with a sane humor and one that was based on truth. She had responded with the arms at her disposal: newspaper scandals and clever lies. I had discredited her artistically, but she had demolished me socially. I recalled her words spoken with great conviction during the night of our mezcal drunken session: "A small, weak boxer is in the ring with a big, strong adversary. The big guy starts to beat up the little guy. Now that little guy is me. When the big guy rushes at me for the KO, I pull a pistol out of one of my gloves and shoot him. Never fight an even battle!"

Another attack occurred, whether organized by her or simply a random act of violence inspired by the climate of tension. Late at night, unknown vandals threw rocks at my house, breaking all the windows. I rented an apartment in the suburbs and began to slink down public streets, breathing anxiously. I had the impression that a thug might jump out and shoot me at any moment. But after a few days, I became ashamed of giving way to such panic. I thought of a koan from the secret book: "Master Ungo meditated with his disciples in a place known as the Dragon Door. One day, one of the monks was bitten on the leg by a serpent. Master Botsugen said to Ungo: 'How can your disciple be bitten by a serpent at the Dragon Door?' Ungo replied by jerking up his leg, as if he had been bitten by a serpent, and calmly saying, 'Ouch.'"

In China the mythical dragon is the guardian of hidden treasure. In order to attain immortality, the hero must conquer this powerful adversary. The terrestrial dragon grows wings and is transformed into the celestial dragon. In other words, the self cannot prevail until it has integrated and tamed unconscious drives.

Botsugen's question insinuates that the perfect dragon (the enlightened monk) should not fall victim to the evils of the material world (the serpent's bite), but Ungo avoids this trap, suggesting that awakening does not exempt us from animal nature. When he imitates being bitten, he demonstrates that it is a mistake to think of awakening as an escape from pain. When in pain, the awakened human being accepts it with an untroubled mind.

My understanding of this koan enabled me to accept my symptoms of fear without shame. I remembered another koan: "The

Diamond Sutra* says that when a person is ridiculed by others, the sins of their previous lives are the cause. Yet at that moment, by submitting to ridicule, the sins of their previous lives are erased. Is this so?" The response: "Repulsive idiot born through an anus!"

The sutra interprets evils of the present as the result of sins committed in previous lives and affirms that redemption and liberation reside in these very evils. Yet the disciple's insulting reply means that it is useless merely to justify an evil by looking for its cause in previous lives. We must face the present difficulty before us immediately, without stopping to wonder about its causes or worrying about the consequences of our present actions. When confronted with an attack, what counts is a response that is unencumbered by mental doubts. If we allow even a hair's breadth to appear between being and nonbeing, we lose our life.

This second koan returned me to myself. I understood that feeling fear was natural, but that this fear need not become cowardice. So I stopped slinking around and made a phone call to ANDA, the national actors union. Invoking my union rights, I demanded a meeting with the Tigress to decide who had the legal right to produce the show.

At ten in the morning the very next day, a noisy crowd was gathered around the entrance to ANDA. My actors were there as well as the actors of the rival troupe and a swarm of journalists. The diva did not deign to appear, but she had sent two muscular bodyguards. They gave me menacing looks and showed me the machine guns they had hidden in golf bags. As her representative at this dispute (which she felt certain of winning because of her political connections), she had sent the Argentine singer. Parroting his boss, he proclaimed my dishonesty

---

*Sutras are sacred texts in Indian traditions. In Buddhism, they refer to accounts of talks by the Buddha. The Diamond Sutra (Vajracchedika Prajñaparamitrasutra) was translated into Chinese around 400 CE and into Tibetan sometime between 800 and 900 CE. It speaks of the nonexistence of a separate self in Boddhisattvas (destined to become Buddhas only through fulfilling a vow to help as long as there are beings who suffer), spiritual evolution, and other themes.

in front of the union officials. When I realized that these bureaucrats were looking at me with ill-concealed contempt and that the mocking journalists were harassing me with their flashes, I decided to resort to the weapon of lies myself—but on a grander scale. Instead of limiting the scope of the scandal to a simple dispute among theater people, I decided to make it into a political affair that would affect the whole country.

"The Tigress has informed me that every two months, carrying a diplomatic passport, she travels to Switzerland in a Mexican military jet. She delivers a trunk full of gold, which the president has stolen from the public treasury, to be deposited in a Swiss bank."

This caused such a stir that all the officials left their desks and went off to consult with their superiors. A deadly silence filled the building. Little by little, the journalists left. The Argentine was summoned to the telephone. He listened, nodding his head several times, and hung up. Looking toward me as if I were invisible, he left the building, followed by his associates and the two gorillas. The union officials finally returned with the verdict: Both rival theater troupes would perform the premiere of *Lucretia* on the same day at the same time with the same music, costumes, and sets. The public would decide which performance was the most deserving.

I understood what had happened. The Mexican people had long been whispering that their presidents stole the country's money. A scandal involving the head of state could trigger a national crisis. I was certain the Tigress had received orders from very high up to put an end to this farce. As if by magic, the newspapers stopped attacking me and nothing more was heard about the affair.

An ambitious impresario signed a contract with us to open at the Teatro Lirico, a swank hall with more than a thousand seats. Because my actors were terrified by our enemy's reputation as a witch, I asked a friend who was an expert in popular sorcery to "clean" the theater. He purified the orchestra pit and balcony with vast clouds of incense.

Then he sprinkled holy water in the corridors, on the chairs, and in all the corners with a brush made of the fresh leaves of seven herbs. We were all relieved, but fear returned when we learned that in that same evening, my friend had to have emergency surgery to remove an enormous boil that had appeared on his anus.

I was lucky to find a very respected and talented actress for the role of Lucretia. She agreed on condition that she never be required to dress in tight clothing. We rehearsed at least ten hours a day and were ready with an impeccable show on opening night.

As for the Tigress, things went badly for her at first, because she hadn't bothered to rehearse and wandered around the stage like a blind animal, listening to a prompter whose voice was so loud it could be heard all over the theater. But then, in defiance of censorship rules, she suddenly took off every stitch of clothing, sporting only a fluffed-up mass of pubic hair dyed green. This audacity brought her resounding success. Avid voyeurs flocked to the theater every night. My *Lucretia Borgia* ran for four months. Hers ran for two years.

When our run was over, I sent a telegram to the Tigress congratulating her on her success. She replied with another telegram inviting me to have a cup of coffee and pastry with her at the Frou-Frou.

The actors of both companies were bewildered by this, for they saw us as mortal enemies. For the occasion, I wore a white suit. The Tigress was "a bit late"—an hour and forty minutes, to be exact. She also appeared dressed entirely in white! We both burst out laughing, sensing that something miraculous was concealed in this apparent coincidence. We drank our coffee calmly and shared a *tarte aux pommes*. Public life was one thing, private life another. Now that the battle was over, we could communicate as simple human beings. A current of sympathy united us, like two old enemy soldiers reminiscing about the war.

"That was one glorious scandal!" she said. "Thanks to the war with you, I made a fortune. Please allow me to offer you a little gift."

I knew I could not refuse, and I allowed her to put, on my left ring finger, a gold ring ornamented with a skull.

6

The Donkey Was Not
Ill-Tempered after
So Many Blows
from the Stick

—✦—

*"Steel-tipped bullets will explode the head from eleven
yards away, Chief."*
"Good. That way the corpse will be less heavy."
SILVER KANE, *TEMPORARY SHERIFF*

When I got home, I struggled in vain to remove the ring. I felt that if I
caressed my wife while wearing it, the golden skull would give off toxic
vibrations. My hand was as cold as ice and my arm hurt.

At five o'clock in the morning, I jumped out of bed and drove very
fast to the zendo. When I arrived, I found Ejo Takata meditating on
the terrace under a dawn sky streaked with red clouds. I stood facing
him, waiting for the incense stick to burn down. Finally, he seemed to
notice my presence. His look went not to my face but directly to the
gold ring. I made a helpless gesture. Smiling, he arose and removed the

ring from my finger without the slightest effort. The pain in my arm vanished.

"If you see it as a skull, your arm will hurt, but if you are unattached either to its form or its name, it is simply pure gold. Clear your mind and this ring will be a ring—and you will be yourself."

Hearing these words, which I only half understood, I began to complain. "I can't help it, Ejo. I'm unable to adapt to this vulgar world. I thought I would find roots in Mexico, but I feel like a chicken in the wrong pen—and my consciousness only increases the pain."

Ejo began to laugh so hilariously that it infected me, and I found myself laughing as well. Seeing that my distress had gone, he fetched the secret book and read a new koan: "A monk asked Master Sozan:* 'Snow covers a thousand hills, but why is the highest peak not white?' Sozan answered: 'You must know the most absurd of absurdities.' The monk asked: 'What is the most absurd of absurdities?' Sozan replied: 'To be of a different color than the other hills!'"

"The first commentary is: 'In the pine branches, the monkey looks green.' The second commentary: 'The disciple, shaking imaginary snowflakes from his head, says: My hair has begun to turn white.'"

No matter how I wracked my brain, it seemed impossible to decode the koan and its very different commentaries. Anxious, I kneeled before the master. "I can't do it!"

With a roar of "Kwatsu!" that came from his belly, Ejo seized his stick and dealt me six blows on my shoulder blades.

"Change yourself into a hill!"

His voice was like a strong gust of wind blowing away my mental images. I saw myself as a hill covered with snow amid a thousand other hills covered with snow. The high, bare peak was only an illusion. Who

---

*Caoshan Benji (840–901 CE) was known as Sozan Honjaku in Japanese. A Chinese Ch'an master who studied Confucian teachings before he encountered Buddhism, along with his master Don-shan Liangqie (Tozan Ryokai), he founded the Caodong (Soto) school, which became very influential in Japan due to his disciple Yunju Daoyin (Ungo Doyo).

is exempt from being covered with snow in a storm? Who can escape aging and death? How could I imagine that developing my talent would exempt me from the sufferings of life? In winter, we are cold. The pine tree is a plant, the monkey is an animal. They are different, surely, but the monkey takes on the tree's green color in leaping from branch to branch. A different skin color, a different culture, a different level of consciousness—it was absurd to feel that any of this sheltered me from the assaults of our common reality. If the thousand hills are covered with snow, then the highest summit is also white.

The slashes of the Tigress's claws had taught me an important lesson. When she first agreed to collaborate with me, I would have done better to put aside my director's vanity and simply incorporate her into the performance without any attempt to change her style. Working together like two hills covered with snow, we could have achieved a fantastic *Lucretia*. She was an actress who never tried to be different from her audience, but I, feeling that I had a superior art to offer, separated myself from her spectators, whom I considered vulgar. In this way, I lost them. The infantry must fight its battles on known ground, not in the air.

"Ejo, I now see that when the Tigress gave me this valuable gold ring, she was saying that popular art is also noble."

When he heard these words, he exclaimed: "Give it to the first beggar you meet!" And shouting "Kwatsu!" again, he gave me six blows.

Then we had a frugal lunch together and meditated for two hours. Afterward, he had me read a new koan: "Joshu visited a hermit. He asked the master: 'Is there? Is there?' The master raised a fist. Joshu said: 'In these shallow waters, I do not wish to anchor my boat,' and left. Then he visited another hermit and repeated the same question. This master also lifted his fist. Joshu said: 'He can give, he can take, he can kill and yet give life!' And he bowed. Commentary: The same tree shaken by the spring wind shows two aspects: warm branches on its southern side, cold branches on its northern side."

Ejo crossed his legs and resumed his meditation. I did likewise. An hour passed. Then two hours, three hours . . . no matter how I turned around the koan in my mind, I could not understand it. The silence lay on my shoulders like an elephant. An agonizing pain stiffened my legs. A fly settled into the hollow of my ear. I bore its flutterings without moving. A voice resounded in my skull: "Understand, or die!" As if he had also heard it, Ejo cried out three times: "Is there? Is there? Is there?"

I heard myself answer: "If there is not here, then where? If there is not now, then when? If there is not I, then who?"

Suddenly, I am Joshu. I walk up a steep path toward the distant hermitage. There are monks there, far from the noise of the world, involved in discovering the luminous jewel buried in the depths of the soul. They sit around an old master. He is a realized being—meaning he is himself and not a simulacrum of another. When he hears my triple question, the master (who has already crossed the border where words dissolve into emptiness) lifts a fist to show his present unity. If he is not fully here, he is nowhere. Yet his gesture does not convince me. I find it superficial. In spite of my advanced age (probably more than one hundred years) I climb another hill painfully. Why this extreme effort? I need to be convinced that I am not the only one, that my awakening is not an abnormal phenomenon, that the end of all paths is the same. In the second hermitage, the master also lifts his fist in response to my three cries. And at that moment, in spite of their responses being the same, I recognize myself in the old man before me. The jewel buried in the darkness of our soul can give, can take, can kill, and nevertheless can bestow upon us its own life, which is impersonal and eternal.

"Ejo, if Joshu preferred one place over the other, it was not because there was a difference between the two fists. The difference was in his own seeing. We always have a personal interpretation of other beings, things, and events. Perhaps Joshu perceived no authentic expression of unity in the gesture of the first master. Perhaps he felt that the latter was saying that he would never let go of his realization and that it was only for him. He may even have perceived that he was being rebuked as an intruder, presumptuously questioning a master right in front of his disciples, whom he protected as a hen defends her chicks. If they were to lose faith in him, they would crumble. The fist was actually a physical threat telling him to be gone. With his closed fist, this egoist can hold only a few grains of sand, but if he had opened it, all the sands of the desert would have passed through it. . . . In contrast, Joshu interpreted the same gesture of the second master in a completely opposite way—as a warning of what not to do: If my awakening is mine alone, then it is not mine. What belongs to me can be mine only when it is also for others."

Ejo tilted his head to the right, tilted his head to the left, took a deep breath of the evening air, and let out a long sigh. He clucked his tongue softly several times as if comforting a hurt child. "Some branches are warmed by the sun, others cooled by the spring wind, but they are all part of the same tree. The two masters gave the same answer. They had realized the same emptiness, but with the first, Joshu felt cold from the spring wind; with the second, he felt the warmth of the sun. If all the branches are fed by the same roots, why go from one master to another, from one magical woman to another? When will you realize that others cannot give you what you already have in yourself? As long as you do not find this treasure in yourself, you will continue to project your doubts onto others. One day, the ring will be a curse, another day it will be a noble work of art. You will say that the skull symbolizes death or you will say that it symbolizes eternity—but the beggar you give it to will see only its monetary value."

I felt wounded. I groaned with irony: "Thank you so much, don Ejo. At last I understand: in order to awaken, I must become a beggar, stripping myself of my personal anxieties in order to attain poverty of spirit, transforming myself into an empty bowl and waiting patiently for my essential being, the great Buddha, to grant me the alms of awakening!"

Shouting "Kwatsu!" in a more piercing voice than ever, the Japanese first made me prostrate with my forehead on the ground. Then he administered a flurry of thirty blows of the stick.

When he had finished, he said: "The wisdom of the master depends on your own capacity to use it to find yourself." After this, he recited a Mexican proverb as if it were a holy sutra: "He who has the most saliva eats the most *pinole*.*

Still feeling hurt, I countered with another Mexican proverb: "You can't eat pinole and whistle at the same time."

He laughed heartily, rubbing his belly. "Exactly! Each thing in its own time."

Then he went to the kitchen and soon returned with plates of rice, fried sardines, and a thermos full of bitter, steaming tea. Between bites, he confided to me: "Mumon Yamada gave me a koan. I was never able to resolve it, but you—you can probably do it."

Seeing a mischievous glint in his slanted eyes, I sensed a trap. Probably the koan he was going to give me was meaningless. What is the meaning of life? Life has neither meaning nor meaninglessness. It must be lived!

"Tokusan was the head teacher of a Zen monastery. Seppo was the chief administrator.† One day, breakfast was late. Tokusan, bowl in hand, went into the dining hall. Seppo said to him: 'I have not heard the bell ring for breakfast, and the gong has not been sounded either. What are you doing here with that bowl?' Without a word, Tokusan bowed and returned to his cell. Seppo then remarked to another monk: 'Tokusan may be great, but he has not understood the last verse.'"

As a sort of commentary, Ejo began to hum very softly: "The wind

---

Pinole is a type of grilled corn flour sweetened with sugar. It is difficult to swallow dry and requires abundant saliva.

†Deshan Xuanjian, or Tokusan Senkan in Japanese (782–867 CE), engaged in a deep study of the Diamond Sutra. He headed a monastery and had several famous disciples, including Xuefeng Yicun, or Seppo Gison in Japanese (822–908 CE), who founded a monastery on Mount Xuefeng, the name he adopted.

has blown the clouds away. Now the moon shines on the green hills like a coin of white jade."

I began to reflect. If Tokusan is really a master, he cannot behave as a senile old man, and if Seppo is an awakened sage, he cannot speak of Tokusan with condescension. Tokusan did not simply wander into the dining hall out of blind habit. He was fully aware that the breakfast bell had not rung. When Seppo seemingly rebuked the master's unconsciousness, Tokusan's bow was not an acknowledgment of his forgetfulness. Between these two masters there could have been only profound respect, not some trivial competition between administrator and teacher. When Tokusan went to the dining hall, he knew that Seppo would be there, hurrying his monks to prepare breakfast, because it was late. Without a word, he held out his empty bowl to the administrator, saying: "The vicissitudes of life do not affect the peace of my spirit. Are you trying to accomplish a perfect work? If so, you are mistaken. For human beings, perfection is not possible, though excellence is. Simply do your work the best you can, accepting the inevitable errors." Seppo understood. His own rebuke was very different from what it seemed to be: "Having realized emptiness, do you wish to show the way to those whom you believe are still in darkness? So many years of meditation, and still you hold an empty bowl in your hands. Your great flaw is the power of knowing your own mind and nature. Beware of your vanity; your bowl contains a thorn."

Tokusan bowed his head in recognition that self-consciousness is the last trap. Seppo's words, like the wind blowing away the clouds, enabled Tokusan to realize that seeing his own perfection is an imperfection. To be in unity is to conquer the dualism of actor-observer. Tokusan returned to his cell—that is, to himself. He still had to learn to dissolve himself, to offer his consciousness as the ultimate gift to the eternal void, leaving aside all metaphysical search. The mysterious commentary by Seppo about Tokusan not having understood the last verse refers to a tradition borrowed from ancient China by Zen masters. In their last moments, enlightened sages would write a poem, leaving the essence of their life experience to their disciples or to their children. The Buddhist monk Zhi Ming,* condemned to die, dictated this poem before his head was cut off:

> *Illusory birth, illusory death.*
> *The great illusion does not survive the body.*
> *But one idea calms the mind:*
> *If you look for a man, no man exists.*

I related this interpretation to Ejo: "Empty mind: nothing to wait for, nothing to receive."

His response was to recite another poem by a dying monk: "In this world burns a rootless tree, its ashes blown away by the wind."

At this moment, a gust of wind made our kimonos flap. We had spent the entire day discussing koans. It was already dark, but night always came so softly here that we hadn't bothered to light candles on the terrace. Another gust of wind, much longer, ruffled my hair. Ejo, with his bald head, grinned boyishly. The gust died suddenly and left in its wake a marvelous gift: a firefly! Free of the wind's tyranny, the insect fluttered around the terrace, emitting its phosphorescent bursts of light.

Ejo murmured: "Little star, your language of light offers a teaching to us."

We remained silent for a long time. Then, for the first time since I had known him, Ejo began to speak of his childhood. He spoke in a childlike voice, conveying nostalgia, sweetness, and fascination.

"I was an only child. I was five years old on that moonless night, when there appeared many thousands of fireflies, like a river of stars rushing through time. That was the night when my mother, distraught by the first wrinkles that signaled the decline of her beauty, decided to drown herself in Omi Lake. My father never got over her suicide.

---

*The religious name of the Chinese official Zheng Ting, who lived during the Sui dynasty (589–618 CE) and the Tang dynasty (618–906 CE).

Lacking the courage to kill himself, he began to drink. This slow sui-cide plunged us into abject poverty. Most of the year, we depended on public charity. He emerged from his drunkenness only with the onset of summer, when he wore around his waist a bamboo stick wrapped to a big net sack and took me with him to the willow forest along the shores of Omi Lake. We lived in the region of Ishiyama, a province of Goshu, where several merchants specialized in buying and selling fireflies. They sent them to big cities in little wicker boxes. Rich city dwellers avidly bought these little creatures and then released them for their feasts so that everyone could admire their scintillating beauty.

"The more frightened fireflies are, the more brilliantly they shine. If you startle them, they become paralyzed for a time before taking flight. Kyubei, my father, hated these insects, blaming them stubbornly for triggering my mother's fatal depression. Like a silent cat, he sneaked up until he detected their presence among the willow leaves. Leaping out suddenly, he began striking the leaves violently with the long bam-boo stick. The insects froze, and fell to the ground, shining brightly like countless precious jewels. In order to collect as many of them as fast as possible, my father scooped them rapidly into his mouth. When it was so full he couldn't hold any more, he spit them into the covered net sack that I held open and then closed quickly.

"The night was as dark as this one. My father was dressed in black so that the insects would not see his approach. Suddenly, in the total dark-ness, his cheeks began to shine. The insects inside his mouth were frantic and shone with such great intensity that the light lit up his cheeks like a red lantern. When he spit out his prisoners, a luminous jet spewed from his mouth. I gathered this stream of light into the net sack, which became my soul. I imagined my father as a kind of demonic god, expelling his power into me, the transmission of a mysterious gift of knowledge.

"My father was glad to punish these insidious phantoms who had stolen my mother—he firmly believed that the light of each insect was the burning soul of a dead person. When we returned to our humble home, with me carrying a sack of at least five hundred insects, he would recite haiku passed down to him from his ancestors and I had tears of joy, wishing that this summer would never end."

Ejo paused, sighed deeply, and murmured: "Permanent impermanence." Drying the tears on his cheeks with the ample sleeves of his robe, he lit a candle. Then, after a loud burst of laughter, he recited:

> *Mizu e kite,*
> *Hikuu naritaru*
> *Hotaru kana!*

In a raucous voice, he recited it again, this time separating and counting the syllables of each verse:

> *Mi-zu e ki-te . . . five*
> *Hi-ku-u na-ri-ta-ru . . . seven*
> *Ho-ta-ru ka-na . . . five*

He smiled with satisfaction. "Five, seven, five: a haiku. The first five, like the fingers of a hand, signify ordinary human reality. The seven, like the seven chakras, signify awakened mind, cosmic unity. The third five return to ordinary reality, but this time with something new, the light of consciousness.

Chiding him playfully, I said: "Your poem is beautiful, Ejo, with a mystical rhythm. But remember—I'm not Japanese. Would you be so kind as to translate it for me?"

To my astonishment, this foreigner who did not speak Spanish very well rapidly produced a translation:

> *Llegando al agua*
> *hace una reverencia*
> *la luciérnaga!**

---

*[The haiku translations from the Japanese used here do not retain the 5-7-5 syllabic structure of the original poems. Nonetheless, they preserve the spirit of the originals. —*Ed.*]

Arriving at the water
the firefly dips in a gesture
of reverence!

This was the first time Ejo had ever spoken of his personal life. I was moved by this revelation of the vulnerable, nostalgic child in him who was still there after so many years of meditation. Did he seldom speak of them because these memories were not an obstacle, but an intimate treasure? For an instant my personal limits faded, my body merged with the cosmos, the roots of my thoughts were the stars, and Ejo's past was my own. I ventured to comment upon the haiku.

"The water is that of an ancient pond, calm and undisturbed—no birth or death, always there, like eternity. Halting its labyrinthine flight—in other words, freeing ourselves from identification with our thoughts—the firefly, like the awakened human being, arrives at the border where concepts dissolve in the infinite void before it drinks and communes with the world, accepting the unending change of everything that was thought to be fixed and permanent, making a gesture of reverence in gratitude for its ephemeral life."

As Ejo listened to my interpretation, an invisible bridge joined his mind to mine. His huge grin made me guess that we were about to embark on a new game: he would recite and I would interpret. I was not mistaken. He went down to the kitchen and returned with a bottle of warm sake. After several toasts, he proposed another haiku:

Akenureba
Kusa no ha nomi zo
Hotaru kago!

The dawn returns
Firefly in its cage
Only grass!

I replied: "When dawn comes, the light of the sun makes the fire-flies opaque. No enlightenment, no ignorance, no master, no disciple—drunk all together, we will sing like frogs who swallow fireflies and croak at the moon with phosphorescent bellies."

Ejo gave a loud "Ho!" of satisfaction and executed a graceful little bow. Then, half singing:

> *Ame no ya wa*
> *Shita bakari yku*
> *Hotaru kana!*

> *Night of sudden downpours*
> *Fireflies fluttering on the ground!*

"Ejo, my dear friend, I think that Buddhas must adapt to their circumstances. Even in the mud, fireflies still shine. In adverse circumstances, the awakened mind, true to itself, does not trouble itself or give way to despair."

"Ho! Easy to say, very difficult to realize. . . . My mother and my four grandparents were dead. I was a child whose only family was a father who was drunk nine months of the year. In spite of my young age, I could understand his widower's grief. But he never understood my orphan's grief. Through long nights of pouring rain, forcing myself to smile, performing my filial duties, my heart was fluttering in the mud.

"When I was nine years old, I returned from school one day to find my father speaking with a Zen monk. Shaking a piece of paper in my face, Kyubei said: 'This is a contract that gives Keikisoken Kodaishi the right to kill you if you don't apply yourself to practicing his teachings. Make no mistake: from now on, being a good monk is a matter of life and death for you. Now eat your rice and go to bed. Tomorrow, at dawn, you will leave with your teacher for the Horyuji Monastery. I am unworthy of raising you. If you stay with me, you'll become a beggar. This is the last time we will see each other.' Then he took me in his arms and we both wept. At midnight, I heard his soft steps going outside. I looked out the window and saw him walking toward the willow forest. Taking great care in order not to disturb the sleep of my future mentor, I took a half hour to get dressed and left the house to spy on my father. I found him kneeling near the lake, so motionless in the moonlight that he seemed like a silver statue. To my great surprise, in spite of the winter cold, a solitary firefly appeared. Its great size and brightness indicated it was a female. After circling several times around my father's head, it settled on his forehead. Then, with the slowness of a dream, he began to walk with tiny steps toward the mirror of the motionless lake. Without making any waves, he entered it little by little, until his head finally disappeared under the water. The firefly never left his forehead. In my child's mind, the lake had consumed my mother and my father."

Ejo took a long drink of sake. Then he recited:

> *Moe yasuki*
> *Mata ke yasuki*
> *Hotaru kana*

> *Swiftly, you light up*
> *Even more swiftly, you go out,*
> *Insect of light*

At this moment, I saw us—the Zen monk and myself—in the midst of the river of time, in the center of an infinite sphere, burning like two logs, like two joyous fireworks which leave no trail in the sky, savoring the paradise of the instant, a moment that would never repeat itself. Should we weep because we leaped into the void? With no beliefs to console us, without inventing a destiny for ourselves through compulsive actions, what would we do with this inevitable life?

As if reading my thoughts, Ejo recited two more haiku as a kind of response:

Yo no fukuru
Hodo okinaru
Hotaru kana

The more impenetrable the darkness,
the more your own light shines

Yo ga akete
Mushi ni naritaru
Hotaru kana

Dawn appears.
Fireflies are now only insects

The first rays of sunlight imparted a golden tint to our skin. Sleepy and queasy from all the drink, I nevertheless ventured an interpretation, feeling that my drunkenness would excuse me, even if it were wrong. "If I compare the sublime interdependence of all things—fireflies, dark nights—to my own fixed ideas of the world and myself, I realize that I am not a stranger, but a participant. Nothing belongs to me, not even my consciousness. All places are open doors; my own existence is impossible without that of others. When love—the dawn—appears, we dissolve into the world, becoming nobody."

Ejo, as drunk as I, let out a long "Hooooo!" Then, in a stuttering voice, he related one last memory: "The shop of the firefly merchant was lit by hundreds of these poor insects crowded in small cages. When my father received the money and returned in the night with his empty net sack, he always said to me, with sadness: 'And now we must go forth into this dark night with bodies that do not shine.' Then he would enter a deep sleep while remaining in his meditation posture. I would get up unsteadily and leave him there, like a golden Buddha, snoring loudly."

I drove home, weaving as little as possible. In the early morning hours, the streets were already full of traffic. At every red light, beg-gars appeared, each with their own method of attracting attention. At the first stop, I placed the golden ring in the hat that a skeleton-thin urchin held out to me after he emitted flames from his mouth by spit-ting benzene onto a torch. At the second stop, I gave all the money in my pockets to three kids in clown costumes with enormous buttocks. At the third stop, I gave my coat and shirt to an old man with a small monkey that he had trained to stand on its nose. At the fourth stop, I gave my shoes and socks to a woman who juggled four small rubber skulls. At the fifth stop, I offered my pants to a mother who carried a blind child.

I arrived home in my shorts. Collapsing into bed and just before plunging into a deep sleep, I remembered that my parents had never caressed me.

Ten hours later, I was awakened by cries of pain from my cat, Mirra, who was having a difficult time giving birth. Sensing an emergency, I drove her to the veterinarian. On the operating table, my black angora gave birth to one beautiful kitten with long, soft, gray fur, and then she died. Seeing the little orphan sucking desperately at the nipples of its dead mother, I thought of Ejo.

Although I knew many details of the strict life of a Zen monk, it was with great difficulty that I tried to imagine how this little nine-year-old boy, deprived of his family, friends, childhood games, and favorite places could live in a monastery, far from any contact with feminine tenderness—but perhaps he had already ceased to miss such attention? An austere life of meditation, prayer, work, service, obedience, begging alms, a life in which the negation of himself was considered the supreme good: I imagined him after his arrival at the monastery, before receiv-ing his first meal, trembling with hunger and timidity, walking toward the cell of the severe *shika,* the head monk, to bow to him and thank him for his hospitality. I saw him sitting still, holding back his tears, while an older novice shaved his head. Any illusions that bound him to the world must have dropped away along with the hair. I imagined him scrubbing floors, emptying excrement from the latrines, working in the garden, helping in the kitchen, and taking his place on a zafu in the zendo, having vowed never to cease in his meditation until he attained enlightenment. Amid this group of severe adults, he would never know a moment of privacy. His only personal space was a *tatami,* a rectangle of woven straw upon which he slept, dreamed, and meditated. A block of wood served as his pillow, and he was given a space in the communal closets to keep his bowl; a razor to shave his head; a thin, folded mattress; and a sutra. Nothing else. No toys.

Every time he entered or left the zendo, he could see a wooden sounding block inscribed with large letters: "It is a matter of life or death. Nothing is permanent. Time passes quickly and waits for no one. You must not waste it." In the morning, when the head monk looked at his palm and was able to distinguish its lines, he took a mallet and struck the wooden block. This series of loud, dry sounds woke the child, and he began his day of exhausting tasks. In the evening, when the head monk could no longer see the lines in his palm, he struck the block again. This announced a meager supper, after which the boy must express his gratitude with deep bows and the chanting of sutras. Finally, at exactly nine o'clock, repeated blows on the block announced the end of the day. Before unfolding his little mattress and taking up the required ritual posture of sleep among the other monks, he saw written on another large plank the strict rules of monastic life. He was taught how to bow and salute, how to walk after meditation, how to drink tea, how to take off his sandals, how to urinate and defecate. It was all written, and no spontaneity was permitted. No private conversations were allowed—no comments, no grumbling. He could use only three cups of water to wash himself each morning, holding the cup in one hand and washing his face with the other, like a cat. Once the roshi came by as he was doing this and urged him to learn to do with only two cups, for water was a common good, and this way he would be leaving more for future generations.

Life went on like this for thirty years. There were tea ceremonies, interviews with the roshi when he was given a koan, raking the garden, begging in town for rice or money, communal baths in strict silence, sleeping in winter without heat or wool socks, receiving the ritual blows and remonstrance from the master, the twice-yearly change of clothes: wool in autumn and winter, linen in spring and summer—and the never-ending examinations before senior monks for the purpose of deciding whether he would stay in the monastery or be sent away.

At what point did this orphan child, adolescent, then adult monk realize the awakening that fate had compelled him to seek? Perhaps he saw himself as an instrument protected by the generous arms of the Buddha, to be used by destiny to accomplish a great work. But he must also have been aware that he had no real experience of life in the world (unless he perhaps indulged occasionally in illicit escapades with other young monks, climbing over the walls at night to drink and carouse in a village bar). To have abruptly left this severe monastery for the United States and then to settle in Mexico must have come as an enormous spiritual shock to him. It is difficult to change the habits acquired over a lifetime. Even in a vast, foreign metropolis, Ejo was still enclosed in his Japanese monastery. A life of strict control over his speech and gestures and the discipline of meditation and purification had caused him to lose contact with much of the natural animal tenderness of life. He still knew little of caresses and the pleasure of spontaneous gestures of love.

I decided to offer him the little gray kitten as a gift.

As could be expected in the morning hours, I found Ejo sitting in meditation. I approached slowly and put the little animal between his legs. The kitten immediately settled there, purring, and fell asleep. Ejo sat immobile until the incense stick had burned out. Then he yawned, stretched, smiled, and caressed the kitten's soft fur.

As he was doing this, he proposed a koan: "One morning, the monks of the eastern hall got into an argument with the monks of the western hall over the possession of a cat. Seeing this, Master Nansen took the animal and a large knife and held them up. 'If one of you can tell me the meaning of this, I will not cut the cat in two.' The monks could not reply, so Nansen cut the cat in two. (Here Ejo imitated the harsh sound of a cat dying.) That afternoon, Joshu arrived at the monastery. Nansen told him what happened, asking him for his opinion. Joshu took off one of his sandals, placed it upon his head, and left the monastery. Nansen said: 'If you had been there, you could have saved the cat.'"

Ejo now made a soft mewling sound, imitating a cat being born. He went to the kitchen and returned with a large knife. Holding the kitten up by the nape of its neck, he said, with an implacable glint in his eye: "If you can tell me the meaning of this, I will not cut it in two."

I began to sweat and breathe hard. I felt as if I would suffocate. What were Nansen and Ejo talking about when they said the meaning of *this?* Did holding the cat up with the knife mean that life and death are the same thing? Or did *this* refer to the illusory, dreamlike reality in which we believe we exist? Or did it refer to the illusory *I,* disputing possession of something equally illusory? Or was it the emptiness beyond words? And why that absurd sandal on the head and Ejo's two cries imitating the death and birth of the kitten?

Seeing my state of incertitude, Ejo escalated the pressure on me by raising the knife, as if to give a fatal blow. The kitten began to meow in protest.

I lost control. Leaping upon Ejo, I grabbed his hand, forcing him to drop the knife, pushing him to the ground, and wresting the cat away from him. Holding it protectively against my breast, I backed away, horrified. To me, this act had been a sacrilege. In that moment, the Buddha had been knocked off his pedestal and my mystical illusions were shattered into a thousand pieces. My friendship with this monk was obviously at an end. I was certain that when he had recovered, he would formally expel me from the zendo.

Old, painful memories were surging through my mind like an irresistible flood. On my fourth birthday, a neighbor had given me a beautiful, gray cat named Pepe. This animal and I established a deep love. He became as attached to me as a dog, came when I called him by his name, and sat waving his paws in the air when he wanted me to share my food with him. He played with me often, never using his claws on me, and spoke to me in a language of meows that I understood. Every night, he came to sleep with me, snuggling under the sheets.

My father was convinced that cats who breathe near the face of a child transmit tuberculosis. One day he killed him in the garden, putting a bullet through his head. My happiness with Pepe had lasted only six months. Only four and a half years old, I found out how empty the world becomes when a beloved friend dies—or rather, how full of his absence the world becomes. This sadness flowed right through the marrow of my bones, and I harbored an impotent bitterness toward Jaime, my father.

Now, even with my sense of guilt at having physically attacked my master, I could smile with relief. I had accomplished something of which I was incapable as a child: saving my cat's life.

And then, to my utter astonishment, I watched Ejo get up from the ground, grinning from ear to ear. He stood in front of me and exclaimed: "You resolved it! When Nansen spoke of *this,* inviting the affirmation that there is no difference between life and death, Joshu put his sandal on his head, ridiculing the ability of the intellect to resolve it. And you also did this, putting ordinary reality in your mind. Because you love the cat, you wrested it from my hands. Joshu was also saying that if you have to kill cats to lead your monks to awakening, your Zen makes no sense. Kwatsu! Kwatsu! Kwatsu! What joy! Life is only a fleeting dream, yet a living cat is not the same as a dead cat!" And then he embraced me heartily, bursting with laughter and compelling me to do a little dance with him.

I was still holding on to the cat, which was purring contentedly. I felt a certain reticence even as I participated in this merriment.

Perceiving this, Ejo took the cat from me gently, murmuring "Arigato," and caressed it with surprising tenderness. Then I followed him into the kitchen, where he give it a bowl of milk. Looking around this impeccably clean and ordered room, I could not help feeling that every object in it exuded the sadness of an orphan. The joy of a little kitten lapping milk only accentuated the coldness of the atmosphere there.

I could not help blurting out: "Ejo—I think you need a wife."

"It's true!" he exclaimed, stretching his left hand toward the ceiling, making a fist.

The next day he took a plane to Japan to search for a companion.

7

From Skin to Soul

"Every man you hang requires a different technique. It all depends on his physique."

SILVER KANE, *VERDUGO A PLAZOS*
(EXECUTIONER ON CREDIT)

The forty days that my master was absent made me realize how important his presence was for me. I needed him near me to verify all my words. Without his counsel, I had the feeling that my footprints were already erased before I even took my steps.

None of us students were really sure that he would return from Japan. Considering the poverty of his life in Mexico (he lived mostly on vegetables, fruits, and fish that he scrounged from leftovers at the market) and the small number of his disciples, it sometimes appeared absurd that he would come back. Nevertheless, to remain in communion with his spirit, we continued our daily practice at the zendo.

Considerably irritated by Ana Perla's assumption of the role of sensei, or teacher (on the pretext that she was the only one able to sit in the full lotus position) and her presumptuousness in directing

the meditations, I retaliated by coughing and clearing my throat constantly. No one seemed to notice me. Everyone had surrounded themselves with small and medium-size Buddha statues, vases with flowers,
and reproductions of Mayan objects. Ana Perla, a 100 percent lesbian,
wore Tibetan bracelets that could not hide the large scars from the
numerous suicide attempts that resulted from her unhappy love affairs.
Now, having shaved her head, she seemed to believe she had become
saintlike, immune to such passions. To guide us all in the sublimation
of hormones, she had us engage in chanting endless repetitions of the
famous mantra from the Heart Sutra (Gate, gate, paragate, parasamgate, bodhi svaha*), like frogs croaking at the moon on the edge of an
ancient lake. And she offered a translation that was as original as it
was deceitful: "I thrust, I thrust, deeper inside, deeper into the depths,
orgasm, blessing."

Convinced that Ejo had disappeared for good into his native land
and disgusted by the idolatry of his disciples, I decided to leave the
community. I wanted to take the cat with me but realized that it would
provoke a serious scandal. They had elevated the feline to the rank of
a representative of the master. Ana Perla swore that she could see a
golden aura around its head.

Once again, I found myself walking down Insurgentes Avenue fum-
ing with rage. At an intersection, I noticed the boy that I had attacked
several months earlier. This time, he was accompanied by several others who, like himself, were dressed in tight jeans and sleeveless shirts
and who attempted to attract the attention of men in passing cars. I
thought of changing sidewalks but did not. One of Ejo's koans came to
me: "Why do you not see what you do not see?" And I thought: "What

---

*Like the Diamond Sutra, the Heart Sutra (Prajñaparamitahridayasutra) was translated
from Sanskrit to Chinese around 400 CE and into Tibetan sometime between 800 and
900 CE. The famous mantra (a sequence of sacred syllables whose chanting strengthens,
protects, and awakens) from this sutra is: Gate, gate, paragate, parasamgate, bodhi svaha.
One widespread English translation is: "Gone, gone, gone beyond, gone beyond going
beyond, awakening, so be it!"

I see, I see only from my point of view, depending on my good or bad mood. The world is an extension of my mind. If I totally ignore them, these kids will ignore me. I will walk past them, invisible."

But either I had not been able to erase them from my mind or else my interpretation of the koan was wrong. As soon as I drew near them, they all leaped upon me, knocking me to the ground, and kicking me repeatedly. "You macho turd! We'll teach you some respect!"

What could I do, with five against one? I protected my head as best I could and allowed my body to receive the punishment without protest, taking refuge in my spirit. The blows did not prevent me from remembering another koan: "A monk asked Master Ummon:* 'What happens when the leaves wilt and fall from the tree?' Ummon answered: 'An autumn wind blows from my heart.'"

What is irremediable deserves to be loved. With this in mind, I accepted the beating that I could not avoid—partly because I deserved it and also because I felt my life was not in danger, though I would have some bad bruises to deal with later. These boys would not take the risk of committing a serious crime, but my calm evaporated when they started to drag me into an alley, pulling down my pants. In the stinking shadows of the place, I could see their penises were out. My hair stood on end. No koan could convince me to let myself be raped! I started kicking back and screaming, but they immobilized me, holding me flat on the ground, my face against the pavement and my legs spread. Accompanied by a chorus of mocking hoots and insults, a deft hand was rubbing saliva into my anus—but their laughter died suddenly at the sound of a female voice.

"Leave him alone! He belongs to me!"

Obeying this order instantly, the aggressors desisted and left, making the sign of the cross as if confronted by the Holy Virgin herself.

---

*Yunmen Wenyen, or Ummon Bunen in Japanese (864–949 CE), founded the Zen school that bears his name. His responses, often consisting of a single word, are famous for their precision, penetration, and adaptability to different disciples.

I had thought that all my Zen meditation had rid me of the pride of ego, but as I lay in that stinking, dark alley, my pants down to my knees, limp and crumpled as a dead mollusk and shaking with nervous tension and pain, I found myself suddenly sobbing like a humiliated child.

"Don't be ashamed, my boy. Don't give so much importance to being penetrated. These kids aren't evil. I know them well. They always come to me when they get sick. They attacked you because you offended one of them. Anyway, they're professionals—even if they had done it to you, they wouldn't have hurt you. Perhaps they wanted to make you accept your yielding side, which men suppress beneath their hairy chests because of their contempt for women. Come now; get up and come with me. I live very close by, near the taco shop. Look, your knees are raw and bleeding. I'll disinfect them for you."

The woman before me was dressed with stark simplicity, and the dignity of her bearing and gestures made me trust her. As we walked toward the taco shop, she spoke to me.

"That day, when you attacked that poor boy, you were talking out loud to yourself without realizing it as you walked down the street. You walked right past me, but you didn't even see me. I heard you insulting yourself [here she produced a perfect imitation of my voice and accent]: 'I'm a spiritual whore, inviting the Buddha to possess me and offer me enlightenment as payment.' You despise yourself and you despise those boys—but you don't understand that they, just like you, are offering a service. They help their clients (most of them husbands and fathers) to discharge their homosexual impulses, and you serve the goddesses. By meditating, you develop consciousness, and that is what the goddesses created us to have. Their divine game is for the entire material universe to become conscious. At the end of time, this cosmos is to become pure spirit. In making your body more subtle, you help the supreme Mother Creators accomplish their task. You were right when you said [and again, her imitation was perfect]: 'I've had enough! Meditating, immobile as a corpse, serves no purpose!' When you transform your body into a statue, you are following the wrong path. It is one that the goddesses have already exhausted: the materialization of spirit. All that your eyes see, all that you hear, taste, and touch are petrified divinities. Within every stone, plant, and animal, a consciousness is trapped and must be liberated—not through destruction, but through mutation. You may not believe it, but what you call reality is essentially a song of love. Everything—even excrement—must have wings. You must realize that even these prostitutes are, in a sense, saints—as saintly as that beggar woman sleeping next to the garbage cans. The Other is the one you see in yourself."

Next to the taco shop, between high, peeling walls, an alley appeared. At its end we arrived at a dilapidated spiral stairway. Filling my nostrils was a greasy cloud of smoke that came from the chimney of the taco kitchen, where tortillas were cooked over coals. I began to cough. The stench was unbearable. Without seeming to notice it, doña Magdalena climbed the stairs with the dignity of a queen. We arrived at a steel-plated door. It was so low that we both had to bow our heads in order to enter. I heard her murmur: "Humility is the key that opens all doors."

In her small apartment, a sweet perfume filled the air, banishing the greasy odor. "It is copal," she explained. "It is used in temples and also in tombs."

The room was rectangular, with one small window and bare white walls. Instead of electric light, there were long, thick wax candles placed in each corner. In the center, under a small awning, was a massage table. Behind a curtain, there was a small toilet. Behind another, there was a small kitchen. A medium-size wooden case served as a closet.

Doña Magdalena invited me to sit on the massage table. No sooner was I sitting upon the cotton padding than she was rubbing the bruises on my face with a cream that smelled of benzoin. My pain was soothed quickly.

She seemed to have changed personality. I felt as if she came from another world. Her deep, pure regard had an intoxicating effect on me.

I no longer heard the noise of the streets outside; voices and odors faded
and reality became like a dream. She spoke in a slow, careful monotone,
as if dictating to me.

"For the moment, you do not know who you are, but you are
searching for yourself with such intensity that we have decided to help
you . . . we, the elementary particles of eternal consciousness. What we
are going to teach you is not just for yourself. Seeds are given to he who
sows in order for him to fructify the earth. What you will be given will
also be for others. If you keep it, you will lose it. If you give it, you will
finally be able to have it. Until now, you have worked by immobilizing
your body, considering as ephemeral everything that does not belong
to you, thinking to find in a corpse the immortal spirit that you are.
Yet, my son, your mind is also on loan to you, and it too is doomed to
disappear. Just as the body does, it must abandon all hope of immortality. They both must cease to live as separate beings and must unite the
male and female, free from the tyranny of time, plunged into a now
without end, giving totally to the work of creating a sublime state of
happiness. When you dissolve the opposites that you have coagulated
and, having been two, become one, then a star will shine in the dark
night. . . . This happiness in being alive nourishes the divine eye that
has been watching you from the center of your ephemeral existence. If
your joy is authentic, if you have burned away all hopes, if you cease
to be a body carrying a mind or a mind carrying a body, if you are at
once dense and transparent matter, you will be received in the heart of
the goddess like a lost sheep who returns home. Your individual luck
will be the same as the luck of the cosmos. Until now, you have been
traveling the way of the intellect, but we shall guide you in the way of
the body.

"If you are in agreement with this, return to see me tomorrow at
noon."

As I left the alley for the street, I was overwhelmed with a fatigue so
profound that I could barely lift my arm to hail a taxi. At home, I col-

lapsed on the bed without having the energy even to remove my shoes. I slept from four in the afternoon until eleven o'clock the next morning. Leaping out of bed, I washed myself and brushed my teeth in minutes and ran out of the house in order to arrive on time. As soon as I knocked at the steel-plated door, my anxiety vanished and I was filled with a strange calm.

Doña Magdalena, completely naked, opened the door. Normally, my reaction to a naked woman was either arousal if she was beautiful or disgust if she was ugly, but the naked Magdalena seemed to be dressed in her very soul. Her calm, dignity, and harmony of movement and the even brown of her skin made her seem like an ancient idol made of baked clay. She was so natural that I felt ashamed of my own embarrassment, aware of the contempt I carried in my own body and the sexual labeling I projected upon my flesh. The truth was that I had always considered my body as a kind of tumor of my intellect, doomed to degenerate into a wrinkled shell, a nest of maggots.

"That's enough, young man. Stop torturing yourself. We shall begin the work with the ornaments that cover you. Your costumes are your dark night, and by removing them, you will see the first gleams of dawn. Now take off that watch and stop measuring time!"

The authority of her command put me in a sort of trance. I lost any sense of haste and was filled with the slowness of a dream. Floating as gracefully as a dust mote in a sunbeam, Magdalena began to remove my leather jacket. She opened it inch by inch, as if peeling off a skin, making each second an eternity. As the articles of my clothing came off piece by piece, they took on diverse forms, like black amoebas. I was aware of the multitude of movements that were involved in taking my arm out of a sleeve. Undressing at this extremely slow pace became an art, a combination of dance and sculpture that gave a sense of the sacred to the clothing itself.

"You arrived covered with the remains of a murdered animal. Its pain has mingled with your body, invading your flesh and settling in your soul. The entire skin is an eye that absorbs the world. Be careful of the materials you use to cover yourself. Every object has its own history. Linen, silk, cotton, and wool are pure materials that will not stain your mind. The others are full of a guile that attacks your cells, unbalancing your nervous system and injecting suffering into your blood."

Entranced by her extremely slow gestures and her voice, as delicate and deep as a lake, I felt that I was becoming lost in a labyrinth of clouds. . . . When I awoke, I was standing naked. Magdalena finished arranging my clothes, folding them with as much care as someone making origami figures.

"Clothing used without consciousness is a mere disguise. Holy men and women do not dress in order to appear, but in order to be. Clothes possess a form of life. When they correspond to your essence, they give you energy and become allies. When they correspond to your distorted personality, they drain your vital forces. And even when they are your allies, if you do not care for them and respect them, they will retaliate by disturbing your mind. Now do you understand why we fold our garments so carefully, as we might fold a flag or a sacred vestment? Follow me; I'm going to give you a bath."

"But Magdalena, I washed my entire body before I came here."

"Which one? You have seven, and the one you take for real is a corpse . . . so come with me and behave like a corpse!"

I didn't know how to respond. I did as she asked, abandoning my own will and collapsing on the floor. She took hold of me in a very precise way and, lifting me up with no difficulty, carried me into the other space behind the curtain, and put me into a bathtub full of lukewarm water.

"Your ancestors followed the custom of washing their dead before burial. This was not because they saw them as dirty, but was followed in order to free their physical and six nonphysical bodies from distorted attachments to matter."

She rubbed me vigorously with soap and rinsed me from head to toe seven times. She did this with such strength and meticulous care that I felt lighter with each washing and breathed more easily. Then she took me out of the bath and applied a perfumed oil that smelled of incense.

"This is galbanum, my boy. Jewish priests used it to anoint their golden altars. Every human body is an altar."

I stood on my tiptoes, filled with a sense of happiness. I felt like dancing.

"Don't celebrate your victory yet. You feel good now, but you'll feel much better when I've finished scraping you."

Scraping me? Ignoring my astonishment, she had me sit on the massage table. She took a bone knife and, using its dulled point, she proceeded to scrape my skin, inch by inch, as if removing an invisible crust.

"Over the years, countless fears have condensed under your skin in the form of tiny grains: the fear of dying, of seeing loved ones die, of losing your identity, your territory, work, health. . . . Also, the auras of the six subtle bodies have been inhibited in their expression, which makes them fold in on themselves, forming an invisible armor attached to the skin, preventing us from union with the true world—not the world we think of, but the one that thinks us. This armor encloses you and separates you from others, from the planet, and from the cosmos. It makes you live in the darkness of hell instead of the light of the soul, which is union. You will come to realize that the human soul is immense. This scraping will take at least three hours—and even then, one session will not be enough to rid you of fear and free you from your fleshly prison. We will have to do this at least nine times."

Humming a lullaby and with infinite patience, she scraped my entire body, including my scalp, teeth, tongue, palate, ears, nails, penis, testicles, and anus. She was so sure and precise in her actions that I never felt the slightest tickle, even on the soles of my feet. She dug the knife in with confidence at just the right depth to dissolve the grains. It was painless, neither too soft nor too hard. Her hands seemed like those of a master sculptor who removes only what is unnecessary in order to reveal the work of art already contained in the material.

It was night when I returned home. I had only a mango for dinner, and I was so full of energy that I did not fall asleep until dawn. I arose at eight o'clock the next morning, feeling not the slightest lack of sleep.

For the next nine days, doña Magdalena repeated the scraping, digging a little deeper each time with the dull point of the knife. My opacity was disappearing; I began to feel more and more transparent. I saw the city and its inhabitants in a different way. I had ceased to criticize, ceased to feel my own guilt. Like a huge breath of wind, the joy of life had swept away my habitual anguish.

Every time I visited her, Magdalena's personality—and even her physical appearance—changed like the clouds. I was incapable of grasping her mind. Once, I heard her say: "I am an empty chair." With her hands, she infused me with the sublime, injecting her humble wisdom into my heart. I thought of certain insects who place their larvae in the body of others so that they can feed on their blood and emerge later into splendid offspring. After a total of ten scrapings, she cleaned my ears with a little stick, anointed them with perfume, and finally rubbed honey in them.

"Now I can really speak to you, for your ears are softened to hear my words. Concentrate yourself. Realize how you treat yourself: like a machine or a donkey to be punished. We allow our body to see, hear, feel, and savor things—but its touch stirs up unwholesome associations. Even when we are naked, we are wearing gloves. Civilization has turned our hands into tools, weapons, fingers made to push buttons. Like clever animals, we serve words, but our words serve only concepts. They have ceased to communicate soul. My son, you do not have two hands; you have two guilt-ridden pairs of pliers. Whenever you touch, you steal. You must relearn to feel your hands. Let me see you open them . . . spread out your fingers, stretch out your palms fully. You see? You can't do it completely. You have trouble letting go of what you think is yours. You are lugging around an invisible corpse: your security, your fears of possessing nothing, of losing what you think is necessary. You content yourself with a handful of coins, not realizing that all the money on the planet belongs to you.

"Open your hands so wide that you feel they are losing their limits, that they contain the whole earth, the infinite sky, the eternal universe. . . . Don't try to hold on to anything, to possess anything. Accept giving away everything and receiving everything. See how your hands breathe in and out, following the rhythm of your lungs. Feel the ebb and flow of your blood, let your hands participate in the beating of your heart, let them nourish themselves from the warmth of life. It is a life without end, for its essence is pure, imperishable love. . . . Now close your fingers. Feel the noble, transcendent force in your wrists. They are like two warriors, ready to the end against death, and then unfold your hands like two sacred flowers, opening their palms from which springs the perfume of a new life. . . . I beg you, my son: Recover your memory! Now feel your hands growing smaller . . . smaller and smaller . . . more. . . . They are becoming very tiny, the hands of a baby, a fetus. Feel the sensations of a fetus in your tiny hands. Feel the divine fluid around you in your mother's belly, feel the innocence, the immense tenderness that resides in every cell of your body, the recognition of the mystery that formed it, the pleasure of energy that once more is offering the gift of matter to the world, the soul coming into the midst of your flesh. . . . Become the mother of your hands, promise them the world, teach them to go beyond density, help them understand the secret poetry of space. Create sculptures in the air. Visualize the forms you are creating little by little so that your touch is not alone in knowing these forms.

"Now let yourself grow up. Let memory return; remember that from these hands your first caresses were born. At that time, you had no sensual experience; everything was new. You groped to discover what distance meant, you knew no separation, you knew that you could touch the stars with your hands. In those hands, you now carry your entire past. Feel them—they are still claws, hooves, even tentacles. Go deeper, all the way back to when they were earth, stone, metal, primordial energy. Now come back, grope in the direction of the future, feel your fingers growing longer, becoming transparent, becoming wings, luminous waves, angelic singing. . . .

"Do you now understand the power that you can transmit? If you can get rid of those mental gloves, your hands will radiate a golden aura."

Then Magdalena opened her own hands in front of my face. I saw that they were indeed surrounded by a golden aura. She pressed them against my heart. I began to weep. I realized that what I was receiving did not come from her. With this apparently simple yet magical gesture, she was transmitting a knowledge that my heart had lacked ever since my parents conceived me: the knowledge of divine love.

"You don't yet have a frame—you are like a man without a skeleton. How can you caress without bones?"

She had me lie on the small bed and began to palpate me. I felt as if her fingers were digging into my flesh and taking hold of my bones. I had always preferred to forget this essential part of my body, because of my fear of death. She worked upon all my bones, pressing into the most hidden corners, tracing forms, making me feel their medullar strength. Never again would I move in my old ways. Until then, my movements had always been superficial, centered in the flesh. Now my movements had a solid base full of life. In the whiteness of my bones, I no longer saw death, something to be swallowed by the earth, but a concentration of time—I had a skeleton. It was like other skeletons yet different, for it was now impregnated with a personal soul.

"You know how to ask; you have done so since you were born. Open your arms, stretch out your hands, and open your mouth to the sky, waiting for manna to fall into it from heaven. My son, you forget that the earth teaches us to turn as the galaxy, the universe turns. If you lack an axis for turning, you become a festering swamp, a morass of hopes that never rise up, like a vine that has no wall to climb upon and grow. Your bones develop by being used as an axis for turning. Both leaning and moving in all directions have their origins in rotation."

Her hands working like pliers, Magdalena grasped and moved one bone after another with endless patience—the fibula, the humerus, the cubitus, the femur, the patella, the tibia. . . . Slowly and relentlessly, she made them all turn outward, as if opening a coffin that had been closed for ages. At first, I was tense and felt a number of minor pains. Then I began to feel as if I had been freed from a shell that began in my bones and reached all the way up into my mind.

"Without realizing it, your arms, legs, and spine have turned inward upon themselves from fear of others. This goes all the way back to fetal memories. Your skeleton has learned to react as a porcupine reacts, rolling up into itself at the least sign of danger. But the clock cannot be turned backward—you cannot again become a fetal ball, separated from the world. Your bones know that someday they will float in the cosmos. Your skeleton, attracted to the future, has the capability of opening as a flower that you have kept closed like a bud. Enough of walking with a black wall in your back, carrying the darkness of the world in your neck! Turn your head and let your eyes shine into the unknown . . . more, do it again . . . to the left now, like that, until you forget you even have a neck . . . now to the right. . . . You see, you don't move forward when you drag darkness behind you. Your body has no front, no back, no sides. . . . It is a shining sphere."

Little by little, Magdalena had me turn my head around until there was no place I could not see. I ceased to feel threatened by an enemy hidden in the night that I had harbored in my back.

"Now another matter: If bones are beings, then joints are bridges across which time must pass. Every one of your ages continues to live in you. Infancy is hidden in your feet. If you leave your baby stuck there, he will impede your walk, dragging you into a memory that is both cradle and prison, cutting you off from the future and trapping you in a demand that cannot give or act. Let the energy accumulated in your soles, toes, and the underside of your toes rise up into your legs so that you become a child: dance, play, kick your feet around as if they are a giant you control—but don't remain there. Invade that seemingly impregnable fortress of your knees. In front, they present an armor to the world, but behind, they offer the intimate sensuality of an adolescent. Knees conquer the world, allowing you to claim your territory as a king claims his. They are the fierce horses of your carriage, but if you don't persist in rising and maturing further, you will be stuck in your castle. Now move the energy up through the length of your thighs and become an adult. In the joints between your humerus and your pelvis, discover the capacity of opening your legs.

"Now, my hero, you are in front of the sacred column. Every vertebra is a step that leads you from earth to sky. From the grandeur and power of the lumbars, climb toward the emotional dorsals until you arrive at the lucid cervicals to receive the cranium, a treasure chest which culminates in ten thousand petals opening to the luminous energy pouring down from the cosmos. . . . Now that you have learned to open, don't go back to being closed."

At this point, she began to pinch many parts of my skin, stretching it: my chest, shoulders, legs, arms, back of the neck, head, eyelids . . . even the scrotum. I felt this last open like a large fan, releasing its blocked energies. This little sack that had always been wrinkled up like bark seemed to let go of its anxiety to protect its sperm and open joyously to the world in an immense smile without fear.

"Toward the outside, now: Stretch into the air, with its hidden perfumes; feel how it reaches into infinity. Let your shoulder blades become wings, offer the skin of your belly like a magnetic cup, absorbing mortal destiny without fear. Your skin is not a prison separating you from the world. You do not live enclosed in the illusion that you call 'inside.' Let 'inside' merge with 'outside' so that the hell of separation is finished. Let your body reach out to the six directions: in front, where plans dwell; behind, where ten thousand holy hands are pushing you into life; to the right, where numberless suns arise; to the left, which is both setting and promise of return; below, to the abysses illuminated by the inextinguishable torch; and above, beyond the stars, to that luminous absence where all words fail. Continue to stretch yourself in this way to arrive at the boundary that dissolves into invisible will. Now you feel like an expanding sphere and you discover your center. Recognize this diamond, this eye of fire, the mystery that feeds both good and evil according to how you use it."

I lost all sense of time. When she had finished stretching my skin, I felt as light as a cloud. I noticed with surprise that it was already midnight.

"This is the hour when the owl's vision becomes perfect. The earth appears to it like a living creature made of waves of love. One of these waves is food. The mouse knows this and offers itself to the owl without trying to escape. Its essence is immortal; being devoured only changes its form. Like a raptor, you will see the world of love offering you all kinds of nourishment for both body and soul. Accept them without demanding to know what they are, for they come from the deepest part of yourself. On the path, do not speak to anyone. Be content with listening to yourself."

I left, walking down Insurgentes Avenue. The entire neighborhood was dark due to a power failure, yet I felt no fear. Some thugs walked past me like strips of black velvet, without noticing me. My reality was no longer theirs. In contrast, a huge moth as large as my hand flew up and settled on my chest, beating its wings as if trying to get inside. Was it because it saw my heart shining like a small star?

When I returned the next morning, doña Magdalena was heating a jug of thick liquid immersed in a larger pan of hot water. When the liquid began to boil, she poured into it some plants that she had ground in a mortar. While the liquid cooled, she stirred the mixture until it became solid.

"This is Vaseline to which I have added savory, ylang-ylang, sage, rosemary, and especially marijuana. With this balm, I shall conquer your willfulness. You do not yet want to let go of the rage of your painful memories. They accumulate in your muscles in the form of contractions and these give you the sensation of existing. If you let go of them, allowing your demand to be loved to disappear along with your fears of abandonment and your bitterness, you will feel yourself disappearing. My sad child, you believe that your suffering is who you are. My balm will give energy and pleasure to your skin. You will know physical well-being, which will bring peace to your soul. The world will finally cease to be your enemy, you will feel inviolable, you will accept matter as a friend and feel the cosmos is your cradle. Now forget the male; allow the female to appear. . . . Surrender yourself; do not resist . . . cease all activity; become water molded by the form of my hands."

I was naked and lying on my side as she massaged the balm into my muscles one by one.

"Now be aware of the real sensation of your muscles. Stop seeing them through a mental image of yourself. Every time you catch yourself returning to your mind, return instead to your body sensations. You are not a character in a movie. If you flee the body to take refuge as a mental observer, the mind immediately becomes a dungeon. Come now . . . come in further . . . more than that! Come into your flesh and stay there to learn humility. You understand? Until now, you thought that humility meant lowering your values, hiding them behind a mask of submission. You must realize that you have been walking through the world without seeing it directly, distracted by what you believed was worthy or unworthy. My child, humility means ceasing to defend your beliefs and prove to others that you have a right to be alive. Let it all go; you have no need to prove anything! Go into your body, uncover it once and for all, relinquish your doubts and defenses, surrender yourself—even if vultures devour your entrails, even if you rot, even if you turn to ashes, let go; every one of your muscles is like a closed box, and I'm going to open them."

The Vaseline mixed with herbs gave me a physical well-being I had never felt before. With her skillful fingers, Magdalena went over every inch of my muscles, massaging them as if they were the tissues of the fetus of a higher being about to be born. Using her thumbs to push down as she lifted from beneath with her fingers, she stretched them to their sides, as if removing the invisible shell of a huge prawn. This sensation of opening spread throughout my body, causing me to break into sobs. I had kept my most painful memories locked up in these muscles. In my calves I hid the vicious kicks my mother gave me under the table to make me shut up when my grandmother came to eat, because everything I said was apparently some sort of expression of disrespect to this caustic old woman. My right arm harbored the rage against my father, the suppressed punch in the face I had wanted to give him, covering his face in blood for having terrorized me for so many years under the pretext of teaching me courage. In my back, between the spine and shoulder blades, I kept the unbearable absence of caresses during my childhood. And in my ankles, like slashes from a scythe, I hid the sadness of being uprooted from my native village when I was nine years old. In one day, I lost all my friends, my favorite places, the cloudless sky, the smell of the sea and the arid hills, the perpetual caress of the dry air—and acquired a tension in my legs that transformed my agile, light-footed steps into foot-dragging through the streets of strange cities.

"Do you see? You were full of closed boxes that contained all your sadness, suffering, anger, frustration. . . . When I revived your bones, it made you go deeper inside. When I stretched your skin, it made you go farther outside. In opening all of your muscles, I have pushed you to the sides, toward both dawn and dusk. Now that I have emptied you of these memories trapped in your tissues like flies in a spider web, your viscera will appear. These are your ignored friends, always working for you in darkness, day and night, without the slightest thanks from you. Now feel them as I insert my fingers into the upper part of your abdomen, like this, on the right side. Feel as I palpate, caress, and move my fingers around; feel its large and generous form. This, my son, is your liver. It is a powerful, honest, faithful organ. It is vibrating, because it knows that you acknowledge it. Listen to its deep voice: 'I am the doorman, the one who works to prevent the passage of toxins—not only those you ingest with your mouth but also those that infect your mind. Every cruel word makes me work to combat it, every repressed anger eats away at me, and unexpected attacks from the outside world strike me. I do my best to keep you alive, sending little pains or increased bile to get your attention. I also store vitamins. I wish you to live in innocence; I wish for words to descend from your ears to your soul like pure water; I wish for you to uproot criticism so that your blood flows like a limpid river. Allow me the strength to forbid entry to the demons of gluttony, jealousy, and deceit! Do not become my enemy, attacking me with substances I cannot assimilate. Not only are you what you eat but also you eat what you are. If you allow my temple to be invaded by substances, thoughts, feelings, or desires that are alien to you, they will be transformed into toxins.'"

When Magdalena spoke as the liver, her voice seemed to me like the purring of a black panther. Little by little, her repeated manipulations and caresses caused me to feel this great, soft organ, flat like a fish, pulsing all over with waves of faith and energy, like the love of a dog. I realized that my body, distorted by the icy indifference of my parents, had always received a rejuvenating elixir from this valiant organ, fatiguing it greatly. For the first time in my life, I felt pity for my liver. I asked Magdalena to liberate it from its suffering so that it could rest.

"My dear soul child, what you ask can be obtained only by going into your heart. Second after second, this friend, like a waterwheel of pure devotion, causes life to circulate in you. It beats in a rhythm that originated the instant the ancient ancestral spirit first manifested. If you concentrate, you will feel that primordial word in your breast, the resounding thunder that brought forth all existence, the dance of matter obeying the incessant demand of multiplicity. Under your ribs you bear a stubborn motor, as vigorous and sure of itself as an arrow flying through the empty sky like a giant bird bearing you toward eternity. This is why you must never go against it, no matter the frustration that may cause one or another of your muscles to contract—for the heart is the king of all muscles and it feels their slightest tensions, accumulating them over time. Little by little, this can cause it to lose interest in leading you to the divine portal. Then it will begin to punish you. It will weaken, beat out of rhythm, stutter, and get stuck. This wrong rhythm announces that the celestial doors are beginning to close for you. Allow my massage to give your heart confidence again, and have faith in it so that it has faith in you. Send your blood to it full of love. Do not reject it by trying to ignore its presence. Do not treat it as a clock that ticks out the minutes until your death. The heart never threatens; nor does it keep accounts. Its essential work is to circulate hope through your arteries and veins. Allow it to palpitate; imagine it as an eagle; climb onto its back; see how it opens its immense wings, carrying you toward a miraculous future.

"You are so used to living like a victim that the happiness you are now receiving makes you cry. You must finish once and for all with this orphan's suffering. I am now going to awaken the consciousness of your lungs. They know the pleasure of air, of singing, the victory of having emerged for good from the sea. Three lobes on the right are male, two lobes on the left are female. They inhale the transparency of the world, inviting you to rise up beyond the stars. Allow all the air to come in and go out; never indulge in thinking you are suffocating; enjoy feeling these two friendly sponges, even when they are empty, and you will understand little by little that they love infinite space. Let them relax; don't strain to breathe—be as calm as possible, as you observe your skeleton, your flesh, and your skin also drinking in this invisible nourishment. Gently let this vital oxygen, this exquisite food, enter into you. Now hold it as long as you can, transforming it into an elixir that penetrates your every cell, enriching its nucleus of consciousness. Then breathe out slowly, and feel how you are feeding the world: when the lungs receive the gift of the sky, you give back air to the energies of the earth. You are a bridge between them; for you the angels come and go, arise and descend as in the dream of Jacob."

I now felt myself to be an essential part of the world. My breathing gave life to plants and to the earth, my heart rhythm was part of the total rhythm of animals everywhere. There was no separation between me and the clouds. Inhaling and exhaling, I could even create stars in my hands.

Seeing my face flushed with ecstasy, Magdalena began to laugh joyously.

"You understand? You have lived your whole life unconscious of the immense pleasure, the miraculous exchange involved simply in breathing. When you purify your mind, the air you exhale purifies all beings and all things. Your passage through this world will be a continuous fertilization.

"Now listen closely, my dearest soul child. There are two ways of sculpting: the way of artists and the way of the gods. Artists take a block of material and shape their creation from the outside to the inside, but the gods begin inside, from the center, the original source. From there, they concentrate and develop their creation of the body, from the inside to the outside. The viscera that spoke to you today are properly called *viscera,* not *organs,* because they live in the interior of your body. If they were on the surface, they could be called organs. For us women, our internal sex is visceral. But for you men, this viscera has become an organ. We feel our vulva as a creative center, whereas you feel your phallus as a sort of companion, a pleasurable tool, and you separate it from your emotional center. Now lie down. I am going to show you the roots of your sex."

The massage that Magdalena now gave me had absolutely nothing to do with masturbation or erotic caresses. She had warned me before beginning: "Don't misunderstand. Look at how I am massaging this foot—feel the quality of my hands. They are full of tenderness, you see? I am holding it as a mother holds her baby. . . . Now feel how I hold your genitals, and how the quality has not changed. It is the same maternal tenderness, protecting and caring. Don't be afraid; let go of your defenses and any sense of shame. It's perfectly normal to have an erection. Allow yourself to be handled, but do not seek pleasure. Instead, seek understanding."

Magdalena took my penis with her right hand and pressed the index finger of her left hand onto the hole of the urethra. She exerted a vibrating pressure concentrated in the tip of her finger. I had the feeling that she was creating a tiny sun there that did not burn but radiated life. She then moved her finger down the upper part of the glans, tracing a line down to the pubis and up the body to my navel. Then she moved up to the solar plexus and continued upward the whole length of my body, finally stopping at the crown of my skull.

"That is the first root of your organ. It goes up to the summit of your skull, and there it absorbs the nourishing energy pouring down from the heavens."

Then she returned her finger to the urethra, took several moments to re-create the intense point, and moved her finger down the lower part of the glans and penis, passing over the barrier of the foreskin to the testicles, down the perineum, then up between the buttocks to the sacrum and the spine, up the vertebrae to the back of the neck, and finally, again, to the crown of the skull.

"The first root absorbs luminous energies, but the second one enters into the night that dwells in your back, arriving at the will constructed in the back of your neck and finally meeting up with the other root at the highest point, which links you to the stars. These two are the main roots, but I also want you to feel the multiple other sexual roots embedded in different parts of your body."

Tirelessly, Magdalena now began to trace out lines all over my body, always beginning at the head of the phallus. They went to the palms of my hands, the soles of my feet, my ribs, the base of my throat, my eyes, my ears, my forehead. . . . Little by little, I perceived that between my legs was something like a tree, with powerful roots passing through my body and leaving through my feet and my head to reach to the center of the earth and every star in the universe.

"My beloved soul child, a woman does not need to search for her roots, for she feels them already at her birth. Instead, she needs to make them branch, pushing from the ovaries, in order to grow a labyrinth of energy toward the vastness of the world. In order to be in union with his sexual organ, a man must make it move its roots toward the primordial seed, whereas a woman must make hers spread into branches that reach toward the ultimate fruit. Just like your phallus, you have been living apart from the roots of your body. You believe that ultimate freedom is liberation from the flesh, detaching consciousness from the body as we remove a hand from a glove or a sword from its scabbard. At first, of course, the body, with its mysterious life, its sensations, its uncontrollable urges, appears like a heavy curtain blocking contact with the light of the soul. But are you merely flesh that possesses consciousness—a consciousness exuded by that flesh? Are you not also consciousness that exudes flesh? The sky symbolizes spirit, the earth symbolizes body. Between sky and earth is the human being, like the god Set of ancient Egypt, separating sky and earth at the beginning to realize finally that the stars above and the roots below are part of the same tree. Certain energies decrease as others increase. If there is no individual self after death, then consciousness and the body are an ephemeral unity that must accept the marriage, the coagulation, with joy. When you meditate, sitting motionless, you go toward the branches. When you abandon yourself to my massage, you enrich your roots. But is this body you offer me a whole or a fragment? Recognize that you have been living it as a fragment. You concern yourself with the matter you can feel, but never with your aura.

"Now come, stretch yourself out on the ground. Concentrate. Feel all your matter, push down from under your skin, move through it, spread out upon the ground like an invisible pool of blood. I begin by massaging your chest and move toward the ribs. Feel how my hands follow the energy down to the floor, caressing it, because your aura is also stretched out there, about six feet out, though you cannot yet feel this. Refine your sensitivity. If my pressure on your invisible body is prolonged, it means you are feeling it, and this will bring you serenity. By entering into the invisible pool of your aura, I feel knots, confusions, and tensions. It feels like tangled hair that has not been brushed for years. Now stand up. I am going to comb your aura so that it will be smooth and orderly."

Using her hands like combs, Magdalena passed them repeatedly all around me. Though she never once touched me, I felt my mind coming more and more into order and harmony. Old resentments dissolved and disappointed hopes were dispersed. My habitual, constant state of anxious expectation—as if my life were always in the future instead of now—was calmed. Like a squid floating tranquilly in the ocean, my mind surrendered to the present, to the world that is instead of the world I thought.

"Now that your aura is well combed, I shall have to wash your shadow."

She opened the only window. The afternoon light flooded in. She had me stand with my back to the light so that my shadow was projected inside the brilliant rectangle of light on the floor.

"My son, stand very still and do not move for any reason. Here you see your companion, the one who—though you never condescend to listen to it—tells you what you actually are: a sundial. Every instant, your body tells the time—and this is important, because every hour has a soul, a different energy, that demands that you use it in a different way. If you force your hours by doing what does not suit them, then you live badly and you become ill. Most people care nothing for their shadow, dragging it around as if it were a dirty animal. This poisons their steps."

Magdalena was now kneeling and washing my shadow vigorously with lavender-scented water and soap. She brushed it, wiped away the water and suds with a sponge, dried it, and then seemed satisfied. But still she forbade me to move, inviting me to look at my shadow as if at a work of art.

"There—it's all clean now. Look how beautiful it is! Now return home while there's still plenty of sunlight, so you can feel your shadow. I'm sure you'll notice the change."

As I walked with the sun to my back, I felt my shadow as a pleasant companion. Even more, I began to see it as an ally worthy of respect. It pleased me to watch it, to observe how this black stain flitted like an immaterial bird over objects, people, and walls, leaving an invisible trace that bestowed purity and joy upon the tortured material of the city. I saw that the other pedestrians were totally unconscious of their own shadows. This neglect made their shadows seem like heavy, black rags, filthy and sad, dragging on the steps of their owners, adding more impurities to the objects they fell upon.

My experience with Magdalena lasted forty days. With patience and devotion, she overcame my resistances little by little, showing me different ways of massaging the body.

"Darling child of my soul, you don't live in a body; you live in a unique wound. In order for you to feel the spiritual matter that you truly are, I must give priority to healing you. You remind me of one of those blackened shrimps they sell at the taco stand down below. You are enveloped with suffering—not just yours, but that of your parents, your brothers, your uncles, your grandparents, and distant ancestors. It is the carbon that hides your diamond. I shall heal you. I am woman and I am serpent. I can give to you not only with my hands, but with my whole body."

And Magdalena began to undulate in waves, adhering to me, wrapping herself around me, slithering from my feet to my head, rubbing me with her hair, her face, her breasts, her back, her belly, her legs, her feet. Using precise pressure, she focused on certain points and then joined them to other points, covering me with meridians and circuits. I had the sensation of becoming like a tightening net, with each node linked to all the others. She pressed her lips upon these points one after another, sucking at them and then vigorously spitting out some mysterious, toxic energy. Then she blew upon each point with such extraordinary intensity that her stream of air cut like a knife. After rendering them extremely sensitive by biting them with her teeth, she used a sweet and powerful voice to inject them with words from the Mayan language. Were these the names of their androgynous gods or words of love? It made no difference.

Then she used all her weight—increased perhaps by the weight of entities from other dimensions—to crush me completely against the ground so that I became an amorphous mass.

Vibrating me with a shifting combination of rhythms—fast, slow, trembling, explosive, delicate, and brutal—she caused me to relive my fetal memories. I felt my eyes, mouth, and limbs growing and felt the palpitating center that must have been my heart. Above all, I saw my soul. It was like a rose opening abruptly, emanating its immense, anguished desire to live.

Then she brought me through infancy, childhood, adolescence, adulthood, middle age, old age—and onward to a sort of millennial androgyne, an angel, a limitless god.

She awakened my vital energy by causing my navel (which she called Eden) to spout four intangible rivers branching into thirteen centers in my body, which she called temples. Through mysterious pressures, she opened these like jugs, giving a list of the different gifts that they were able to pour out.

The forty days had come to an end. "That is enough," she said. "You have received it all. You no longer need to receive. What I have given you, you can give to others."

She placed her palms on the back of my hands with such firmness and assurance that I felt as if we shared a single skin. Then she directed me in self-massage. The more confident I became, the more she relaxed the pressure of her hands until, without my even realizing it, her hands seemed to have flown away like a pair of doves. Everything she had been teaching me came back little by little: I palpated my bones, stretched my skin, made contact with my viscera, planted my feet in the ground after having calmed my shadow, combed my aura, traced out meridians and circuits, centered myself in my spinal column and from there sent out energy to the sides with the sensation of unfolding two immense wings.

"Yes, fly, my son! Spread your wings; your body doesn't stop at your skin. It extends out into the air, filling all space. It grows with the cosmos, embracing the divine creation. The earth is yours, the galaxies are yours, you are eternal and infinite. In the shadow of your reason live countless goddesses, and they are also yours. Humans, animals, plants, the unborn, the legions of the dead—they are all yours. Make your decision! Become master of your life! You are a flower whose number-less petals open and close every instant, surging like an explosion of light from the black matrix that is neither matter nor energy but the creative womb. And you live in all this, in the corolla that is collective consciousness, like a diamond scintillating with rays of love from conscious beings. Other diamonds form a necklace that shines eternally around the mystery that none can name."

As I walked the streets, I no longer felt that the weight of my body was a burden. Instead, it was a link of union with this mirage I called reality. Every step was a caress, every breath of air was a blessing. These sensations were so surprising that I felt as if I were living in a new body and a new mind. The thought of receiving any further massages from Magdalena was distinctly unattractive—a bird does not need extra air to fly, a fish does not need extra water to swim without limits. I allowed a week to pass, during which my eating habits changed. I could no longer tolerate meat, coffee, or dairy products. Rice best suited my stomach. It also reminded me of Ejo Takata. On the same day his image came to mind, I received from Ana Perla a postcard with a Hindu-style Buddha on it announcing the imminent return of the master.

I bought a bouquet of white roses and went to say good-bye to Magdalena. Her door was open, but the room was empty.

I went downstairs and asked the taco merchant where she had gone. The people working there only shrugged their shoulders. Noticing one of the boys offering himself in the street nearby, I asked him about her whereabouts.

"Doña Magdalena is like the wind," he answered. "She arrives bearing her seeds, sows them, and then leaves. No one can pin her down."

I murmured to myself: "Under the motionless clouds, the wind carries away the city."

Left: The curandera Pachita

Below: Maria Sabina, the mushroom priestess

Right: Chilean singer Violete Parra

Below: Spanish writer Francisco Gonzalez Ledesma, who used the pseudonym Silver Kane

Left: Mumon Yamada, the master of my Zen master. He was an elegant Buddha.

Below: My own master, Zen monk Ejo Takata, after his arrival in Mexico

"Intellectual, learn to die!" Myself, about thirty years old

Above: Me with Ejo Takata. I'm reflecting on the austere staging of my theater production Zarathustra, *based on Nietzche's work.*

Below: During Zarathustra, *my Zen teacher agreed to sit motionless on stage, meditating during the entire two-hour performance.*

Above: Surrealist painter and artist Leonora Carrington

Right: Carrington's husband, Chiki, who wore this beret day and night

Above: The actress Maria Félix

Left: Leonora Carrington's painting of Maria

Above: The Tigress with her tiger, Salgari

*Right: Later, the Tigress produced a performance of
Lucretia Borgia in competition with my own. She was
naked on stage with her pubic hair painted green. This
performance ran successfully for two years.*

*Below: A poster for my own production, which ran for
only four months*

*I acquired a dubious notoriety
because of my relationship with
the Tigress, before we had a major
falling-out.*

The only known photo of doña Magdalena

Above: In my film El Topo, *I played the title role.*

Right: "I am the daughter of Gurdjieff," Reyna D'Assia told me. Here, as a child, she is pictured with her father.

Above: I went with Reyna to Monte Alban, a Zapotec ceremonial center built on a plateau more than sixty-five hundred feet high that was located on a mountain that had been leveled to build the center.

Right: In an envelope sent from Bali by Reyna D'Assia, I found this photo with these words: "Me and my daughter, Ivanna. I don't know whether her father is you or don Prudencio."

Above: I played the title role in my theater piece Hamlet Gonzalez—*an apocalyptic version.*

Left: Me and producer Allen Klein, after our reconciliation.

8

Like Snow in a
Silver Vase

～✷∩✷～

*"OK—and by the way, why do you talk so much, you son
of a bitch? I told you to shut up! I may get so tired I'll put
a bullet through your balls!"*

SILVER KANE, MADISON COLT

Ana Perla, as the head of the group of disciples, received the master
at the airport. He was accompanied by a sweet nun named Michiko
(who would later become his wife) and her ten-year-old adopted daughter, Tomiko, an orphan. Exhausted and irritable from lack of sleep on
the long trip, Ejo cut short any talk with a brief bow and asked to be
taken directly to the zendo to rest. Ana complied with this but decided
that while the family was sleeping all the disciples must meditate until
the master awakened. This lasted for about two hours, but then we all
began to fall asleep. In the early hours of the morning, everyone was
awakened by a piercing shout of "Kwatzu!"

The master was standing before us, indignantly pointing his finger
at the cat. The disciples had decided to shave the top of its head to

imitate a monk. They had also dressed it in a brown robe and had trimmed its ears and its tail. Ejo Takata stood frozen in the center of the zendo, which was now decorated in a kind of hippie-Aztec style. It was clear that he was barely able to control his rage. The disappointment of witnessing this grotesque perversion of his teaching was soon to be amplified by the humiliation that would be inflicted upon him by Fernando Molina.

I had been meditating with Ejo for about two years. Very late one night, someone rang my doorbell, which made me nervous. My cottage, though in a central part of the city, had no near neighbors. In front was a vacant lot where pitched battles between cats and huge rats took place. The buildings next to mine formed a solid, connected row of tottering, ruined houses that were barely held up by rotten beams. They were home to so many scorpions and spiders that even the most desperate alcoholics dared not sleep there.

Mastering my fear, I unlocked the chain and opened the door. Before me was a slender youth with tiny eyes that glittered like coals and teeth so large he looked like a horse. He held a bouquet of sunflowers. It was Fernando Molina, a standup comedian who worked in variety theaters, appearing between striptease acts with a stream of salacious jokes and stories. I invited him to enter.

After giving me the bouquet, he raised a fist in front of my face and, with an extreme disrespect indicating madness, said: "If you tell me, I'll punch you in the mouth! And if you don't tell me, I'll punch you in the mouth! . . . What?"

A multitude of thoughts raced through my mind at the speed of light. This guy was clearly a raving barbarian who learned vaguely something about koans and wanted to test me in a stupid and vulgar way. If I was to give him the correct response to this koan, which I happened to have learned from Ejo, he wouldn't understand and he would try to punch me anyway, so I decided to apply the deeper lessons I had learned from the master. Conquering my fear, I relaxed my muscles and emptied my mind of all thoughts, looking deeply and steadily into his eyes, asking nothing, offering nothing, simply being there, like a stone or a bird.

With churlish contempt, Molina drew back his arm to hurl the punch. Without blinking an eye, I stood with perfect Christian mildness, ready to receive the blow.

And then the unthinkable happened. It was one of those incredibly precise synchronicities that arrive exactly when they are needed: the entire row of dilapidated neighboring houses collapsed! It resounded like an explosion, and a cloud of dust billowed in through the window, covering us. I took advantage of the shock, pushing Fernando away from me, and shouted:

"*There* is your answer to your 'What?'"

The comedian was so agitated that his horselike teeth were chattering. He then burst out laughing, hesitated for a few seconds, and finally kneeled before me.

"Tomorrow, I was supposed to take a plane to Peru to see a master who lives there. But tonight, I dreamed about you. You were seated in meditation like an ancient sage. I prostrated before you, gave you a bouquet of sunflowers, and begged you: 'Save me! Give me the teaching that I lack. Enlighten me!' And you answered: 'Wake up and come see me immediately.' So I did. On the way, at Rio de Janeiro Plaza, I noticed a large bed of sunflowers planted around a copy of Michelangelo's *David*. I stole eleven of them and brought them to you. Do you understand? Eleven sunflowers plus myself makes twelve disciples turning around the central sun. That sun is you, who are able to make a whole street collapse!"

"Hold on there, Fernando! Those houses have been in ruins and ready to collapse for a long time. It's an accident that it happened now. Your dream was corrrect in telling you to come see me—but not because I am your master. Instead, it told you to come so that I can introduce you to a real master, which will make your trip to Peru unnecessary. His name is Ejo Takata. He's an authentic Zen monk who can give you the teaching you desire. Now it's two o'clock in the morning. In three hours, Ejo will begin his meditation. Let's have some coffee, and then I'll take you to the zendo."

Sadly, the comedian pointed to his teeth. "I broke all of them in a motorcycle accident. They gave me these huge false teeth, which make me look like a horse. No master would take me seriously."

"Don't worry about it. Ejo sees your essential being."

At the zendo, Ejo took Fernando by the chin affectionately, looked at his teeth, sighed deeply, and said, "One day, you will have very beautiful eyes."

From that time on, Molina kept his mouth shut tightly, decided to remain mute for the rest of his life, and moved into the zendo, sleeping on the meditation platform. He kept the place impeccably swept and mopped, whitewashed the walls, and cooked rice. Later, he helped Michiko rid the plants of parasites; accompanied Tomiko to school; cleaned the cat box; was allowed to walk among the meditating disciples, brandishing the kyosaku and slapping the shoulder blades of the drowsy ones with slumping backs; made trips to the market to scavenge leftover fruits and vegetables; and did many other things.

Touched by such devotion, Ejo was full of hope, imagining a future in which the ancient cultures of Japan and Mexico would come together in a religious embrace. When Fernando's head was shaved and he donned the robes of a monk, Ejo wrote a poem:

> *He who has no arms*
> *will help with his arms*
> *and he who has no legs*
> *will help with his legs*
> *in this great spiritual work*
> *where many beings*
> *will lose their hair.*

Shortly afterward, Ejo decided to send his first Mexican monk to the same monastery where he had been trained. At this news, Molina let out a great neigh of pleasure, showing his teeth for the first time in a year. All of us contributed money to help purchase the airplane ticket, most of which had been paid for by a contribution from the Japanese embassy.

A month later, the master received a card from Mumon Yamada congratulating him on having trained such an exemplary monk who outdid even his Japanese disciples in his devotion to daily tasks and meditation.

Later, Ejo returned again to Japan. When he arrived at the monastery, it was as if he was drenched with a huge bucket of cold water. The very day he went to visit his old master, the monks who had the job of supervising the letters and packages that novices received from their families had made an unpleasant discovery: concealed in the boxes of chocolates that Molina had been receiving from Mexico were several types of drugs, including opium paste, heroin, and LSD. Worse, they discovered that a part of the package contents had been set aside for the purpose of selling drugs to the other novices.

Thus the first Mexican monk was expelled in disgrace and forbidden to enter any Zen monastery or temple in Japan.

Judging from the terrible rage that Ejo manifested in the zendo upon his return, his shame and disappointment must have been immense. Molina had already returned from Japan, taking a plane that left only two hours before his. Acting as if nothing had happened, Fernando was still wearing his monk's robes and sleeping soundly next to Ana Perla. Mingled with the fragrances of incense—sandalwood, patchouli, and myrrh—was a strong odor of marijuana.

Standing motionless for a moment before this spectacle, Ejo suddenly burst into a flurry of raging action. Swinging his stick, he smashed all the flower vases, the pre-Columbian sculptures, the Shivas and the Shaktis,* and the gilded Buddhas. He ripped from the walls

---

*In Tantra, awakening happens through the union of male (linga/Shiva) and female (yoni/Shakti) energies. The classic Hindu representation of this is the figure of Shiva in sexual union with Shakti: both are seated face-to-face, and she has her legs wrapped around him. This image recurs in Buddhist deities represented with Tibetan tantric imagery.

all the kabbalistic and astrological posters and removed the cat's robe and tossed it out the window. He also tossed out all the zafus, which, formerly black, had been covered with white cloths and embroidered with Huichol designs.

Then he proceeded to expel Ana Perla and the others who were in the zendo, threatening them with fists and feet. Terrified, they all fled in haste. Only Fernando Molina remained, sitting hunched in a ball, his head between his legs and his arms clasped tightly. Ejo rolled him out the door, into the middle of the street, but Molina refused to budge. He remained there in a ball, with cars swerving to avoid him, and there he stayed for hours, yet the master's compassion seemed to have vanished. Finally, an ambulance arrived. They placed him on a stretcher, still rolled in a ball, and took him away.

We never saw him again. (Three years later, I learned that Molina had appeared in a "happening," now endowed with normal teeth. His new act consisted of burning a monk's robe and copulating with his wife upon its ashes before a large audience.)

Late that night, Ana Perla sneaked back to the zendo, accompanied by six of her acolytes, and painted this graffiti upon its facade in huge red letters: BUDDHA IS A WOMAN.

During this dismal period, I decided imprudently to read to the master the following essay, which I had just published in the cultural supplement of the conservative periodical *Heraldo de Mexico.*

Donald Duck and Zen Buddhism

There exists a Donald Duck comic that corresponds exactly to the message of koans 42 and 44 of the book of Mumonkan.*

---

*A collaborative work by Mumon Ekai (Wumenguan, "the doorless passage," in Chinese). It is a collection of forty-eight koans plus a commentary and poem. Mumon Ekai's collaborator was Wumen Huikai (1183–1260 CE), whose own master, Yuelin, gave him as an exercise the famous koan "Does a dog have Buddha nature?" The famous response— "Wu" (Mu in Japanese)—was given by the Chinese master Shaoshou Congshen (Joshu Jishin). Wumen meditated on this response for six years, when an experience of awakening led him to compose the repetitive quatrain that introduces this book.

The city fire chief invites Donald to join the volunteer firefighters. He tells his three nephews about it. They want to join too, but their uncle considers them incompetent and orders them to stay at home. Donald is provided with a complete uniform on condition that he rush immediately to the scene of the fire as soon as he hears the alarm. If he arrives in time, he will receive a bronze medal. Proudly, Donald empties a chest, saying he'll need the space for all the medals he is bound to receive. That night, the alarm rings, but he sleeps through it. His nephews drag him out of his sleep. He hurries to the fire but forgets his helmet. He also forgets his hatchet and his pants. When he finally arrives with these items, it is too late. The house he was supposed to save is a mass of smoking ruins, and the other firefighters have left.

The next day, the chief demotes him, taking away his hatchet and replacing it with a small extinguisher. That night, the alarm rings again, and once more, his nephews have to drag him out of sleep. This time he dresses more carefully, but in his haste, he grabs a can of insecticide instead of the extinguisher. When he sprays it on the fire, it only makes the flames worse.

The chief demotes him again. From now on, he has only a sack to use against the fire. Wanting to help him, his nephews decide to set a small fire so that he will not be too depressed and will have work to do. Meanwhile, Donald discovers a package of fireworks, including rockets. Thinking they are dangerous, he stuffs them in his coat pockets.

"Uncle Donald, there's a fire in the street! You must take your sack and save the town!"

Donald succeeds in putting out the flames, but his coat catches fire and he runs home. The rockets explode there and his living room catches on fire. The nephews put it out with a hose.

The chief arrives and is impressed by the nephews. He invites them to join the firefighters. The next night, when the alarm sounds, the nephews wake up, shouting: "We must go quickly!

Nothing can stand in our way!" They rush off toward the fire in a modern, fully equipped fire truck. Meanwhile, poor Donald is left standing in the street with his pathetic sack, watching the truck speed away. "They have all the luck," he mutters.

Several esoteric teachings point out the error that causes us to link all our ordinary states of consciousness, forgetting that they are separated by vast lakes of sleep. Zen is based upon a total awakening known as *satori.*

> *Satori* is the alpha and omega of Zen Buddhism. It may be defined as intuitive insight into the nature of things, as opposed to logical or analytic understanding. In practice, it signifies the discovery of a new world heretofore unnoticed because of the confusion of a mind educated in dualism. When we experience satori, everything around us is seen with a kind of perception that has never before been known . . .
>
> (*Essays on Zen Buddhism,* D. T. SUZUKI)

In koan 44, known as Pa-tsiao's stick, the master says to his monks: "If you have a stick, I will give you the stick. If you don't have a stick, I will take it away from you." . . . Let us analyze this koan in the light of the Donald Duck story. He first receives a "mystical call" to put out a fire. Yet in receiving the call, Donald is blinded by his pride. He is already congratulating himself on the honors he will receive: a position of great responsibility and bronze medals to gratify his narcissistic self (though if they were of real value, they would be gold, not bronze). Furthermore, he intends to store them in a trunk, a symbol of his closed ego. His nephews, on the contrary, represent collective wisdom and the priority of social good over selfish good. They are both three and one. They pronounce one sentence, dividing it into three parts: 1) The alarm has rung, 2) . . . and our uncle must be, 3) . . . asleep. These are the nephews who disdain egoistic thought. They awaken when the alarm sounds and set about extinguishing the fire selflessly, expecting no reward and thinking only of the task at hand. Finally, it is they who try to help the Other. They have a stick, and this is why they are given the best fire truck. Uncle Donald does not have a stick, which is why even what he has is taken away from him little by little. . . .

In koan 42, a nun is deep in concentration beside the Buddha. The other disciples complain because she alone has the honor of sitting next to the master. The Buddha tells them to bring her out of her meditation, but they are unable to do so. The Buddha calls out: "Ignorance!" Then he approaches the woman, snaps his fingers, and she immediately wakes up.

The content is clear: Neither knowledge nor discussion nor study can give satori. Only mind which is not conscious of a separate self can trigger it.

. . . Donald Duck, a modern Prometheus, receives the call to extinguish his petty mental fire, then he discovers some rockets and becomes submerged in the great Fire-Unconscious universe. It is clear that the abnormal excess of dualistic thought causes us to suffer. This is why the duck cries out when his house catches fire. He needs satori but is afraid of it. He loses his chance, and sadly, lugging his intellectual sack, he watches the new generation disappear in the distance. His pathetic consolation is to exclaim how lucky they are. He does not see that such luck is the result of constant inner work (the necessity of being responsive to all calls) and that it is because of their work that they have been given this blessing.

Poor Donald! Everything is taken away from him. His rigid concepts cause him to expect something without working to obtain it. And how to obtain it? For Donald, the path is shown in the story: He must clean his trunk, emptying it of all those bronze medals.

After I had finished reading the article to Ejo, my contented smile froze as he began to fan himself, muttering, "Like snow in a silver vase."

His tone left no doubt as to his meaning. In spite of their cleverness, my words were destined to vanish without a trace.

After a seemingly interminable silence, Ejo spoke in a very low voice: "The moment you open your mouth to speak 'the truth,' you betray yourself." Blushing with shame, I understood. However accurate my Zen interpretation of the Donald Duck story might be, I rendered the teaching useless by such an attempt to explain it.

Ejo passed me the secret book. "Read the first koan of the third part. It is not for novices; it is only for those who aspire to become masters. When this and the forty-three other koans are received after three years of novitiate, the aspirant must confine himself to the monastery and practice for at least ten years. Only someone who has succeeded in becoming a Zen master has the right and the capacity to ask these koans of a new generation.

"That night, when Señor Molina came to your door and asked you that koan, not even knowing its correct form, and threatened to punch you violently in the mouth—the same place where he had done violence to himself, breaking all his teeth—he was giving a sign of inexcusable vanity, pride, stupidity, and unconsciousness. I should have seen this, but I was blinded by his childlike ambition and I ordained him as a monk. My real wish was for my own 'fathers' to congratulate me for helping the Dharma take root in Mexico. I deserve a hundred blows of the kyosaku. Please administer them to me."

He gave me the stick and kneeled, bowing his head and back. I hesitated. He slapped the ground loudly with his palm. "One hundred!"

What else could I do? I knew it would be useless to try to persuade him to abandon this plan. It would make him only angrier—and if I refused, it would be a further insult and humiliation to him. I began to strike him with three rather soft blows.

"Harder!" he shouted.

So I continued striking him vigorously. After a while, a bitter sob of grief rose from my belly to my throat and finally emerged from my mouth, a long, serpentine wail of lamentation for both of us, for his childhood and mine, two children who had never been allowed to play with abandon, imprisoned inside ourselves by the adults around us, two islands who had lost hope of ever meeting another pair of kind and understanding eyes that would accept us just as we were, as innocent souls, with no strings of religious or social duty attached.

After the hundredth blow, I kneeled down beside him. I attempted to embrace him, but he would not allow it. Arising with great dignity, he handed me the book.

"Read aloud!"

"Zen master Kyogen* said: 'Suppose a man climbs a tree and holds onto a branch with his teeth. He hangs there without his feet touching the ground. From below, a monk questions him on why Bodhidharma, founder of Zen, came from the west. If the man does not answer, he will be shamed for eluding the question. But if he opens his mouth, he will fall and die. What should he do?'

"A monk named Koto replied: 'Once the man is up high, hanging from the branch, he cannot reply to any question. If the monk had something to ask him, he should have done it before the man climbed the tree.' Hearing this, Kyogen burst out laughing. Later, Master Setcho commented: 'It is easy to answer while hanging from a tree. It is more difficult to answer while standing under the tree. Therefore, I must hang from a branch. Come, ask me a question.'"

"First, the classic responses," Ejo said. "There is one for when the man is hanging from a tree and another for when he is on the ground. In the tree: The disciple places a finger between his teeth, imitating a branch, wriggles his body, and grunts 'Ooh, ooh,' imitating someone trying to answer without being able to. Under the tree: The disciple imitates falling from the branch and lands on his bottom. 'Ouch, that hurts!' he says. Now answer me without opening your mouth!" Ejo said.

---

*Xiangian Zhixian, or Kyogen Chikan in Japanese (died ca. 898 CE) appears in example 5 of the Mumonkan (Wumenguan). The story of his awakening is considered edifying and is often quoted.

I offered the classic response: "Whether or not I can reply, you try first!" And I covered his mouth with my hand.

He pushed it away. "You see? Whether or not you speak, your brain is stuffed with words. Can you climb the tree and hang by your teeth from a branch? The monk Koto saw the smoke but not the fire. Human beings give more importance to knowing in advance how to answer a question with grand words that reveal the truth of the teaching than they do to the ferocious effort between life and death that they must make to realize their true nature of emptiness. Master Setcho understood this, demonstrating clearly the difference between thinking and experiencing. Under the tree, man seeks the Buddha's meaning without understanding that this Buddha he talks about is not an external being, but a level of consciousness that must be found beyond concepts. Being suspended from the tree means putting an end to intellectual discourse, to the search for ideals and goals. It means entering into a vital process, an agonizing struggle like that of a larva twisting itself to become a butterfly."

Listening to this—with my mind organizing Ejo's fragmentary phrases, because of his modest command of Spanish—I felt I had understood the two responses. In the tree: if I speak, I intellectualize and lose myself. Under the tree: if I answer by trying to translate the truth into words, I destroy it and I wind up with sentences that, however elegant, are no more than snow in a silver vase.

"Ejo, I want to hang from the tree!"

"Can you take it? Zen is not a game. It is not a mystical pastime for privileged hippies. Awakening cannot be bought or sold. It is earned by losing everything, sometimes even your reason and your life."

"Teach me, I beg you!"

"I can teach you only how to teach yourself." Now Ejo Takata seemed to undergo a change. It was as if he had rid himself of a coat of lead. He stood more erect, vibrant with energy, a huge smile lighting up his face. "We shall do a *rohatsu*. We will meditate for seven days."

"What is a *rohatsu*?"

"A Zen technique equivalent to hanging from a branch by your teeth. You are allowed only one bowl of rice a day, forty minutes of sleep, and fifteen minutes to go to the toilet. The rest of the time, you must sit without moving."

"But Ejo, this is the rainy season. The mosquitoes will devour us . . ."

"And they will enjoy a fine feast! Enough discussion. If you agree to do it, remove your shoes, and we'll start immediately. If you don't have the courage to do it, then go and burn your secret book. Koans are not poetic games. Resolving them means surrendering to a mutation. That woman you spoke of in your essay: meditating next to the Buddha, she realized ignorance ignores itself and she discovered that she is the Buddha. Do you want to awaken? Yes or no?"

"Yes!"

I removed my shoes, kneeled, took the only remaining cushion, and put it between my legs, bringing my feet together behind my back with my knees planted upon the wooden platform as if they were anchors fastening me to the center of the earth. I straightened my spine as much as possible, imagining that I was being pulled upward by my hair. Suspended between heaven and earth, I was like a strung bow ready to shoot an arrow. I placed my hands so that they were lying flat on my lap, right upon left, letting my two thumbs touch with very slight pressure, neither too much nor too little, "neither mountain nor valley." I did not close my eyes, but instead let them focus upon the floor about three feet in front of me, the corners of my mouth in a faint smile. Ejo Takata took up the very same position. Nevertheless, compared to him, I was like a pile of jelly next to a block of granite.

He lit a stick of green incense, struck a metal bowl with a wooden mallet to produce a peaceful ring, and with no further ado, my course of torture began.

We were in semidarkness. The closed window barely muffled the noise of the traffic—cars, trucks, cries from the street. From the kitchen on the ground floor we could hear the delicate movements of the master's companion. We could also hear the faint sounds of Japanese-style rock music that Tomiko had brought with her, but at a very low and discreet volume. All these noises were as nothing compared to the buzzing of a mosquito that appeared next to my ear.

Valiantly, with an almost delirious enthusiasm, I intensified my meditation, deciding to become a statue. After an hour, I began to flinch. The pain in my legs was growing worse every minute. When I could no longer take it, I tried to change my position. Ejo let out a lion's roar, which paralyzed me. To flee my body, I tried to take refuge in my mind. I imagined landscapes, interstellar voyages, multiformed clouds, zzzzz. . . . I was awakened by another terrifying roar. Ejo got up and gave me three blows of the kyosaku on each shoulder blade. This had a refreshing effect, and I was once again filled with enthusiasm and felt rested. I meditated. An hour . . . another hour . . . another . . . another. I was thirsty and hungry and my entire body was in pain. I had gas in my stomach. Ejo leaned to the right, lifted a buttock lightly, and let out a string of the loudest farts I've ever heard. Then he returned to his granite posture of meditation. With deep shame, I also let myself fart aloud. As I was in the midst of this odoriferous occupation, Michiko entered, dressed in a sober kimono. Before each of us she placed a bowl of steaming rice with bits of carrots, chopsticks, and a glass of green tea.

"Eat quickly; don't waste time," Ejo commanded. "The important thing is the meditation."

Like him, I had to wolf down the rice, to the great displeasure of my tongue. In order not to waste a single grain (waste is forbidden to monks), I poured a bit of tea into the bowl and shook it, then drank the burning mixture containing the last grains.

When Michiko removed the bowls, Ejo lit another stick of incense and we continued as before, mute and motionless. Now, though, we were allowed to interrupt the sitting once an hour, walking in a circle for five minutes to free our legs of swelling. Mine felt as if an army of ants had invaded them.

At midnight, Ejo said: "We will now sleep for forty minutes, no more." Suddenly, without changing his position, he began to snore. A mood of desperation overcame me as I noticed my shoes. Their openings seemed like two generous mouths inviting me to place my feet inside them and escape for good, abandoning this monstrous folly. Yet it was my pride that held me back—a monstrous pride that, until then, I had not even known existed in me. The only movement I made was to lie down on the floor. I felt like a dog. I was used to soft mattresses and had difficulty finding a comfortable position on the hard floor. I had trouble falling asleep. Suddenly, a terrifying noise brought me out of deep sleep. Ejo was pounding on a flexible metal plate with a steel bar, which produced sounds like thunder. I had trouble rising, and he gave me several kicks to wake me up.

"The forty minutes have passed! Quickly, quickly, don't waste any more time! Sit up and meditate." I felt like killing him.

The first two days passed. Not even a glimpse of wisdom had come to calm my mind. These days were simply hours of struggle—with my body and its swelling, cramps and pains right to the bones, mosquito bites, hunger, sleepiness, burning in my stomach, feelings of suffocation, claustrophobia, and rage against this accursed Japanese who endured such torture impassively. There were brief moments when the physical suffering miraculously disappeared, but then a profound boredom appeared, plunging me into unbearable anguish.

On the third day, my knees were swollen, my eyes were burning, my skin was covered with a rash, my vertebrae felt like fists, and my bowels were full, because the pressure to rush to the toilet and defecate in only minutes had constipated me. Feeling as if every nerve in my body had become an electric needle, I suddenly allowed myself to collapse on my back. In a plaintive voice imitating agony, I whined: "I have a sharp pain in my chest. I'm having a heart attack. Call an ambulance."

With ferocity and contempt, Ejo snapped back at me: "Then die!" Without deigning to help me, he maintained his posture, more granite-like than ever. I rolled on the floor, stamping my feet, crying. I grabbed a shoe and threw it at his head. But Ejo merely ducked slightly, just enough to avoid the projectile, and returned to his meditation.

Suddenly, my rage became like a kind of nourishment. Possessed by a new kind of energy, I sternly told my body to go to hell and resumed my meditation position, straightening my spinal column, forcing the corners of my mouth into a slight smile, fixing my eyes upon the floor in front of me; I was transformed into a statue. I felt very distant from this abominable, animal suffering. I had the impression of floating in a diaphanous sky. After an hour of deep calm during which I felt I was the Buddha, a profusion of images invaded my brain: sexual fantasies, lust for great wealth and fame . . . and then a parade of delicious food, meats, desserts, drinks, yet also succulent morsels of human flesh. Then I imagined all sorts of tortures inflicted upon men, women, and children with naked, bloody, mutilated bodies—and me floating safe and sound above this hell. I spent hours trying to vanquish this diabolical dimension of my being, but as soon as I thought I had succeeded, there arrived painful memories of the mother who never caressed me, the infantile and competitive father who used terror as a means of education, the selfish elder sister who did everything to expel me from the family so that she could be the center of attention, the cruel and intolerant classmates, the neurotic schoolteachers, and the loneliness and humiliations. It came like a tornado, causing streams of tears and mucus to run down my cheeks. Yet my enforced immobility prevented me from drying them or hiding them. To escape this morbid cemetery of the imagination, I began to compose poems, which then became stories, theater pieces, films, novels. Stories arrived, opened themselves like flowers, and then dissolved into the void. I took a long voyage into my brain, discovering a delirious universe that constantly produced images of all sorts—shapeless forms, beings, mandalas, complex geometrical designs, explosions, vast shiftings, beams of light, changing whirlwinds of madness.

When I returned to myself, I discovered illness, old age, and death.

In spite of the revelations that doña Magdalena had worked in my human organism, partly through the contact of her holy hands and fingers, I now realized that I was still identified with my mind, seeing my body, frankly, as a coffin—a beautiful coffin, certainly, full of so many riches. Nevertheless, it was not my being. It had its own life, its own mystery, its own union with the cosmos. I vegetated inside this cage, and however marvelous it might be, I was condemned to age and rot there, under constant attack from millions of microbes, viruses, inflammations, cancers. . . . Sleeping only forty minutes a day, eating only one bowl of rice, shut up in this dark room where the odor of incense mingled with the stench of thousands of farts and burps, my mental defenses were in ruins. I saw myself as covered with wounds, hacked, peeled, suffocated, burned, devoured, bleeding through my mouth and my anus. I imagined a thousand and one ways of dying: fires, hurricanes, floods, earthquakes, atomic bombs, leaping out of the window of a high building, filling my pockets with stones and jumping into a lake, taking a cocktail of poisons, swallowing a pound of nails, piercing my skull with a dentist's drill, vaulting into the murderous embrace of a wild bear, being crushed by a frozen cow that falls from a freight plane, being devoured at the summit of a mountain by starving alpinists. . . . Finally, I came up with such complex forms of suicide that I could not help shaking with suppressed laughter. Ejo, still the block of granite, made no sign.

When I stopped laughing, time and space descended upon me. I felt the immensity of the microcosm and the macrocosm and saw myself between them like a speck of dust between two suns—so small, so small, so small, so ridiculously little, floating in this immeasurable past and this interminable future. Infinity and eternity, like two spears, were thrust through my breast; oceans of universes in expansion, imploding only to start all over again; immense galaxies that, like me, were doomed to disperse into the void. It was terrifying. In front of me and within me I saw death. What I was, what I felt, what I thought I possessed, my memory, my individuality—all went down the black hole in a few seconds. I was obsessed with three words I had read in the notes left behind by Frida Kahlo: "Everything for nothing." In sum, no being possessed anything whatsoever. Everything was on loan to us for a few years—but in the end, all goes down the black hole. I felt caught up in a universal delirium. . . . In an attempt to calm myself, I focused on my shoes, those modest and useful friends with their open mouths, just waiting for my feet. An impotent rage possessed me once again: "What the devil am I doing here with this mad monk, torturing myself in this way? I'm not a samurai or a Buddha. I'm a free man. No one can oblige me to stay here any longer. That's enough!"

It was two o'clock in the morning. I stood up, picked up my shoes, walked into the street, took a taxi, and went to Globos, a cabaret on Insurgentes Avenue where many people—actors and actresses, painters, writers, singers, politicians, drug dealers, prostitutes, and so forth—went after hours to eat and dance. A Puerto Rican band was playing. The moment I entered the place, my sense of freedom vanished into thin air. I felt like an extraterrestrial who, after a long interstellar voyage, arrives in a prison. The dancers seemed like galley slaves, going through their motions; smoking their tobacco and marijuana; ingesting their alcohol, cocaine, and pills; aware of only this tiny sliver of time and space. They seemed like walking corpses that wore masks of immortality and were chained to a deafening rhythm, accepting the world that was offered to them and swallowing it whole, imitating each other, devouring each other, carrying a burden of limitations that were transformed into solid identities. This ceiling, with its cement stalactites, blocked any possible vision of the dance of the myriad stars above. The consciousness of these people was opaque, and, in reality, each of them was tragically alone in the midst of this false festivity, sporting their sunglasses, their phallic pistols. . . . I saw nothing but swollen mouths and breasts, a herd of animals driven by thirst for money, power, fame.

I found a waiter, tipped him, and asked him to loan me a pair of scissors. I locked myself in the bathroom and cut off all my hair. I returned to the zendo with shaven head, but Ejo Takata had not moved. As I entered, he slowly murmured, without lifting his eyes from the ground: "Master Ummon said: 'The world is so vast. Why, at the mere sound of a bell, do you don the clothes of a monk?'"

I removed my shoes, pants, coat, and shirt and put on a black robe that was hanging on a hook. Taking my place on the meditation cushion, I recited the response I had learned by heart. "When the king calls for us, we go immediately, without waiting for a coach. When our father calls our name, we answer without hesitation."

As I pronounced these words, I experienced a strange acceleration of thought and this insight: to be free in a world so vast does not mean taking advantage of its many options; my freedom means to be who I am. And at that moment, I was a monk. Having responded without hesitation to my inner bell, I had no reason, sitting in this cramped room, to feel like I was a slave of this master before me.

Ejo murmured with satisfaction: "The branches of all trees hold the same moon." At that instant, it began to rain in torrents. On the roof the drops rebounded with a deafening noise. Raising his voice in order to be heard over the din, Ejo gave me another koan: "Master Kyosho* asked a monk: 'What is that noise outside?' The monk answered, 'The sound of rain.' Kyosho commented: 'People live in immense disorder; they blind themselves by pursuing material pleasures.' The monk asked him: 'And you, Sensei?' Kyosho replied: 'I can understand myself almost perfectly.' The monk asked him: 'What does it mean, to understand yourself perfectly?' Kyosho declared: 'To awaken is easy. To explain it with words is difficult.' According to the secret book, the disciple resolves this koan by hissing to imitate the sound of the rain. Will that also be your response?"

I did not reply. Instead, I arose, went outside, and allowed myself to be drenched by the rain. I returned to my meditation dripping wet, as if nothing had happened. Ejo gave a sigh of pleasure. Clearly, he had

---

*Jinquin Daofu, or Kyosei Kyosho Dofu (ca. 865–937 CE), a Ch'an master and disciple of Xuefeng Yicun.

accepted my return to complete the remaining seventy-two hours of the rohatsu.

Due to lack of sleep and fatigue, my brain was functioning as if under the influence of a strong drug. The rapidity of my thoughts had a delirious energy. As soon as the master had given me that koan, I understood it in the same way that an explorer, borne aloft by a condor, understands the valley below, where he has previously walked. I was at once Kyosho, the obtuse master, and also the disciple who understands the koan by imitating the sound of rain. When the master asks about the sound outside, he sets a trap for the monk, who falls into it by answering intellectually. For Kyosho, there is no "outside" or "inside." Because he is awake—that is, living in reality—he knows that the monastery where they are meditating is not separate from the universe, which is one. The monk feels that he is meditating in the limits of a protected, sacred space. For him, the ten thousand things of the world are separate, outside, like the sound of the rain. For the master, the noise of the rain arriving is that of the whole world, inseparable from the eternal and infinite cosmos. He tries to indicate this to the monk by speaking of the millions who live in forgetfulness of the spiritual quest. The two of them are meditating amid all of this. This is why he omits any mention of the rain itself in his seemingly absurd commentary.

How could I have understood all this without verifying it by my visit to Globos? I believed I had escaped the frivolous absurdity of such cabarets, freeing myself from trivial material pursuits by plunging myself in meditation in the zendo with Ejo. Yet Kyosho showed me that no one escapes anything. We live in a world that includes an ocean of minds that are asleep. To be conscious is to become the eyes of this blind world. When the monk asks, "And you, Sensei?" he shows that he still does not understand. He still separates the world of materialism from the world of the master, who is free of desire. With great patience, Kyosho explains: "I can understand myself almost perfectly." Who is this self? A limited individual? Not at all. This self is all of humanity, the entire cosmos and that which gives it life. The "almost" refers to the limitation of the human point of view, which is necessarily subjective and imperfect. Perfection can be only divine. Humanity, including all matter, permanently impermanent, can only approach perfection.

But the monk stubbornly persists, trying to grasp everything with intellect and words instead of direct perception. "What does it mean, to understand yourself?" It means precisely to see beyond words, allowing yourself to fall into the abyss of the unthinkable. Kyosho administers the coup de grace by pointing out that awakening is easy, but putting it into words is difficult. The disciple imitates the rain, leaving behind the prison of intellect to plunge into the natural phenomenon so that it reaches all the way to the heart.

We continued the rohatsu. After two hours, my body temperature began to rise. My robe dried little by little, emitting a slight cloud of vapor. With tenacious will, I strove to prevent words from distracting my mind, but each time I seemed about to succeed, the absurd words "I'm about to succeed" spoiled it. So I chose a word at random: *guarisapo,* meaning "tadpole." I repeated it endlessly in my mind for a time that seemed an eternity. Even during the forty minutes of sleep, I hung on to guarisapo as if it were a lifebuoy. When Ejo woke me, I did not wait for him to shake me, but resumed my sitting position quickly, straightening my spine, lifting the corners of my lips slightly, and disintegrating the word *guarisapo* with a mind that was finally empty.

It was a moment of absolute peace, though it was quite brief, unfortunately. As soon as I ceased to produce thoughts, my heart filled the vacuum with loud beating, like a drum resounding in my chest. A slow, pulsing flood began to beat in my temples, the tips of my fingers, my genitals, my calves, my gums, my tongue, my feet. Everything was flooded with this reverberating rhythm. Ultimately, there was not a single part of my body where it could not be felt. Then I felt the constant ebb and flow of my blood circulating. To this was added the song of air moving back and forth from my sinuses to my lungs. Finally, there came the incessant gurgling of my digestive tract. Perhaps it was an auditory hallucination, but I then began to sense that even beyond what was happening in my body, everything that was around me emitted a sound. The floor, the roof, the walls were vibrating as were the zafus, clothes, everything—different tones and rhythms joined together in a chorus that sounded like the sound of a beehive. This sensation extended to include the noise of the city outside and then the earth, the air, the sky. It was such a colossal impression that I began to tremble and felt as if I would faint.

At this point, Ejo shouted: "Don't fall! Recite the four vows along with me. Though sentient beings are numberless . . ."

". . . Though sentient beings are numberless . . ."

". . . I vow to save them all. All passions, even the inextinguishable ones, I vow to extinguish them. All Dharmas . . ."

"What are Dharmas, Ejo?"

"Even if you don't understand, be quiet and repeat after me! All Dharmas, though infinite in number, I vow to fulfill. All truth, though immeasurable, I vow to attain . . ."

I repeated everything after him. He recited them again and again, louder and louder. Though I followed suit, he shouted constantly, "Say it louder!"

Finally, I was shouting as loud as I could—but he urged me on: "Louder still!"

I felt that my vocal cords would burst. My shouting felt like vomiting, but he was still not satisfied and I began to despair. Seized by a fit of rage and screaming like a madman, I threw my zafu at him. It bounced against his chest, but he did not flinch, continuing to repeat the vows and demanding that I repeat them louder. Seeing red, I leaped at him, intending to throw him to the ground. I don't know whether it was hallucination or the effect of extreme fatigue, but I could not budge him so much as an inch, though I was shoving him with all my strength. It was as if I was pushing against a stone statue planted in the ground. I even drew back and rushed at him several times, but he was imperturbable. I let out a final yell so loud that a piece of plaster fell from the wall in pieces. Then I collapsed, empty.

At first, Ejo did not cease his recital, but soon he stopped, took a stick, and struck a small bell.

"Now at last you have succeeded in shouting with both halves of your brain and with all your guts! Before, you were doing it with only one hemisphere. *That* is how koans are resolved! And now it is midnight. The rohatsu is over. Sleep until tomorrow."

I fell like a feather into an abyss. When I awoke, sunbeams were filtering through the window. Michiko entered, bringing me a cup of coffee and some sweetbreads. Smiling, she spoke in her rudimentary Spanish: "Sleep fourteen hours. You come down, take breakfast. Ejo wait you. You go Oaxaca . . ."

It was the first time I had seen Ejo without his monk's robes. Impressed by the way he looked in ordinary clothes, I would never have been able to guess his age. He seemed like a being out of time—but now, seeing him dressed in jeans, a T-shirt, and tennis shoes, wearing a large backpack and smoking a cigarette, I could not resist the temptation:

"Master, how old are you?"

"I was born on March 24, 1928," he replied without hesitation. This surprised me. This spiritual guide I had chosen was only a year older than I. He was a young man, not an old one, as I had imagined. Dressed like this, he seemed more like a traveling companion, a friend, a peer. Some inner devil made me change my attitude as a result, and I began to speak to him with less respect. Ejo did not seem to notice. When I complained about the weight of my backpack, he pointed to his: "Twenty-two pounds." Then he pointed to mine: "Eleven pounds."

"Pounds of what, Ejo?"

"Soybeans."

"What are they for?"

"We are going to teach the Indians how to grow them."

"It's a waste of time. Only corn interests them."

"That's what the industries say. They want to keep the Indians in misery, growing only corn so that they can buy it from them at a low price."

"Ejo, you don't know Mexico. It's a country of very ancient customs."

"If you want to recover the wholeness of your spirit, you must decondition yourself. You see my face? You hear my voice?"

"Yes."

"Are you conscious of your eyes? Are you conscious of your ears?"

"Yes."

"If you are conscious of your eyes and your ears, then maybe you are sick. Are you coming with me or not? Sickness is curable. Destiny is incurable."

I was flustered. Was he trying to tell me that I should not form a self-concept in my consciousness? I did not know what to answer, so I followed him in silence.

A taxi took us to the train station. We traveled to Puebla in a third-class car stuffed with packages, baskets, chickens, children, and dogs. Ejo smiled as if it were paradise, and I tried to get some sleep. I was not used to such intimate contact with the poor classes. After my head had nodded several times, I was startled awake when a duet began: two blind men sang and pounded at their small guitars. Ejo elbowed me, pointing to himself, and whispered: "When a blind man guides another blind man, they both fall in the water." Then he laughed like a child, but I was in a bad mood and stuck my fingers in my ears.

At Puebla, we took a battered old bus that was even more full than the train and headed toward the mountains. The trip lasted several hours. It was impossible to sleep with all the noise of people chattering, chickens clucking, dogs barking, children crying, and the engine roaring and the flies, the dust, the stifling heat. I made a titanic effort to calm my nerves and said to Ejo:

"Why don't we take advantage of this time to study another koan?"

"Time is not a thing. Ten thousand rivers flow to the sea, but the sea is never full. Ten thousand koans fill your mind, but you are never satisfied. Adapt your mind to the circumstances in which you find yourself. Look around you, look at yourself, and take advantage of that."

Yet seeing how tenacious my boredom was, he shrugged his shoulders, as if dealing with a hopeless case. Without enthusiasm, he recited: "When the Buddha was being born, he pointed with one hand to the sky and with the other to the earth. He took six steps in a circle and looked in the four directions, saying: 'I am the only honored one in the sky and under the sky.' Master Ummon commented: 'If I had been there, I would have beaten him to death with a stick and thrown his body to the dogs. It is important for the world to be at peace.' Commenting upon that, Master Ryosaku said: 'Ummon believes that we must offer our body and soul to the world. This is called repaying the favor of the Buddha.' And you—what do you say?"

I reflected on my response, but before I could say a word, the bus was shaken by a violent jolt, probably because of a pothole. A package fell on a child, making his forehead bleed. The boy began to scream, his face covered with blood. Ejo got up calmly, took a tube of powdered green clay from his sack, and rubbed it on the boy's wound. A scab formed immediately and the blood stopped flowing. The child stopped crying. Through the open windows, the silence of the Cordillera entered. Ejo came back and took his seat next to me as if nothing had happened. I felt the clouds in my mind disperse, allowing a ray of light to enter. With deep respect, I murmured: "It is important for the world to be at peace."

Ejo smiled, closed his eyes, and began to snore. I was ashamed. I saw myself as a seeker of gurus, gods, worlds beyond, and other sorts of metaphysical aspirin, all for the lack of a kind father. Through the words attributed to Ummon, the koan gave very clear advice to uproot all those legends, fairy tales, infantile venerations, and grandiose hopes that are inspired by fear of death. I was not a safe little bird waiting calmly in its nest for my mother to drop a tasty worm into my mouth.

To follow after the Buddha slavishly was no better than rolling in dog shit. As long as I seek the light outside myself, the world will never be at peace. I observed my body invaded by nervousness, I saw my insatiable appetite for knowledge, my desire to plunder the secrets of all the masters instead of realizing myself, instead of repairing the self-esteem that my father, like a competitive child, had destroyed with his sarcasm.

Ryosaku affirmed that everything we have attained must be given in return—"Nothing for myself that is not also for others." To find yourself is to give yourself to the world, body and soul. To be an integral part of the world, let things happen naturally, without useless effort, surrendering confidently to the present. In accepting Ejo Takata as my teacher, I had moved from *me* to *you.* Yet because I still saw others as *them,* I had rejected the *we.* In wearing the label "artist," I had tried to make Ejo into an ideal refuge. There, like a blind and deaf mole, I had distanced and alienated myself from the world. Nevertheless, however alienated I was from this world, I was still more than ready to steal food from it in the form of applause, love affairs, rewards, diplomas, and fame. I was neither more nor less than a thieving parasite. I was always taking, and in return, I offered only autographs, literary portraits of my navel, photographs through an artist's mask, and distractions to capture the attention of the whales of social admiration. Meanwhile, the world was proliferating more and more war, misery, sickness, child abuse, murderous industries, inhuman bankers, toxic disinformation, political corruption. . . . And I, in the safe island of my mind, created an art that amounted to buffoonery, a brilliant veneer to hide the darkness of other thieves like myself—thieves who pillaged the earth, robbing others of their health, transforming their time into a hard personal shell, dividing others' space into dog kennels in which these citizens, befuddled by the walls, accepted the obligatory blindness.

I saw that nothing was really mine; everything was on loan to me, and anything that I do not give back amounts to thievery. Now I am carrying a sack of grain. Thus is my mind. If I am really an artist, I must sow it. And if I am to be a master, I must teach others to sow, to make it grow, to harvest it. If I remove my selfishness from the world, the world will find peace. Things will then cease to be as I thought they were and will become the truth that they already are.

We hitchhiked from Oaxaca, crossing endless plantations of corn and finally arrived at Santa Maria Mixi. It was a small hamlet of houses with roofs made of grass and palm leaves and with cobbled walls covered with a light coat of plaster and with only one door and several windows.

A group of Indians came to welcome us. There were men, women, and children. Probably all mixed-race, these people had abandoned their ancestral tribal customs to become "peasants" grouped into families. Our visit had caused a sensation—it had been a long time since anyone had bothered to visit these sad lands. With a friendly smile, Ejo made a respectful bow, and I did likewise. The Indians removed their straw hats in return. Ejo looked around for a clear space between the rows of corn and sat on the ground with his legs crossed. He rubbed the earth with care, ridding a large space of its small stones, and then let the soybeans pour out from his sack into a heap. The little yellow spheres seemed like magical jewels lying upon the reddish ground. This did not fail to arouse the curiosity of all the people. In his rudimentary Spanish, the master began to speak. What he said was so interesting to the peasants that several of them ran into the fields to fetch the others who were working there. Ultimately, a circle of about fifty people had formed around us. Because Ejo's pronunciation mixed up *r*s and *l*s, I improvised a kind of translation.

"This is a powerful variety of soy that comes from Japan. Its roots go down three feet. It resists freezing and drought. It is very rich in protein and in oil. It can be harvested several times a year and grown in any season. It does not need rich soil and will grow even in infertile soil."

For about three hours, Ejo explained how to plant soybeans, how to grow them, protect them from parasites, harvest them, and use them. He gave a description of almost two hundred products that could be derived from them: oil, milk, cheese, flour, yogurt, animal fodder, and lecithin, and they may be simply grilled like peanuts.

Then, drawing on the ground with a stick, he showed how to orient houses in relation to the sun, opening the windows and moving the stoves outside, because their presence inside was the cause of pulmonary diseases. He showed them how to build the stoves outside. He also showed them how to weave sandals using only plant materials. He taught them techniques for making butane gas with their excrement.

Then he told them: "These lands belong to you, not to the corn. You grow corn and sell it for a low price to industries that are growing rich behind your back. If these buyers ever stop coming here, you will die of hunger. This is the danger of letting an economy grow without limits. Become independent of these industries. Instead of planting to sell, plant first to feed yourselves and meet your own needs. Soybeans are much more useful than corn."

It was three o'clock in the afternoon. When Ejo had finished his lesson, the sun was going down behind the mountains. The peasants were very grateful. They brought us two bottles of beer and some tortillas stuffed with refried beans. An old newspaper served as a picnic cloth.

As Ejo ate, the peasants all kneeled before him. It was clear that they recognized him as a holy man. This reverent silence was interrupted brutally by the noise of an army truck arriving. Ten soldiers, ordered by a civilian, leaped out of it. About forty years old with a potbelly, the civilian was dressed in a coat with enormous epaulets, a black shirt, a green tie, a large sombrero, dark sunglasses, and a holster with a revolver on his belt. He introduced himself in a loud, barking voice: Salvador Cepeda, official of the Mexican government.

The soldiers began shoving and striking the terrified peasants with the butts of their rifles, herding them all into their houses and shutting the doors. Then they all aimed their rifles in our direction as the potbellied man shook a finger with a large brass ring at us and shouted.

"Filthy communists! Guerillas of the great whore! Go fuck your-selves! We're going to smash your skulls to teach you a lesson about stirring up rebellion among our workers! What we grow here is corn, not this soybean shit! I'm the man in charge here, and I can kill anyone I decide to kill. Show me your papers! I have a notion to have you both shot to set a good example for all those assholes who might want to imitate you."

Revealing not the slightest fear and without even uncrossing his legs, Ejo calmly searched in his sack and brought out a few papers. I remembered that he had told me that when he was a child during the American bombardments of Japan, he was ordered to continue meditat-ing without flinching, even amid the noise of the bombs falling. One child monk could not take it and fled from the meditation hall. He was killed by an explosion. After telling me this story, he had added: "Fear is useless."

The fat man was having some difficulty reading the documents. "Monk . . . What? Zen? . . . Minister of Education, embassy of Japan . . . bishop of Cuernavaca. . . . Well, it seems you have some very good recom-mendations, don Baldhead! I can see you're not a guerilla, at least, but your friend looks suspicious to me. Get moving, hombre, show me your papers!"

Though I knew my pockets were empty, I pretended to search them, trembling. I had nothing on me to prove my identity.

"Aha! So you're traveling incognito, you asshole, trying to get these stinking Indians to revolt! Show me an ID or a passport *pronto* or I'll have you shot by this firing squad!"

I realized that the fat guy was serious, convinced that I was some kind of communist. No doubt he considered communists more danger-ous than scorpions.

"Señor Governor," I addressed him humbly, trying to quell the tremors I felt in my body from head to foot, "I am a very well-known artist. My death would create a huge scandal. Please do not make this terrible mistake."

"You shitty little worm, how dare you tell me I'm making a mistake? You communists have no respect! A well-known artist? You? Skinny, filthy, and with that ridiculous chopped-off hair? You're a liar and a coward as well. You don't deserve to live!"

He pulled out his revolver and pointed it right in front of my nose.

"Be thankful that my gun isn't loaded, otherwise I'd just shoot you right now, like a coyote. Instead, you'll have the dignity of being executed properly by a firing squad, though you don't deserve it."

The soldiers formed a line and aimed their rifles at me. Ejo stood up and stepped between us.

"Señor Governor, this young man is my student. I assure you, he is a very famous theater director."

"Shut up, don Chinaman! You're a monk—of course you want to save the skin of this dangerous person. Sit back down and cross your legs! If you try to interfere again, I'll consider you his accomplice and have you shot too!"

Ejo sighed. Then, with a beatific smile, he told me: "Death is an illusion. Life is an illusion. You will cross through the lake of the mirror. You will come to rest on the ground of emptiness."

"Is that all you have to say to me? These guys aren't joking! They're really going to shoot me! I'm an intellectual, I still haven't learned to die! You, who know no fear—teach me how to do it."

Ejo sat once again in his meditation position and with absolute calm, recited: "Truth can never be attained by us, for we carry it forever within us."

It was incredible. I was in the midst of a nightmare and I had to wake up! At this moment, an intense, immeasurable, unconditional love of life descended upon me. Everything was vibrating: the red of the earth, the yellow of the corn, the blue of the sky, the white of the clouds, the majesty of the mountains, the warmth of my body, the transparence of my consciousness, the song of the birds, the odors dancing in the air, the uniforms of the soldiers repeated ten times like a musical motif, the sugary glint of their rifles, and above all, this love for myself. I understood why Ejo had spoken of a mirror as vast as a lake. . . . I was this immense mirror, and my soul was rooted in the ground of emptiness.

Suddenly, a great gust of wind covered us in a thick cloud of dust, interrupting the fat man's orders to fire. The wind scattered the old newspapers we had been using as a tablecloth and one of them landed next to me. As my eye fell upon a large photo that covered half a page, I shouted: "Wait! Right here is the proof of my identity!"

I grabbed the paper, and feverishly showed the fat man the picture of myself and the Tigress. A banner headline announced our future marriage.

Taking it, he removed his hat, scratched his head, and finally let out a long, noisy breath. Then, breaking into loud laughter, he patted me on the back. "Well, well! So you were the one who fucked the ex-mistress of the president? You must have a golden dick, you rascal! Why didn't you tell me before? Well, no matter. That's enough joking for now. Of course, I already recognized you—I just wanted to give you a little scare, that's all. Just a little joke of mine—a pretty funny one, right?"

I emitted a phony laugh. "You have quite a sense of humor, don Salvador. Now can we be on our way?"

"Of course, my boy, of course! But don't ever come this way again, you hear? I don't want you stirring up trouble in the henhouse. In these lands, we plant corn, and that's how it's been for centuries. I'm willing to admit your ignorance of that. One mistake is forgivable—but not two. If you come back here, you'll hear the sound of a different rooster—and his crowing will sound like rifle fire."

The soldiers doused the soybeans with gasoline and set them on fire. Then they got back in the truck and started the engine.

Cepeda called to us: "You can ride with us—we'll drop you off near Oaxaca."

The Indians came out to say farewell, giving us a half dozen oranges and waving their red bandanas as we drove out of view. Inside the truck, the soldiers, with insolent grins, stole the oranges from us. I felt humiliated.

Later, as we rode the bus toward the train station at Puebla, I said not a single word, though Ejo's silent calm exasperated me. When we sat in the crowded third-class, I found nothing intelligent to say, but I wanted to speak. "After such a painful experience, no commentary comes to us. Where is the error?"

Pointing out the window, Ejo contented himself with a grunt: "The mountain!"

I was furious and fed up with this Japanese style. For every emotion, for every doubt the masters reply, "Mount Sumeru," implying that this silent monolith is never submerged by mere feelings, that it never wonders about life and death, that it imperturbably allows the seasons to pass, never forcing nature, never prey to the dualism of actor–spectator. In sum, it is a panacea—just cross your legs and sit as still as a corpse.

I was so upset I squeezed my lips shut tightly, slammed my fist into my other hand, turned red, and breathed heavily through flaring nostrils, like a bull about to charge. Seeing this, Ejo pulled a white fan from his sack and, fanning himself with an air of disdain, gave me a koan: "Remedies heal sickness. The entire earth is a remedy. What remedy is your true being?"

These words fell like rain on the lips of a thirsty wanderer. In a sudden clarity of consciousness, I realized that I was alive for a duration of time that was infinitesimal within the eternity of the cosmos, and what a privilege, a gift, and a miracle this life was. This instant of my existence was the same instant in which the stars were dancing, in which the finite and the infinite were united, in which were united the here and the beyond, the perfume of the air and the memory within all matter, the gods of imagination and unimaginable energy, lights and abysses, colors and blindness, the humble sensitivity of my skin and the ferocity of my fists—but also the miserable peasants, the soldiers, the imbecilic fat man, the passengers in the train chattering like monkeys, the cloud of dust following the bus: all of this was a remedy if I accepted it as such so that it was transformed by my vision. The world is what it is: a remedy instead of the poison I had believed it to be.

Yet I saw that I was repeating constantly the same mistake: setting up a mental border between "inside" (my conception of myself) and "outside" (the world that is not myself). I was living as a subject confronted by an object. Even in saying that the entire earth is a remedy, I was still subtly trying to use an external object to heal my individual self, not realizing that this very separation of myself from the world is its sickness. "The world is my life and essential being. Inasmuch as I do not dissolve this border, I am dead."

When we got off the train in Mexico City, Ejo made a little bow to me and said: "Yosai, the founder of the Shofukuji Monastery where I spent my youth, was a simple man. He said: 'I do not have the virtues of an ancient Boddhisattva, but miracles and wonders are useless for teaching Zen.' One day, a poor peasant begged him: 'My wife, my children, and I are dying of hunger. Have pity; please help us.' In those days, there was no spare food, clothing, or valuable objects in the Yosai monastery. Nevertheless, the monk found a piece of copper that had served to make the rays of the halo of a statue of the Buddha. Yosai gave it to the peasant, telling him to trade it for food enough to feed his family. The disciples complained, saying that it was a sin to make personal use of sacred material consecrated to the Buddha. Yosai replied: 'The Buddha offered his own flesh and limbs to starving beings. Even if I had given the entire statue to this peasant dying of hunger, it would not have been a violation of his teaching, and even if such acts cause me to suffer a dire fate, I will continue to help starving beings.'

"Do you understand now? It isn't Zen for intellectuals that Mexico needs. I'm going to put away my kyosaku for good. The zendo is finished."

With a sense of a huge abyss between us, I watched him walk away with long, energetic strides. Remembering this scene, I thought of a phrase from Silver Kane's novel 953 in the collection *Bravo Oeste:* "Mounted upon a black horse which seemed to embody the mourning of his master, he lost himself in the shadows."

For reasons of security, I had to leave Mexico for France. Very little news of my master arrived there. I learned that he had stopped dressing as a monk and had moved. On Insurgentes Avenue he had opened a consultation office called IMARAC, and in 1975 the director of research at the Ryodoraku center in Tokyo officially named him professor of electro-acupuncture in Mexico. He treated sick people, gave courses in acupuncture, and used a Japanese device known as the Tormenter: instead of having traditional needles planted in acupuncture points in the skin, the patient was connected to battery-powered electrodes. For this treatment, a few seconds sufficed instead of the twenty minutes required for the needles.

Many patients came to the clinic to be treated, and a sizeable group of students formed as well. Dressed in a white nurse's shirt, Ejo offered his teachings at no charge. The institute thrived until certain Mexican professors of medicine learned that epileptics had been cured in a few sessions. They had Ejo charged with the illegal practice of medicine, and he was forced to cease all therapeutic activity. Following this, he filled his small truck with bags of soybeans and left the city to live with the Indians in the Sierra Tarahumara. For many years, I lost all trace of him.

9
Work on the Essence

~~//∩\\~~

*And he hugged her tightly in his arms, because he knew
that this person, condemned to death, was the woman of
his life.*

SILVER KANE, *VERDUGO A PLAZOS*
(EXECUTIONER ON CREDIT)

When I saw her at the Ethnology Museum of Mexico, Reyna D'Assia
was explaining the Aztec solar calendar to a group of Americans, men
and women dressed in an Eastern style, like the figures in the paintings of Jean-Léon Gérome. That same morning, in the conference hall,
I had given a screening of my film *El Topo* for a group of journalists.
In a humorous mood, I had dressed as a cowboy: black leather pants
and overcoat, black silk shirt, large hat, and a belt with a white-handled
revolver in its holster. When the screening was over, the critics treated
me to insults: pernicious, foreign vermin; raving egomaniac; donkey
murderer; and so forth. I left the room, wandering the halls, trying to
calm my rage.

From afar, I was attracted to Reyna D'Assia's outlandish group. Her eyes met mine and held them. She let out an exclamation of surprise, opened her arms, and ran toward me. I actually thought she was running toward someone else until she embraced me with great warmth. I was disconcerted. In spite of her crazy turban, her lacy blouse, her bangled vest, her multilayered gauzy skirt, and her frizzy hair, which spread out like an aura of black tar, she was a woman of irresistible charm, with proud breasts, a luxurious bottom, and two azure wells for eyes. Holding onto me, she spoke with a deep voice and warm breath.

"Three days ago, I saw your film in New York. I fell in love with El Topo, that bandit who is at heart a visionary rabbi. I decided to come to Mexico. My excuse was to teach my group about the secrets of the Aztec calendar, but my real goal was to meet you. So you see? When your mind formulates a wish with true passion, it appears before you in the mirror we call reality."

Her strongly perfumed skin stirred up a kind of madness in me. I allowed her to take me by the hand out into the street, where she hailed a taxi. During the drive, she kissed me with passion. When we arrived in her hotel suite, she undressed hastily, kneeled on all fours with her back turned to me, and lowered her head to the floor, forbidding me to undress. Then she asked me to penetrate her still dressed in my leather cowboy outfit, hat, and boots.

With mad excitement amplified by the intense wetness of her vagina, I entered her with a fierce thrust of my thighs. I was about to begin the back-and-forth when I was paralyzed by a sudden cry of, "Stop! Don't move! I want you to serve as the axis of my passion!"

With amazing agility and a precise use of my own body for support, she turned around so that she was facing me, her thighs around my waist, her feet crossed behind my back, and her own forehead pressed against mine. In this new position, I was overcome once more with the desire to thrust inside her Eden, but she nipped this in the bud with a "Stop!" so imperious I had no choice but to obey.

A minute passed; it seemed longer than an hour. My whole pubic zone was trembling, aching to move inside her. In this tormenting immobility, the walls of her vagina suddenly began to shake with a gradually increasing tempo. Finally, her entire vagina was convulsing, squeezing, and vibrating like a quivering glove. Inside this muscular tempest, I had no more need to move. A few seconds later, my semen flooded her. I had three successive ejaculations.

I told her that I had never before met a woman of such mastery. She confided: "I had a great master myself. I wish you to know that I am the daughter of Gurdjieff.* In 1924, the master visited New York with a group of disciples for a demonstration of his sacred dances. My mother, who was thirteen years old at the time, brought him some food that he had ordered from a Russian restaurant. He seduced her and taught her these vaginal techniques, which I learned from her. Gurdjieff said that through laziness, most women have a dead 'Athanor.' From childhood on, girls are taught that only the phallus is powerful, active, and vital and that what they have between their legs is a mere receptacle, a kind of swamp whose function is to be filled by sperm. People take it for granted that the vagina is a passive organ. But there is a world of difference between this kind of passive nature and that of a deliberately trained vagina. Gurdjieff taught my mother to awaken and develop her soul by developing a living vagina."

Deciding to offer me a demonstration, Reyna spread her legs, contracted the lips of her vulva, and, with a soft airy sound, began to pump air into her vagina. Then she expelled it with a powerful hiss.

"Phase one: learning to breathe in and eject with the vagina, as if it were a lung. When this is mastered, a woman can go much further . . ."

She set four olives in a row and, scooting up to them with her perineum on the floor, she swallowed them one by one. Then she lay

---

*George Ivanovitch Gurdjieff, the famous esoteric philosopher of Russian nationality and Greek and Armenian ancestry. In 1922 he founded an experimental center in Fontainebleau, near Paris, devoted to the study of consciousness: the Institute for the Harmonious Development of Man. He also traveled and taught in New York and in Chicago. He spent most of the latter part of his life teaching in Paris, where he died in 1949.

on her back and expelled them with such force that they bounced against the ceiling. She lit several candles and blew them out with one gust from her vagina. She drew a thread up into her organ and then deposited it, knotted, in my hand.

"My vagina has the same agility of movement as my tongue. What's more, I can will my lubricant secretions to increase or diminish."

She concentrated with effort. Then, from the base of her lips, she expelled an oval of small, transparent jets of fluid, which covered her thighs.

Finally, kneeling and concentrating with a queenly air, her knees spread far apart, she inhaled a very large quantity of air into her vagina. When she expelled it, a quasimusical sound was heard, both metallic and organic in tone, which recalled the song of whales. My hair stood on end as I thought of the legend of the sirens of Homer's *Odyssey,* who attracted sailors with their wails in order to shipwreck them. Fascinated and overwhelmed, I laid my head on her lap and began to whimper like a child remembering a lost paradise.

In a very soft voice, she said, "In the most ancient times, women chanted lullabies with their vulvas to make their babies sleep, but as this art became lost and forgotten, children ceased to feel they were loved. An unconscious anxiety settled in the souls of human beings. That whimpering of yours expresses the pain of having a mother with a mute vagina, but we are going to resolve that."

She undressed me with precise, delicate movements, had me lie on the bed, and began by embracing the soles of my feet, moving all the way up my body—countless, deep kisses given with all her soul, patiently, over every square inch of my body. For two hours, from my foot to my head, without neglecting the slightest place, she bestowed upon me that ineffable caress, murmuring each time: "You are loved." I had been kissed by women in many ways, but never over the totality of my skin. I surrendered to it.

When she finished with a final kiss on my nose, I gave a great sigh of happiness mixed with deep sadness. "You have shown me nirvana . . . but

I would have preferred you to say 'I love you,' instead of 'You are loved.'"

Her blue eyes flashed with utter disdain.

"As I multiplied my kisses, I perceived you moving back through time. From thirty years you went to twenty, to fifteen, to ten, to five, and suddenly you were six months old—a baby marveling at having found a universal mother. That is what you are feeling right now. Should I accept such an unworthy role in saying 'I love you'? What do you want? By soliciting my love, what you are really saying is: 'Because I never had the tenderness of a mother, I'm confused and lost in my life. You are my only emotional refuge. That's why I cling to you. Be authoritarian, guide me, possess me, ground me, nourish my soul. Never abandon me, satisfy my desires constantly, amuse me when I'm bored, make delicious food for me, forget yourself, and admire me more than anyone else. Become my audience.'

"You deceive yourself by seeing me as a projection of that inner woman that you call 'soul'—but in no case will you accept me as the portrait of your mother. When you say, 'I love you,' which one of your multiple selves is speaking? The mental *I*, the emotional *I*, the sensual *I*, the moral *I*, the cultural *I*? What is the profound *I* that is independent of age, sex, nationality, or beliefs? When you define yourself, which part of yourself is making this definition? Can you say, without dividing yourself in two: 'I am what I am'? Do you realize that you are not an individual organism? Do you realize that this body that you believe is yours is all men—all who exist, have existed, and will exist—and that I am all the women from the beginning to the end of Creation? Your essential self is the cosmos manifesting itself through you. When you enter into contact with me, it is for you to unite yourself with the totality of time through our minuscule present.

"By wishing to have me, centering yourself in possession, you go astray. Love is an infinite energy that surges within you and has nothing to do with the image you have of a separate self. In the *we* there is no *me*. Love goes beyond all desire of possession. When you prefer 'I love you,' to 'You are loved,' you fail to realize that the only reason you are in this world, born in a body of flesh and bone, endowed with consciousness, is because that mysterious force that creates the universe every instant loves you. You are obeying a divine destiny. Right now, every moment, cell by cell, atom by atom, you are loved—you, just as you are, with your particular form, your style, your limitations, and your irreproducible aura. The universe thirsts for this consciousness that your organism can produce. A grain of this consciousness has been given you so that you can make it bear fruit to prevent it from disappearing without leaving a trace in time.

"My blessed father said: 'Whoever does not create a soul lives like a pig and dies like a dog.' You have been taught that you were no one, that no inner god lives in the center of your dark psyche. Your parents, seeing you as only a projection of their selfish plans, never saw you. Not seeing you, they never knew you and forbade you to be who you are and permitted you to be only who they wanted you to be. They did not love you. This is why you brew all this emotional muddle around women, who will never be able to love you as you would prefer. In a state of perpetual neediness, your 'I love you' actually means: 'Mean mommy, you don't love me. I search in vain for your look. If you don't want to see me, then I don't want to see me and I must be as you imagine me to be. If you do not tell me who I really am, then I am not. I remain a child. I cannot become an adult, because in order to do that, you would have to see me as I really am—and that's impossible, for then you would have to be able so see yourself as you really are, which in turn is impossible because your parents—my grandparents—never saw you. Because I am afraid you will abandon me, I'll distance myself from you first, before you can do it.'"

Suddenly, losing control of my rage, I seized a chair and smashed it into a mirror. Walking heedlessly over the broken glass, trying to hide the limp from my injured foot, I dressed, lashing out at her with insults. "You insolent, didactic charlatan! You've read a handful of books on psychoanalysis and think you can pass yourself off as a master! Daughter of Gurdjieff? Don't make me laugh!" I was still hurling these insults as I opened the door, a shoe still in my hand, and I was so furious that my voice rose to a scream at the last phrase.

At that precise instant a blind tourist passed in the hallway with a guide dog. Startled by my scream, the dog sensed aggression and began to bark loudly. The blind man was frightened and began to call for the hotel police. I jumped from the corridor back into the room and closed the door.

Reyna D'Assia received me with hilarious laughter. "You see? You can't escape so easily. A blind man's dog stopped you. In English, *dog* spelled backward is *god*. The god of the blind, the ignorant like you, obliges you to listen to me.

"Now open your ears: We always fall into a rage for reasons other than what we believe. You think mistakenly that I have offended you. The truth is that during these hours in this room, you have received something from me that you have never before received in your life. It has brought to the surface all the hatred you feel for your mother. You are reacting as a psychological barbarian might react. You have aspired to a relation between man and woman that is as simple as that between animals, never imagining that love between a man and a woman is also the expression of a neurosis of two genealogical trees.

"You must understand this: The only true couple is not a symbiosis, but a collaboration between two free, conscious beings. Cease to beg for love! I am not your solution, still less your crutch. The purpose of our meeting is not to share the sublime pleasure of an existence that is neither mine nor yours. An alchemical text says: 'From one substance, two are made and from these two, one is made that bears no resemblance to the first substance.'

"You and I shall establish a meeting of soul and soul so that this androgynous energy expands into the eternal and infinite present. It is marvelous to meet someone who exists at your own level of consciousness! This has not yet happened for you. Your intellect is like a wild horse that you have never tamed. It does as it pleases, dominating you, directing you under the influence of insane ideas implanted in it by your ancestors ever since your birth. Instead of being the slave of its desires, you must teach it to obey and develop it into a machine without limits."

"Your theories are just words," I retorted. "You brag about this power, but it's impossible for you to demonstrate it to me!"

"It is possible, and I will demonstrate it! Psychological barbarians such as yourself find it entirely natural to spend hours training their body in sport, yet it never occurs to them to train their mind. My blessed father rarely had the time to come see me himself, but he appointed one of his major disciples, Alfred Orage, to take charge of my education until I was thirteen. This remarkable man taught me psychological exercises that permitted me to realize what you shall now hear and see."

Then, like a monkey entranced by a cobra, I watched a fascinating spectacle. Standing on her left leg, Reyna D'Assia traced a figure eight in the air continuously with her right leg. Meanwhile, her left hand continuously traced a square and her right hand a triangle. All the while, she recited a seemingly chaotic succession of numbers. In continuous movement, Reyna paused only briefly in her reciting, explaining the different exercises. They were so complicated that I could not remember all of them, though I do remember a few. I heard her recite, very fast and seemingly nonsensically, the multiplication tables from 2 to 22. For example, $8 \times 1 = 8$; $8 \times 2 = 7$; $8 \times 3 = 6$; $8 \times 4 = 5 \ldots 8 \times 12 = 6$; and thus onto $8 \times 100 = 8$. It sounded to me like a computer gone haywire.

"Listen carefully: $2 \times 8 = 16$. If I add the 1 and the 6, I get 7, you understand? No? Another example: $8 \times 12 = 96$ and $9 + 6 = 15$ and $1 + 5 = 6$. Therefore, $8 \times 12 = 6$. How much is 7×7?" Without giving me time to think, she replied, "$7 \times 7 = 4$."

I was feeling dizzy. Relentlessly, Reyna continued the exercise and then complicated it even more. While continuing to recite the table in ascending order, she interspersed it with an alternating descending order:

"8 × 1 = 8; 8 × 100 = 8; 8 × 2 = 7; 8 × 99 = 9; 8 × 3 = 6; 8 × 98 = 1 . . ."

As she continued her reciting and movements, I did manage to verify one part with a laborious mental calculation. Multiplying 8 by 98, I obtained 784. 7 + 8 + 4 = 19; 1 + 9 = 10; 1 + 0 = 1. Indeed, 8 × 98 = 1 . . .

For an interminable hour, Reyna held me spellbound with further mental juggling. Some of it was absurd, such as mixing two tables together: 7 × 1 = 12; 12 × 1 = 7 . . . 7 × 2 = 24; 12 × 2 = 14; 7 × 3 = 36; 12 × 3 = 21; 7 × 80 = 960; 12 × 80 = 560. . . . And she went on like this to 7 × 100 = 1,200 and 12 × 100 = 700. As if this was not enough, she once more interspersed it with alternating ascending and descending tables: 7 × 2 = 1,188; 12 × 99 = 14 . . . 7 × 3 = 1,176; 12 × 98 = 21 . . . 7 × 4 = 1,164; 12 × 97 = 28 . . .

A feeling of terror began to grow in me as this woman began to dance as a sinister machine—with very complex and sinuous movements that had not the slightest hint of seduction—to a music that did not exist for me. The more complicated the dance became, the more insanely complicated her numerical exercises became.

In her trance, she shouted, "Number 1 is Tom, number 2 is Dick, number 3 is Harry!" And then she counted: "Tom, Dick, Harry, 4, 5, 6, 7, 8, 9, Tom-0, Tom-Tom, Tom-Dick, Tom-Harry, Tom-4 . . ." and so on, substituting, for example, 5-Harry-Tom for the number 531. . . . Then, to complicate things further, she yelled, "Now I'm changing! Tom = 2, Dick = 5, Harry = 7!" This meant: 1, Tom, 3, 4, Dick, 6, Harry, 8, 9, 10, 11, 1-Tom, 13, 14, 1-Dick, 16, 1-Harry . . . and on and on.

I felt as if my brain and my entire body would explode from all these complications. When I could stand it no more, I leaped up, grabbed her, and halted her gyrations.

"Get hold of yourself, you lunatic! Your problem is that you've never been trained to develop your soul; you've been taught to be only a kind of circus performer. It is like the story of the juggler who presented himself to the king. After twenty years of training, he had achieved the feat of juggling a hundred chickpeas at once without letting a single one fall. As a reward, the king gave him a barrel full of chickpeas."

"So! I see that you do not understand the importance of these exercises. You are an artist established in the habit of pulling from your navel all sorts of garbage—which then are qualified as works of art. Yet they are only the expressions of a pack of contradictory egos that you call *I.* Your mind creates one thing, your emotional center wants something else, your sexual center demands still another thing, your body is going its own way, and meanwhile, that which should be your soul is an egg that no one is hatching. You are a chariot pulled by four horses straining in different directions, and the coachman has fallen asleep at the reins. Of course, the inner jewel is still there, but veiled by a cloud of contradictory thoughts, feelings, desires, and actions. There is no real will, no unitary goal—only a chaos of changing objects under which is buried an unchanging subject. You cannot hear the beating of your heart in a city roaring with traffic . . ."

"What arrogant presumption!" I retorted. "How do you know I have not attained inner unity? Every morning, I meditate for two hours with a Zen master."

"What are you seeking?"

"Awakening!"

"Then you're a dreamer. You seem to think you're climbing a ladder with only one rung, but it has many more. You sit motionless on your butt in this zendo, hoping to attain a mysterious state that they've taught you to name 'awakening.' You're like a parrot that salivates when it sees clouds, because it's been taught that they're also called 'banana.' You imagine that awakening is like obtaining a piece of gold or a precious object that you can then keep, like a halo around your head. It's ridiculous. Only when your stagnant ideas become fluid will you experience your first explosion of consciousness. And of course you think that will last forever, but you are mistaken—in this dimension of reality, the only permanence is impermanence. That which does not change stagnates. Acquiring fluidity can be likened to a large stone falling into the middle of a lake. The shock creates a circular pattern of waves that covers the entire surface of the water. The expansion of consciousness is infinite, but the lake of the mind is finite. Once the process begins, you will go from awakening to awakening, from smaller to greater surprises, never ceasing to be astonished before the newness of the world. Do you understand? You have been searching for a static awakening, whereas there is only continual change . . ."

She grabbed me by the shoulders, pressed her face to mine, and cried: "Stagnation is not only mental! It is also emotional, sexual, and physical! Break down your dams!"

A dense anger made my heart pound. "I agree to be your lover, not your pupil!"

"Then why are you so angry? I only want to give . . ."

"Giving has nothing to do with obliging someone to receive! Give me only what I ask for!"

"Very well."

"Then shut up and let's fuck again!"

With an astounding agility, she shoved me so that I fell onto my back on the bed, and she immediately began caressing my penis. Her hands were like butterflies fluttering from testicles to glans without ceasing. Her fingers moved so fast that they seemed to become transparent and multiply. Soon, she interrupted this delight to administer a series of small, authoritarian taps that went from high to low and back again. Then came the deep caresses, spiraling, stretching my organ out toward infinity and then making it soft and burying it in my pubis as if to change it into a vagina, squeezing it like a fruit, moving it from one hand to another, cradling it tenderly like a mother cradles a baby. Finally, after a multitude of different kinds of caresses, she seized it firmly and began masturbating it with a superhuman rapidity for a very long time and with increasing vigor and no sign of fatigue until I could resist no longer and the white fountain shot out.

Seeing that I was exhausted and mute with pleasure, she assumed the schoolteacher role again.

"What you have just experienced is the first technique that every woman should develop to satisfy her lovers: the manual technique. The three other techniques are the oral, the vaginal, and the anal. My blessed father associated these with the intellectual, emotional, sexual, and corporeal centers. The manual technique corresponds to the body, the vaginal to the sexual, and the oral to the intellect. Therefore, it is through the anal technique that we can control the emotional center. Would you like to try it?"

When we did, I went crazy. The dam that had been holding back my emotions, created by the absence of maternal caresses, burst into pieces. Convinced to the marrow of my bones that I was totally in love with her, I begged her not to leave Mexico and stay with me forever.

She laughed. "As I told you before, you are a psychological barbarian. You are weak, because you lack a true will of your own. The result is that any strong emotion can make you change your ideas or even corrupt you. You do not dominate events; they just happen to you in such a way that you have no control over them. A few expert anal contractions and you are ready to be my slave. This is not because you are foolish, it is simply because you have made an error: you have been using your meditation practice to construct a big, fat ego disguised as the Buddha, which serves only to hide instead of reveal your impersonal essence.

"In India, they worship an elephant, Ganesh. He is always accompanied by a mouse who eats the offerings. This image reveals the hidden situation: the real god is not Ganesh; it is the mouse. The elephant, swollen and covered with gold with a great jewel upon its forehead, stretches out its four arms toward symbolic objects. It makes an impressive disguise, hiding the truth that the mouse is really the master. No one can see a true master. He is invisible, like the mouse. He has no favorite disciples, for he teaches all of humanity. He has no church, for the planet and the entire cosmos are his temple. He often hides inside a seemingly unimportant figure. He is the tiger skin upon which the Buddha meditates, the donkey that Christ rode, the black bull that gave Mithra his strength. . . . This truth is a difficult one for you to understand, because you have been trying to transcend the body, whereas you should be submerging yourself within it to become so small that you arrive finally at that inner offering that is our birthright—that indefinable diamond that we call 'soul' but which is beyond words.

"Please don't answer me, don't try to argue with me. I see your ego. I see how you waste your energy, believing that you are who you think you are—a jumble of learned behaviors that began at the cradle. My blessed father called this jumble the 'elephant,' and he divided it into two categories: the stinking elephant and the perfumed elephant.

"The first type is unbearable, living only for appearances, ready to do anything for fame, reward, and recognition. He has contempt for the wise, because he is terrified of their level of consciousness. Convinced that he is master of himself, he has no qualms about assuming or stealing the virtues of others. He is like a pathetic beggar disguised in the suit of a millionaire.

"The second type is bearable and is able to balance his needs and desires. With humility, he kneels before his own essence and recognizes that he does not belong to himself. 'Belong to the Holy Spirit, not to yourself,' says the Bible. The domestication of the ego consists of converting the stench into perfume. In Japan, this process is represented by a series of drawings showing a black ox that, little by little, becomes white. In China it is a horse; in India it is an elephant.

"My blessed father realized that animals were our first teachers. On a trip to Bangalore, he went to live in an elephant reserve to learn about their domestication. The first thing he learned was that the trainers, the *mahouts,* of these great beasts commanded them in a language of two basic words: *ara* and *mot.* To make an elephant move, they would repeat with authority: *mot, mot.* To stop him, they would repeat *ara* with the same tone of authority. This seemingly insignificant fact became the inspiration for the basis of my father's teaching. The two pillars of his temple were called Mot and Ara.

"The stinking elephant is the situation of individuals trapped in the jumble of insane demands that they call 'reality.' They desire, feel, think, and act constantly inside it, forgetting their immortal essence. In order for human beings to recall this essence at any moment, even when they are totally trapped by the world, they must be able to command themselves: *Ara!* . . . or, in other words, *Stop!* Then, in stillness, they can observe the torrent of useless ideas, infantile illusions, impotent desires, and purposeless plans in which they are submerged, and, like Christ driving the money changers out of the temple, they can free themselves of this absurd swarm in which their stinking elephant has been acting as though it was immortal instead of their true essence. This act of stopping is unity in the midst of multiplicity, which leads them to realize that the only permanent thing is impermanence. Thus, little by little, the elephant becomes perfumed. Only when the garbage can is empty can they perceive the jewel inlaid in its very bottom. Only then can their will command *Mot!* The perfumed elephant moves consciously. Then, thought can describe the world without mistaking itself for the world, feelings can form attachments with knots that can be untied, and desires are in harmony with what is possible. And finally, realizing possibility after possibility, we attain the impossible.

"It is like the legend in which the god Pan uses a sheepskin to disguise himself as a cloud in order to sneak up on the moon and possess it. Every action we perform is useful, provided it develops our consciousness. Who are we, here and now? The intellect that seeks only to know more and fill itself with abortions from the past must empty itself to attain ignorance. The heart that craves to be loved is never satisfied, for it feeds on the future. It must accept what can be given, its daily bread, cutting its illusions and vain quests at their root. This sexuality—which invades the present by confusing its animal appetites with life, its children, and its conquests with immortality—must learn by ceasing its doing and discovering how to die in peace.

"Tell me: what is your ultimate desire in life? To be happy? To be famous? Rich? Loved? To live to an advanced age?"

"Well, to be quite honest—all of the above."

"My goodness, you desire so little! Do not content yourself with such modest hopes. Raise your thinking to the level where all living beings desire to be free! You have not transcended personal goals. Your life is that of a separate person, not the life of humanity. Give priority to seeing what is called *God* face to face, without dying and without fear. When you free yourself of all your afflictions, your unconscious and your subconscious become your allies. You must become your own healer and, thereby, the healer of others' sickness. You can acquire such spiritual strength that you will not be taken by surprise; demolished; or defeated by misfortune, disasters, or enemies. You can know the whole cosmos, its past, present, and future. In the dimension of dreams, you can learn how to resurrect the dead. You can develop your consciousness to the point that it is able to pass through countless deaths without disintegrating and live as long as the universe.

"By your simple presence, you can learn to raise the consciousness of any living being. You can teach human beings to use the energy of the divine presence trapped in matter. You can cleanse the planet of industrial filth, speak words that calm dangerous animals, be immune to deadly venoms, and see at a glance into the depths of the heart and soul of a man or woman. You can foresee inevitable events, offer immediate and effective consolation and advice, prevent setbacks from becoming deviations from the path, transform problems into challenges and master them, tame love and hate, enrich yourself without harming others, and become the master of your fortune instead of its slave. You can thrive in poverty without misery or abjection, master the four elements, calm storms, make the sun appear through dense clouds, and bring rain in times of drought. You can learn telepathy, healing at a distance, and being in several places at the same time. No doubt, these and so many other things seem fantastic to you at the moment, but if you take the trouble, you will succeed in attaining them, little by little."

"Reyna, you are telling me fairy tales! Such goals are 100 percent utopian—and even if they were true, what is the first step on this path?"

"Whoever wishes to attain the supreme goal must first change his habits, conquer laziness, and become a morally sound human being. To be strong in the great things, we must also be strong in the small ones."

"How?"

"We have been badly educated. We live in a world of competition in which honesty is synonymous with naïveté. We must first develop good habits. Some of them may seem simple, but they are very difficult to realize. Believing them to be obvious, we fail to see that they are the key to immortal consciousness. Now I shall offer you a dictation of the commandments that my blessed father taught me:

"Ground your attention on yourself. Be conscious at every moment of what you are thinking, sensing, feeling, desiring, and doing. Always finish what you have begun. Whatever you are doing, do it as well as possible. Do not become attached to anything that can destroy you in the course of time. Develop your generosity—but secretly. Treat everyone as if he or she was a close relative. Organize what you have disorganized. Learn to receive and give thanks for every gift. Stop defining yourself. Do not lie or steal, for you lie to yourself and steal from yourself. Help your neighbor, but do not make him dependent. Do not encourage others to imitate you. Make work plans and accomplish them. Do not take up too much space. Make no useless movements or sounds. If you lack faith, pretend to have it. Do not allow yourself to be impressed by strong personalities. Do not regard anyone or anything as your possession. Share fairly. Do not seduce. Sleep and eat only as much as necessary. Do not speak of your personal problems. Do not express judgment or criticism when you are ignorant of most of the factors involved. Do not establish useless friendships. Do not follow fashions. Do not sell yourself. Respect contracts you have signed. Be on time. Never envy the luck or success of anyone. Say no more than necessary. Do not think of the profits your work will engender. Never threaten anyone. Keep your promises. In any discussion, put yourself in the other person's place. Admit that someone else may be superior to you. Do not eliminate, but transmute. Conquer your fears, for each of them represents a camouflaged desire. Help others to help themselves. Conquer your aversions and come closer to those who inspire rejection in you. Do not react to what others say about you, whether praise or blame. Transform your pride into dignity. Transform your anger into creativity. Transform your greed into respect for beauty. Transform your hate into charity. Neither praise nor insult yourself. Regard what does not belong to you as if it did belong to you. Do not complain. Develop your imagination. Never give orders to gain the satisfaction of being obeyed. Pay for services performed for you. Do not proselytize your work or ideas. Do not try to make others feel for you emotions such as pity, admiration, sympathy, or complicity. Do not try to distinguish yourself by your appearance. Never contradict; instead, be silent. Do not contract debts; acquire and pay immediately. If you offend someone, ask his or her pardon; if you have offended a person publicly, apologize publicly. When you realize you have said something that is mistaken, do not persist in error through pride; instead, immediately retract it. Never defend your old ideas simply because you are the one who expressed them. Do not keep useless objects. Do not adorn yourself with exotic ideas. Do not have your photograph taken with famous people. Justify yourself to no one, and keep your own counsel. Never define yourself by what you possess. Never speak of yourself without considering that you might change. Accept that nothing belongs to you. When someone asks your opinion about something or someone, speak only of his or her qualities. When you become ill, regard your illness as your teacher, not as something to be hated. Look directly, and do not hide yourself. Do not forget your dead, but accord them a limited place and do not allow them to invade your life. Wherever you live, always find a space that you devote to the sacred. When you perform a service, make your effort inconspicuous. If you decide to work to help others, do it with pleasure. If you are hesitating between doing and not doing, take the risk of doing. Do not try to be everything to your spouse; accept that there are things that you cannot give him or her but which others can. When someone is speaking to an interested audience, do not contradict that person and steal his or her audience. Live on money you have earned. Never brag about amorous adventures. Never glorify your weaknesses. Never visit someone only to pass the time. Obtain things in order to share them. If you are meditating and a devil appears, make the devil meditate too."

That first night together (interspersed with demonstrations of Reyna's erotic expertise), we talked until dawn. It was more of a monologue than a conversation, for Gurdjieff's daughter was keen to relate her father's teachings with great rapidity.

She analyzed several tales of Mulla Nasruddin. She maintained that the notion of masculine and feminine thinking was obsolete and described what she called androgynous thinking. She criticized the vulgarity of human beings who live by using their senses in a negative way. "They curse what they see, what they hear, what they feel, taste, and touch," instead of blessing everything they perceive. She taught me exercises for learning to love, exercises for giving birth without damaging the seed of the fetus's soul, and exercises to develop creativity. All of this was founded on the principle "Never struggle with yourself." She said, "When the world is not as you like, it is because you want the world to be not as you like."

I wanted to see if Reyna had a true mastery of the secret of symbols. Taking advantage of our intimacy, I asked her about the meaning of the "game of the goose" in which the poor bird has to advance on a path full of traps: it falls into a well, goes to prison, goes to the hospital, goes to the cemetery, is always having to retreat and begin again, and so forth.

"What is the goose seeking with such obstinacy? For years I have puzzled over this without finding the answer in any book."

"I know the answer!" she replied. "How much will you pay me for it?" Offended, I made a gesture that I intended to be exalted, representing our intertwined bodies. But she would have none of this. "How much?" she insisted. Angrily, I grumbled, "Twenty pesos." She began to laugh. "Is that how much you value the secret? You've searched for it for all that time, and now that you find someone who has it, you become stingy. You believe that knowledge should be free, but you are mistaken: if you do not pay for it, you give it no value and it will be useless. Give me everything you have! It's the only fair price."

I glanced at her with the same hatred with which I sometimes regarded my mother because of her lack of affection. From a pocket of my pants lying in a heap beside the bed, I retrieved five wrinkled bills.

"That's all I have."

"Liar! I know you're lying. You have a big wad of bills in another pocket. So much the worse for you—keep it. I'm going to reveal the secret to you anyway."

She put her lips to my ear and whispered: "The goose braves all those dangers because she is desperately looking for a mate." I gave a huge sigh and fell asleep.

When I woke up, the raucous calls of a flock of thrushes living in the courtyard were invading the room. Reyna yawned, then spoke to me with a smile that seemed condescending:

"What do you think about the things I've told you?"

"Reyna, I'll be frank with you. The things you have told me are a revelation that will surely change my life. But there's one thing that makes me wonder about you: Why would a woman as wise as you waste her time with a psychological barbarian like me? And there's another doubt I have: The pain you have undergone in order to live in accord with what you believe to be your realization is enormous. Yet how can we really live in peace while making such strenuous efforts? Where is everyday tranquillity in all this? The simple pleasure of eating a piece of bread next to a river, of doing nothing, or walking in the street, smelling the wet asphalt after a rain, watching a flock of sparrows fly without wondering where they're going? What about simple weeping in grief as we scatter the ashes of a loved one in a beautiful landscape, or speaking of ordinary, unimportant things with a child, an old woman, or a madman? . . ."

"What bad taste! That's quite enough! Do you wish to belong to the anonymous herd of sheep, abandoning yourself to an empty happiness, sitting like a clam with your bread beside the river, sniffing the wet asphalt like a dog, thinking yourself a poet because you admire the flight of a few scrawny, ugly sparrows, reveling in your grief as you scatter ashes that testify that you are mortal, with the misfortune of some becoming the happiness of others, wasting your time discussing trivialities with people of limited intelligence? If so, you are putting off till later—perhaps much later, perhaps hundreds of thousands of years—something important. And what you are putting off is the blooming of cosmic consciousness.

"*Please* realize this: The universe is a being in the process of evolution. Degree by degree, it is rising from inert matter to pure thinking. The consciousness of the human race is a minuscule light in this immensity, a light that is the result of the effort of the entire cosmos. Call it God if you like, this will to go beyond the limitations of form. Then at least you can accept the idea that you are a part of this alchemical process, a process in which, for reasons we don't yet understand, God has imprisoned himself in matter and has been trying since the very instant of his fall to liberate himself. As for us, we are here in this fleeting present in order to help God escape from the organic cell. To fail to develop your consciousness is to betray God."

"But . . ."

"Don't interrupt, don't argue with me, put aside your reason for a moment and just listen. Why did I seek you out? It was because I perceived that you are an artist who will create a different film more ambitious than the first. My blessed father transcended his personal interests in order to become a benefactor of humanity, one who awakens those who are asleep. What ordinary mortals call 'death' did not stop him in the great work that he took upon himself. Dissolved in his ideas, he continues to act. In making love with me, you have been touched by him. Now, whether you like it or not, you carry him embedded in your soul. He will guide you in the creation of your next work. Through cinematic images, you will unite with him to bring consciousness to those who have eyes to see and ears to hear."

At this time I had not yet even begun to think of the adventure of making the film *The Holy Mountain*. In it, a master similar to Gurdjieff promises to reveal the secret of immortality to his disciples. Therefore, what Reyna was telling me seemed to be delirious raving. My analysis was that, in spite of her astounding mental and corporeal techniques, she had not yet overcome her incestuous desires. However much she wanted to appear to me as a mature adult, she was really a little girl in love with her mythic father. With the cynicism of a retarded adolescent, I decided to humor her in her neurosis to take full advantage of learning as much as possible about her four sexual categories. . . .

We had a copious breakfast together and then lost ourselves in a battle of sexual caresses that lasted at least five hours. Exhausted, we fell asleep like two satiated stones.

When we woke up, it was midnight. I felt a kind of indigestion, like a child who has eaten too much candy. I tried to leave on the pretext that I needed to change my clothes.

"Out of the question. The seeds of my blessed father's teachings have been sown only in your intellect. Now we need to undertake an act that will show your unconscious mind how the work of initiation can conquer time, accelerating the unfolding of the soul. Wearing your barbaric costume as a disguise, you must come with me to a sacred place: Monte Alban, a six-thousand-foot mountain whose peak was flattened by the Zapotecs for their ceremonies. I will call the hotel desk right now so they can find us a limousine with a chauffeur. Monte Alban is about 380 miles from here. If we stop to eat, we'll need at least six hours to arrive there. During the trip, we can continue our conversation or perhaps practice certain oral techniques I haven't yet shown you. You can decide."

This promise won me over, and I agreed without protest to this adventure. An amiable chauffeur, don Rodolfo, agreed to drive us all night in his gray Cadillac. In the shadows of the backseat, Reyna showed me how the larynx can perform astonishing movements if it is vibrated simultaneously with the aid of certain Tibetan mantras. After being subjected to this ecstasy several times, I was overcome by a sensation of intense, organic emptiness. I fell asleep like a log in the arms of my lovely torturer.

The day was under way when the car finally arrived at the foot of the mountain. We declined don Rodolfo's offer to accompany us on foot. Hiding a yawn, he settled himself in the Cadillac for a well-deserved siesta.

As we climbed, Reyna told me: "It is called the white mountain— white in the sense of being sacred. Five centuries before the birth of Christ, the Zapotecs were able to cut off the head of a mountain. You understand the meaning? We must dethrone the intellect, transform the brain into a field, in order to see the totality of the horizon. When you live down below, you see only in fragments what confines you, giving a limited image of yourself and the world. From above, you live in communion with all of nature, a circular horizon that is the wedding ring that unites earth and heaven. These pyramids—labeled as tombs or temples by those necrophiles who call themselves archaeologists—are observatories. They have a dual meaning: god-demon entities that the initiate must climb— in other words, master—in order to dance freely at the summit in communion with the stars. Here, there are nine principal constructions, which refer to the nine points of the enneagram:* acceptance–criticism;

*The enneagram is a diagram in the form of a kind of nine-pointed star. It is used as a model to describe cosmic and psychological laws of human consciousness, especially in the study of character and personal evolution. It may have originated in Persia. It is used by some Sufi schools and was used by Gurdjieff. Oscar Ichazo and Claudio Naranjo had a major influence on its current popularity.

humility–pride; sincerity–vanity; contentment–craving; detachment–
greed; courage–fear; sobriety–gluttony; innocence–luxury; and conscious action–self-forgetfulness. . . . Come! Let us climb to the highest
part. It is there where, as they say, thousands of human hearts were
torn out!"

It was early enough in the day so that there were no tourists. Once
at the level top, Reyna led me to the pyramid built upon one side of it
and had me kneel with her at the base.

"Help me dig. We must free a stone."

Plunging our hands in the earth, we touched the stone foundations
of the pyramid. By exerting all our strength together, we were able to
pull out a stone. With a handful of grass, Reyna cleaned the rectangular stone. Its surface was covered with some light fissures. Deeply
moved, Reyna placed the open palm of her right hand next to the
stone's surface.

"In this life that is a continuous miracle, how can we speak of accident? Compare the cracks in this stone to the lines of my palm. They
are identical. This stone has been waiting for me for more than two
hundred centuries. Destiny had already chosen me to bring it out of
darkness. Without me, it would have remained down below for thousands of years. Now we are going to allow this stone to be placed at the
very summit of the pyramid. This is a symbol of all my blessed father's
teachings: if we make the effort, we can take a leap through time, accelerate our evolution, reach the highest consciousness, the meeting point
of earth and cosmos, matter and spirit, the sacred space that is an eye
of God.

"Climb with me now. Slowly, very slowly, with small steps, in a
ceremonial ascent. Support me from behind, holding my shoulders
while I carry the stone against my belly with the feeling of gradual
gestation. When we arrive at the top, we shall put it in the center
of the platform. It shall be the ruler of all the stones that support it
from below. When the sun becomes hot, perhaps it will even open

and release a phoenix. . . . Yes, I fervently believe that these pyramids are life-generating monuments. That is why they have platforms instead of points at the top: so that there will be a space for a conscious being to take wing, a being to which this space will someday give birth."

We climbed extremely slowly, step by step. Chanting as if it were a magic mantra, she recited an exercise: 2; 4; 8; 16; 32; . . . 128; . . . 512; . . . 134,217,728; . . . 8,589,934,592; . . . and so on, arriving at an incredible series of figures recited with dizzying speed.

Finally, we were at the top. It was square, about six feet on each side. The stones were covered with a sort of mortar. Silently, with tears in her eyes, Reyna went to the center of the square. There, she tossed the stone upward as if she wanted to dip it in the sky. Then she kneeled and tried to place it, saying: "After so many centuries, you reach the central place to give your life to the pyramid. . . . You are the chosen one. . . . May our souls do as you do . . ."

She was about to prepare a place in the center for the stone when I suddenly grabbed her arm, preventing her from doing this.

"What are you doing?" she said. "Why do you interrupt such a beautiful act?"

"Look carefully—there is something even more beautiful!" Through a crack in the very center of the earth, a tiny flower was blooming. "You see, the pyramid doesn't need your help in order to produce life. A stone opening to release a phoenix is only a poetic vision—but this little flower, so real, so pure, so fragile, it gives meaning to the entire monument. Reyna, I remain convinced that you give too much importance to effort. Stop carrying so many heavy stones! Allow something to be born in you that is not a product of your will . . ."

She threw the stone straight at my head. If I had not ducked, it would have fractured my skull. Then she let herself collapse slowly into a sitting position, as if she was an ice-sculpture melting. Finally, she spoke.

"What monstrous vanity. To believe that I, this ephemeral little earthworm, am capable of helping a pyramid! And the pyramid, with the almost imperceptible gesture of producing that little flower, has shown me that I am like a mosquito perched upon the horn of an ox, believing it is helping the ox to pull the cart. I see it now: the very foundation of my theoretical edifice is rotten. I have taken a wrong path. In order for my efforts to bear fruit, I must find another way.

"It turns out that someone told me about a curandero, don Prudencio Garza, who lives in a small village only a few miles from here. I had been afraid of undergoing the terrifying experience that he offers, but after this miraculous sign, I must do it if I am serious about dismantling the castle of illusions that I have taken so long to build."

"What experience are you talking about?"

"He is a sorcerer who has pupils eat little mushrooms that produce real, physical death. In the beyond, if you succeed in crossing the river of acid without your essential consciousness dissolving, you come to life again. If not, you actually die. No, stop shaking your head—no one can stop me from undergoing this definitive trial. I am taking the limousine. Either you accompany me there or you leave me and walk six miles to Oaxaca, where you can catch the train back home."

"You are engaging in madness. I feel obliged to accompany you."

We descended the mountain fast, almost running. When we reached the limousine, we were shocked to see that all its wheels were gone! Don Rodolfo was snoring loudly in the front seat. When we woke him and showed him the disaster, he lost all his aristocratic demeanor of tourist chauffeur. "Sons of whores!" he shouted over and over. Finally, he knotted his large handkerchief to make a headscarf to protect him from the sun and walked off toward Oaxaca, still railing against the thieves and the hot sun.

Reyna, as stubborn as her blessed father, was determined to walk however many miles it took to find the sorcerer. Trying to conceal my own anxiety that the village might be much farther than she thought, I asked her its name.

"Huapancingo or Huanotzcan—I don't remember exactly. But stop worrying. All problems are mental illusions. Give yourself to the reality of this moment. We are only a short distance away from something incredible, whether it's a thousand or ten thousand steps from here. Let's go!"

We had been walking for four hours. The sun was beating down more and more harshly and the caresses of the wind had become like knives, cracking our lips. My dry, hard shoes tortured my feet. Reyna walked like a zombie, murmuring mathematical exercises. I sat down on a fallen tree trunk. I had to shout for her to come out of her trance and stop.

"Somebody gave you bad directions. This road doesn't go anywhere. We'd best turn back now."

"O man of little faith! Accept the here and now and stop thinking about the future. Free yourself from the domination of your mind; use the pain in your feet to awaken your consciousness of being and the miracle will happen. Let us go on!"

"Out of the question. Go on if you want to. I'm going back. Your madness is not my madness."

I got up, and with a sudden irrepressible rage, I kicked at the tree trunk. Part of the bark flew off and a swarm of small black spiders surged out. I jumped back in alarm and beat a retreat.

Reyna came up next to me, laughing. "Coward! It is your resistance that produces failure. If you lack fervor, you will miss the incredible transformation."

"This road is very long and it passes only through fields of alfalfa. Perhaps I can be of help to you?"

The voice of the old man resonated in our ears with a friendly seriousness. We had not noticed him come up. Probably he had been resting in the shade of a tree nearby. His deep-set eyes surrounded by many wrinkles and his pupils barely visible within cataracts made us think he might be blind.

Anxiously, Reyna asked him: "Do you know a curandero named . . ."

". . . Prudencio Garza?" he interrupted her. "I am he, my dear girl. The wind blew me the fragments of your shadows, so I came down here to wait for you. Follow me."

We crossed through a pine forest on a winding path between hills, which finally brought us to a small valley. Near a black boulder covered with grass there was a cabin. Its door was framed with vultures' beaks. Not far away, three goats made awkward movements: each had one hind leg tied to those of the other goats. A black dog gnawed at the remains of an iguana, and a pig was snuggling its belly comfortably into a freshly dug hollow in a humid patch of ground.

The dog dropped its prey at our approach and circled around Reyna, emitting ear-splitting barks. It stood up on its hind legs and put its paws on her chest. Fearlessly, she stroked its head.

"Calm down, Mictiani. Let the lady alone."

Obediently, the dog moved several yards away, but it still stared at Reyna with eyes full of love.

"Welcome to my humble abode, and please make yourselves at home."

The interior was divided into living room and kitchen by a fragile wall made of old cardboard. In the center of the living room, under a lantern hanging from the smoky ceiling, there was an altar with a plaster statue of Santa Muerte (St. Death), a skeleton covered with a cloak like that of the Virgin of Guadalupe. There were also some yellow flowers, a small box of cigarettes made of dark tobacco, a bottle of strong liqueur, four stoneware cups full of corn beer, thirteen black candles, and some human bones. Among them was a brilliant, silver-plated gourd cut in a circular fashion to make a kind of coffer.

The curandero made Mictiani lie down at the doorstep, offered me a small bench several feet away from the altar, and invited Reyna to sit on the rug woven of palm branches.

"Sit in front of me, my girl. I perceive that you have decided to visit the land of the dead. It is not an easy thing. The mushrooms will bring you death for three days. You will wander in the four petals of the flower of shadows. In the eastern one, a thousand vultures will devour your flesh and bones down to a dark residue. In the northern one, a boiling river will eat away your memory. In the western one, hordes of the dead will empty your soul. In the southern petal, gluttonous goddesses will devour what remains of you: your vision. If you can withstand all this, you will arrive at the center as one who is blind. In that place, inner and outer are the same. There, you will meet Talocan, your inner God. If you are worthy of him, he will cause you to be reborn. If he considers you unworthy, you will not come back to life. Did you notice the pit I dug when you arrived here? It was for you in case you do not come back to life.

"As for you," he said, addressing me, "because you came here as her protector, you are allowed to stay—but on one condition: that you remain absolutely silent. If you say so much as one word, your friend will wake up as a demon and drink your blood."

I was frightened. I felt like running out of that place, forgetting Reyna and the sorcerer forever. Yet, whether through pride or curiosity, I accepted this trial, telling myself that Reyna could not become a vampire nor could this friendly old man really be a murderer. Probably, the poor fellow was just trying to earn a few dollars by taking advantage of a tourist's desire for exotic experiences.

I made a sign that I agreed to the conditions. Don Prudencio had Reyna undress and lie down on the mat. She did so without the slightest embarrassment.

Then, to our great surprise, don Prudencio seemed to become an entirely different person. No longer was he a bent, humble old man with cataracts. The elder man seemed to dissolve as his back straightened. His movements became elegant and feline as he put on a woolen cape embroidered with Aztec designs. He brandished a green obsidian dagger as he lit three black candles and recited a prayer to Santa Muerte.

"Santa Muerte, because you were created by divine commandment in order to renew life, please have the kindness to rid the soul and body of this poor woman of all trace of suffering, shame, anguish, and fear, which come from the cruel treatments she received as a child.

"Santa Muerte, may the heavenly scythe that you wield cut the roots of bitterness, pain, anguish, despair, resentment, sadness, loneliness, confusion, and other afflictions caused by the venom that has been poured into the mind of this poor woman. Through you, may she thus be allowed to know the one who sees all and can do all."

With the assurance of a high priest, he opened the silver gourd and took out a patty of cow manure upon which were growing about forty mushrooms crowded together. They were white and looked like tiny phalluses. The energy that radiated from these fungi seemed to fill the entire room. With his green dagger, the sorcerer cut them patiently, one by one, placing each mushroom into Reyna's mouth. When she had swallowed the last one, she began to sweat and tremble. A few minutes later, she vomited. The sorcerer examined her vomit, counting the mushrooms there.

"The body knows its own measure. It has rejected only six of these little children. She is a strong woman—she has kept the largest possible number in her stomach."

He kneeled before the altar and recited praises before the plaster statue as Reyna became more and more pale and lethargic.

"Praise to you, Santa Muerte, for your divine beauty is God's reward to the just. Praise to you, Santa Muerte, for without your help, human beings could never free themselves of their pride. Praise to you, Santa Muerte, for your perfection is like that of the life that God has you renew."

The curandero continued reciting prayers and praises until very late into the night. Reyna seemed like a wax statue. Flies buzzed around her, and it seemed that she would never breathe again. I was uncomfortable and trembling from a cold that was not so much from the temperature as from anxiety. Hypnotized by the droning voice of the sorcerer, I finally fell asleep.

Near dawn, I was awakened by the raucous calls of a flock of vultures. Reyna was still dead. The sorcerer was outside, shouting imprecations. I stood up with difficulty and walked out of the cabin with cramped legs. Don Prudencio had a big stick with which he was striking at the vultures who were swarming over the dead body of his dog, Mictiani. The animal's eye sockets were empty, bloody pits. Its guts were spilling out on the ground. Finally, the blows of the stick prevailed, and all the vultures flew away.

"No, it wasn't these devil's messengers who killed him. He let himself die. Help me put him in the grave."

He was a big dog. The curandero grabbed him by the neck, I seized his back paws, and we tossed him into the pit. Little by little, he covered the dog with the dirt piled up at its side, talking to him.

"I never imagined I was digging this grave for you, my brother. You are so good that you decided to die for the foreign visitor. In the afterworld, you will protect her soul. Praise to you! You have sacrificed your own happiness in order to lessen the suffering of the foreigner. Praise to you! You have given everything in exchange for nothing!"

Taking a deep breath, he chanted a final "Amen," which seemed to last interminably.

He looked at me, smiling, but his eyes were sad. I saw his cataracts reappear. His back bent slowly until he had once more become the kind old man instead of the formidable sorcerer.

"Thanks to Mictiani, your friend is no longer in danger. Yesterday, she passed through two petals. Today, she will pass through the last two. Early tomorrow morning, she will arrive at the center of the flower and come back to life.

"Look—somewhere over that way, I have some tortillas, goat cheese, and many prickly pears. Have something to eat—but quietly."

That night was very long. Don Prudencio knelt before the altar again, chanting his interminable series of prayers to Santa Muerte. Lying on the floor, Reyna was still not breathing and her skin was terrifyingly white. I also lay on the floor, my head against the little bench.

Above: El Topo reawakens under the mountain. From El Topo.

Right: One of the four masters before his duel with El Topo. From El Topo.

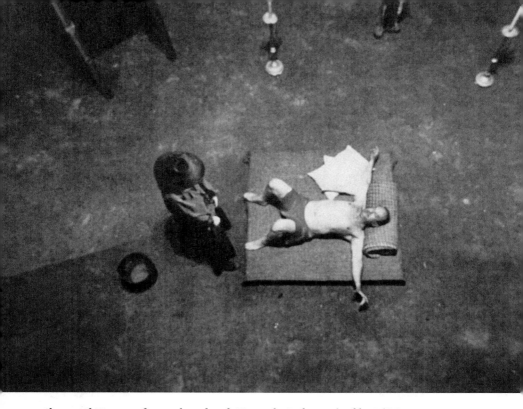

Above: El Topo confronts the colonel. From the Jodorowsky film El Topo.

Below: El Topo rides off with his son, leaving vestiges of their past life behind. From El Topo

Above: The female gunfighter and his former companion gun El Topo down. From El Topo.

Below: Gay cops at a wedding. From El Topo.

Above: Captured monks watch a bandit read the Bible. From El Topo.

Below: The lineup. From El Topo.

Above: The Sex Machine. From The Holy Mountain.

Below: A parade of Santa Claus at the factory. From The Holy Mountain.

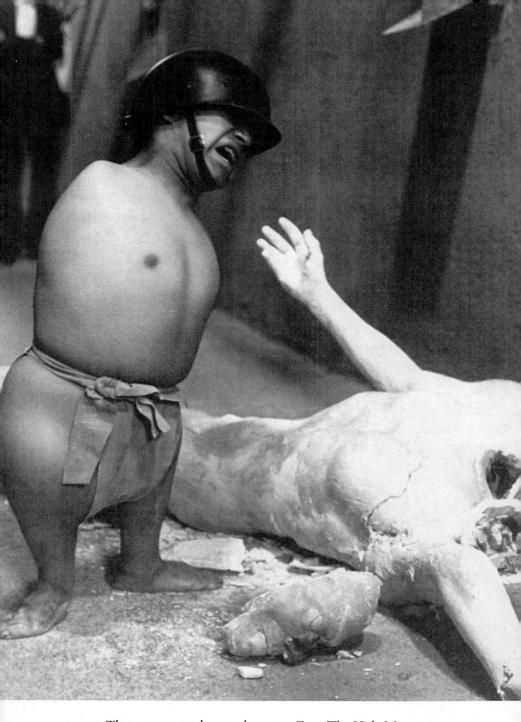

The war monster berates the corpse. From The Holy Mountain.

Above: Christ carrying the cross. From the Jodorowsky film The Holy Mountain.

Below: Christ for sale. From The Holy Mountain.

The tiger ascends the mountain. From The Holy Mountain.

I wanted to sleep, but no matter how I tried to empty my mind, a river of words flooded it. I thought I had solved the koan known as stepping into the abyss; I thought I had realized what the Chinese monk Dazu* was speaking of in the poem he wrote on the day of his death:

> *In face of the real, words and reflections are obliterated.*
> *In true identity, seeing and hearing are gone.*
> *Such is the place of calm peace.*
> *All other study is mere verbal rambling.*

I also thought I understood what the philosopher Seng Zhao[†] wrote after the king sentenced him to death by beheading:

> *As the naked blade approaches my head,*
> *it will be like beheading the spring wind.*

Yet Reyna's courage in putting her life in the hands of a primitive curandero brought about an intense crisis in me. When Ejo told me "Learn to die, intellectual!" was he saying that I must stop identifying myself with my thoughts or was he saying I must learn to accept physical death as my friend was now doing? In any case, was this cataleptic state true death? Could the visions produced by a hallucinogenic mushroom be considered a true exploration of life beyond death? Who was Reyna now, during this long, long night? Was she this inert body or was she a spirit voyaging in a mythic world?

---

*Little information is available about Dazu. According to Sinologist Paul Demiéville (in the book *Poèmes chinois d'avant la mort* also by Jean-Pierre Diény [Paris: l'Asiathèque, 1984]) he is quoted in the *Songjing* in 961 CE and must have lived during the Tang dynasty (618–906 CE) and also during the Five Dynasty period (907–960 CE).
†Seng Zhao (374–414 CE) may be regarded as the first Chinese Buddhist philosopher. He read the Taoists and the Vimalakirti-nirdesa and followed the teachings of Kumarasvira, who died in 409 CE. Later, he was sentenced to death by the sovereign and committed suicide at Zhang'an, where the Kumarasvira school had stirred up jealousy and opposition.

In our readings of the secret book of koans, Ejo and I came across one that might apply to the present situation:* "There was once a woman named Seijo, whose body and spirit separated. One fled her home to marry her lover, Ozu, whereas the other Seijo—sick, silent, and wasting away in bed—remained with her parents. Master Goso Hoen asked a monk: 'If the body and spirit of Seijo are separate, which is the real Seijo?' The monk replied with this question: 'Which of the two is real?'"

At first, it seemed to me that the monk made it clear that it was not a question of the reality of one Seijo or the other Seijo, but of the concepts of *body* and *spirit*. Later, I realized that the monk was referring to the spirit and body of Goso Hoen himself. He was saying: "At the moment when you ask me this koan, trying to trap me in the metaphysics of body-spirit duality, which of the two are you? In reality, you are one. No matter how many different names you give to this unity, it does not change."

In his own turn, Goso Hoen answered the monk's question with another question: "What is Seijo's state of being?"

The answer:

> *Lamentable, desirable, odious, enchanting. . . .*
> *Though my golden ring has grown by an inch,*
> *I will tell others I am not in love.*

Being cannot be divided into parts. It is everything at once.

> *Maitreya, the true Maitreya,*
> *divides his body into thousands, a hundred hundred*
>   *thousand fragments.*
> *From time to time, he appears to people subjected to*
>   *time.*
> *Those subjected to time do not perceive him.*

---

*This refers to case 35, collected in the Mumonkan and presented to one of his disciples by Goso Hoen, or, in Chinese, Wuzu Fayan (1024–1104 CE).

The model of reality is not reality. The growing ring symbolizes growing love, but it is not real love. The word that describes the world is not the world. Existence can be spirit and body united or it can be neither spirit nor body. It is what it is and not what our intellect analyzes and perceives it to be. This cold body lying on the floor is not separate from its spirit and the spirit is not wandering in another dimension. They are one and the same. Tomorrow, when Reyna wakes up, will she really believe she has been traveling in another world in which she arrived at the center where a mythic God reigns? And what if she does not come back to life? Perhaps this old man is really crazy and has poisoned her!

Don Prudencio interrupted his prayers, went to the kitchen, and returned with a little jug full of milk.

"It is from my goats. Drink it and you will fall asleep quickly. Your thoughts are making a lot of noise."

As soon as I drank the delicious milk, I fell into a profound sleep.

I didn't wake up until midday. Reyna was dressed and waiting for me, ready to depart. The curandero had disappeared.

"Don Prudencio has left to put his goats out to pasture. It's time for us to go now."

We walked for three hours without her saying a word. I respected her silence. She seemed changed—even her face was not the same. Before, it had been mobile and ready to grimace. Now it was like a smooth, polished surface from which a mask had been torn away. Her body movements were different too. She walked so softly that her steps, though very energetic, made almost no noise. Her spine was very straight, her chin slightly lifted. She gave the impression that she was wearing a crown.

When we caught sight of Monte Alban and its pyramids, she spoke at last.

"As you have no doubt noticed, I am the same yet not the same. Do not suppose that I believe I have died and been resurrected. I have traveled to myself, entered into the underworld of my reason, and tried to arrive at the center of the unconscious. The process unfolded as the sorcerer said it would: At first, the mushrooms made me lose all sensation of my flesh and bones. I realized then that I had always lived in my body as if it were a prison. As I began to lose it, I felt an intense love and compassion for it.

"Then my memory was gradually erased. As my emotional bonds disappeared, I understood how attached I had been to people, places, actions. Every being, every thing, every act had been grafted onto me to become confused with my essence, thereby covering it. In forgetting all this, I was able to be myself. But even this *"I am"* was annihilated. I lost all form, all content, all definition. I possessed nothing. I was no more than an impersonal point of view.

"And even that did not last long. The perceiving eye was no longer separate from the world. There was no more perceiving self or other, only being. . . . I regained original innocence and purity. I was both the naive creature about to be born and the wise creature after death. Light and darkness were one, all opposites were harmonious. In love with myself, I became a sun. Then, with frightening clarity, I saw that the Other, my body, was waiting for me. The moment of return had arrived.

"It was easy. I simply opened my eyes. I found myself lying on the floor, naked. My legs were spread and don Prudencio had inserted his penis into my vagina. I pushed him away. The old man took it very calmly. Zipping up his fly, he extinguished the thirteen candles. Then he held his open hand toward me. I gave him a wad of dollars. He simply put them in his sack and then left to go take care of his goats."

"That old rascal! He gave me some milk laced with a sleeping potion. Let's go find him! I'll teach him a lesson!"

"No. Hold on there! I don't know what to think about it. It is strange that he was ejaculating just as I came back to life. He may have been doing it in order to revive me. Let us leave him in peace. Everything happened because it had to be that way. I regret nothing. This experience has freed me. I will never be the same.

"The teachings of my blessed father were the boat that helped me cross the river. Now that I am on the other side, it would be stupid to try to continue to live in that boat. The past is dead, and you are part of that past. Let us agree that our adventure has come to an end. I will disappear for a time. One day, I will write you. . . . From now on, let us not speak to each other."

Thus we continued, like mutes. We mingled with a group of tourists and took a bus to Mexico City. We sat far apart on the bus. When we arrived in the city, we did not even say good-bye.

I never saw her again. A few years later, an envelope arrived with a Bali postmark. It contained a short note and a photograph: "Me with Ivanna, my daughter. I don't know whether her father is you or don Prudencio."

10

Master to Disciple, Disciple to Master, Disciple to Disciple, Master to Master

Suddenly, this man sensed that the plain had turned in a complete circle. The sky and its clouds seemed to lie at his feet.
SILVER KANE, *UN COLLAR DE PIEL DE SERPIENTE*
(A SNAKESKIN COLLAR)

"Above the place where his head had been, a small cloud of blood floated. . . . The blood seemed to have a life of its own."
SILVER KANE, *CON PERMISO DEL MUERTO*
(WITH THE DEAD MAN'S PERMISSION)

Ten years later, disguised as a film and theater director, I returned to Mexico. I had been invited to give a lecture in a theater of the University of Mexico. On its facade, nineteen huge letters proclaimed it as the TEATRO JULIO CASTILLO. I realized that this talk represented the closure of a cycle of my life.

Julio Castillo, the same young man who had asked me years ago to teach him about lighting (not spiritual light), had gone on to become the director of many successful plays but had died at the peak of his fame. His legacy to the world of theater was so important that the autonomous University of Mexico had named its largest theater after him. In my own homage to Julio Castillo, I tore up the notes I had prepared and decided to repeat the same mistake I had made with him years ago—but this time deliberately. They wanted me to talk about cinematography, but I was going to talk to them about spiritual enlightenment and my experiences with koans.

In front of the thousand young people who filled the hall, I proposed this: "I am going to give you some riddles to solve. When you've finished offering all your solutions and exhausted your inspiration, I'll offer you mine."

With great perplexity they listened to me clap my hands and ask: "That is the sound of two hands clapping. What is the sound of one hand clapping?"

After considerable laughter, the responses came: snapping your fingers, slapping your forehead, holding out one hand and making the sound of a fart, and so forth. When they had finished and declared their inspiration exhausted, I had them each lift their right hand, as if about to swear an oath. Then I lifted my own and said what I had learned many years before from Ejo Takata.

"The sound of my one hand is the same as the sound of your one hand."

This elicited enthusiastic applause. Inspired by this appreciative audience, I began to invent koans and offer solutions.

"Why do mountains have rocks? ... Mountains don't have rocks. The rocks are the mountain. ... Why is the mouth under the eyes? ... Because the mouth is for kissing the earth and the eyes are for kissing the sky. ... Why can't I stop thinking? ... I don't think—the thoughts think me."

Carried away by their enthusiasm, I even stepped down from the stage and began to mingle with the audience. Suddenly, I saw that their eyes were no longer on me but were fixed on the stage, which was at my back. Something was happening there.

When I turned around and looked, I felt as if I was in a dream. Ejo Takata, dressed in a monk's robe was seated in meditation position, grinning at me.

It had been ten years since I'd seen him, but he looked the same as ever—generous spirit, ageless face, anchored to the ground, head pushing at the sky!

He jumped right into our game, holding his wooden kyosaku in a threatening gesture. (On one side of this stick the characters say: "I can teach you nothing. Teach yourself." On the other side is written: "The plant flowers in the spring.")

"What is the sound of an empty mind?" he asked me.

"The same sound as the voice that asks," I answered without hesitation.

Ejo shouted a joyous "Kwatzu! . . . Where does a thought spring from, and what is it?"

"Ideas have no owners. They are in the world, seeds of action."

He began fanning himself. I realized I had fallen into the old intellectual trap. I prostrated myself three times before the master (sensei), and I recited one of his own proverbs: "A boat can find support on the water. The water can overturn the boat." And I awaited the next question.

"When the mind is empty, what does it see?"

"Everything but itself."

"Kwatzu! When a thought springs forth, where does it come from?"

"Tell me where it is going, and I'll tell you where it comes from."

"Kwatzu! If you see that a thought is excessive and artificial, do you think that there also exists a natural thought?"

"The farmer waits for rain; the traveler waits for good weather."

"Kwatzu! What does your birthday mean to you?"

"There is no birth or death."

He made a sign for me to come on stage. I climbed up and kneeled before him and touched the floor three times with my head.

He lifted me up with a smile. Holding the kyosaku in a horizontal position, he offered it to me. My hands were burning and my feet were freezing. Never had I expected to receive such an honor. Without thinking about what I was doing, I took the stick as in a dream and held it against my breast.

The students began to applaud. I had to acknowledge this with a bow, but as I was doing so, Ejo took advantage of the moment to disappear. After a minute of confusion, I ran outside to try to find him.

By chance, several cars were waiting in line to leave the parking lot. I saw Ejo in one of them, a beat-up old car with an Indian-looking driver. When he saw me, he rolled down the window. I held out the kyosaku to him, crying, "I don't deserve this! You yourself once told me: 'If you have the stick, I will give it to you. If you don't have it, I'll take it away from you.' You must give your stick to someone who already has it. And I do not have it! I demand you take it!"

Ejo lowered the window farther. Instead of taking the kyosaku, he threw his fan in my face and rolled up the window again. The car started moving. I ran after it as fast as I could, but I could not catch up. Breathless, I stood there and began to fan myself. On the paper of the fan was written: "Chapultepec Forest. The usual place, same time, tomorrow."

I couldn't believe my eyes. Deep down, I had always aspired to become a master basking in the veneration of hundreds of disciples. Not only that, but I wanted to be able to sit cross-legged for endless hours in a zendo, a smiling Buddha until I died. I also knew this was an unattainable goal. I knew only too well my shameful weakness, my flawed successes, my ignorance like that of a microbe in the infinite cosmos.

To lose Ejo as a master was unbearable. "A master is for your entire life." By giving me his stick and his fan, he made me not only his peer but also his successor. He must be saying that he was leaving, that he was sick, or that he thought he was about to die. I felt nauseous at this thought. I was losing my support. The axis around which I turned, thinking it always protected me, was about to be taken away. I had countless questions and no real answers. Ejo was the only one who could provide the one answer to all my questions. A cloud veiled my vision. If Ejo perceived in me the value of a master, he was mistaken, and if he could make such a mistake, then he was not a true master. I felt like vomiting. I collapsed, sitting upon a cement bench. I fanned myself with his fan. With the stick I gave myself several blows on my shoulder blades.

"Master . . ."

An exceedingly skinny youth with brilliant eyes came up to me. Feeling ridiculous, I immediately stopped striking and fanning myself. I forced myself to smile at him. He kneeled before me.

"Please allow me to introduce myself. My name is Daniel. I just came from your lecture. I saw your film *The Holy Mountain*. It changed my life. I have made a short film, inspired by your work. I wanted to thank you . . ."

His admiration came at a most inopportune moment, but I replied, simulating a warm friendliness: "Stand up and come sit down beside me. Thank you for your thanks. Would you like an autograph?"

"Well, of course, that would give me pleasure, Master. But if you don't mind, I would like to ask a favor of you . . ."

"Ask whatever you like, but don't call me 'Master.'"

"Actually, I'm a writer as well as a filmmaker. I've been reading ever since I could think. Yet I know nothing about Zen. I've never heard of these strange koans before. When you asked them, I had no idea how to answer, and afterward I didn't understand your answers. Nor did I understand the ones you gave to the monk. Could you explain the meaning of all this to me?"

I had to get a grip on myself in order not to burst into tears. The absurd dance of fate had sent me a boy who took me for a master, whereas my mind was like a mirror broken into a thousand pieces. His desire to understand was so naive and his trust in my artistic mastery was so great that I felt incapable of disappointing him. Mustering a tone of calm and assurance, I improvised a little speech for him.

"Mountains do not have rocks any more than the world has individuals. The rocks are the mountain; the individuals are the world. The totality of the universe is one. The mouth is below the eyes; the birds fly in the sky; the fish swim in the sea. Everything has its natural place, without effort, in happiness. The bird drowns in the water just as the fish drowns in the air. Happiness means being ourselves in the place that is right for us. We think but we are not our thoughts. When we identify ourselves with our thoughts, we cease to be ourselves. Thoughts are, but we are not. The sound of an empty mind is the noise of the words of the one who is asking questions. 'From where does a thought spring and what is it?' That question is a bunch of words that cannot be answered properly by another bunch of words. One thought springs from another thought, and so on to infinity. Yet saying 'bread' does not satisfy our hunger. I should have just screamed at every question and given that as an answer. When the mind is empty, the observer-actor dualism disappears. If we see ourselves, we are not empty—no one arriving, no one leaving, everything just always here. Every thought is a mirage. There is no first cause; it is neither the chicken nor the egg. No beginning, no end. Permanent impermanence, formless present. Accept this appearance of change!"

Daniel tried to thank me, but I left in a hurry.

The trees in the forest were half hidden in a grayish, toxic, morning smog. In a clearing at some distance from the hordes of automobiles rushing like sheep to the slaughterhouse, Ejo and I had established a custom of meditating for two hours at six o'clock in the morning. I found him there, in zazen position. He was wearing jeans and a black

T-shirt. Beside him was a mesh sack. I prostrated before him and placed the stick and fan in front of him.

"You are mistaken, Ejo. I am not a master."

He shouted "Kwatzu!" at me so loudly it must have been heard a mile away. Then he seized me by the shoulders and forced me to sit in his place. He kneeled before me, touched his forehead to the ground, and spoke softly:

"Sometimes we are disciples, sometimes masters. Nothing is fixed."

I did not want to accept this. I took him by the shoulders and sat him again in his place. I prostrated again before him, pressing my face obstinately against the ground three times.

Sighing with exasperation, Ejo recited a text that he had apparently learned by heart: "Are we ourselves? Where are we when we are? If I close my hands, water still escapes from them. When these hands play the lute in the moonlight, they are like the hands of the Buddha. Master Rinzai said: 'Sometimes a cry is like a precious sword molded of the purest gold. Sometimes a cry is like a magnificent lion merged with the bushes. Sometimes a cry is like a fishing pole in the middle of the grass in whose shadow fish gather in a group. Sometimes a cry does not function as a cry.' A monk asked him: 'What is the meaning of the first maxim?' Rinzai said: 'When the seal is removed, the red ink becomes visible. Though the letter has not yet been read, the roles of the guest and host are already decided.' The monk asked again: 'What is the meaning of the second maxim?' Rinzai said: 'Careless one! Why should the work be inferior to the ideal?' The monk insisted: 'What is the meaning of the third maxim?' Rinzai said: 'When the puppet dances on the stage, the movement comes from the hand of the actor hidden in its clothes.' And he added: 'If you understand the first maxim, you will become the Buddha's master. If you understand the second maxim, you will become a master of men and gods. But if you understand the third maxim, you will not even be able to save yourself.' Then he continued: 'Sometimes you remove the man without removing the surroundings. Sometimes you remove the surroundings without removing the man. Sometimes you remove both. Sometimes you remove neither.'"

These words, recited rapidly by Ejo, engraved themselves in my memory. I can regard them from several points of view. Their apparently different elements fit together like pieces of a jigsaw puzzle. An understanding came to me through these words like luminous flashes (I can find no better metaphor for it). Ejo was now showing me the higher level of koans!

Are we ourselves? It is impossible to define ourselves, for we do not belong to ourselves; we are the world. Where are we when we are? Reality is formless and fluid, constantly changing. The dry leaf carried away by the stream is in the water, not in a place. If I close my hands, water still escapes from them. If my intellect identifies itself with a separate self, it does not capture eternal truth. When these hands play the lute in the moonlight, they are like the hands of the Buddha. The Buddha imagined by our intellect lacks any hands. When my hands produce beauty, they are the hands of the cosmos. All things are one and one thing is all things! Sometimes a cry is like a precious sword molded of the purest gold. The master transmits his satori directly to the disciple without words, like an electric shock. Sometimes a cry is like a magnificent lion merged with the bushes. The master seeks to open the stagnant mind of the disciple, who believes the world is dark because his eyes are shut. Sometimes a cry is like a fishing pole in the middle of the grass in whose shadow fish gather in a group. The master penetrates the unconscious of the disciple, trying to bring light to his hidden treasure, his essential being. Sometimes a cry does not function as a cry. The master cries without finality, naturally and spontaneously, from the highest heaven to the depths of the earth. It is thunder resounding in the blue sky with a bright sun. There is no disciple. There are two masters.

What is the meaning of the first maxim? The monk is looking for truth in the meaning of Rinzai's teachings. Rinzai tells him not to ask such questions, but to trust his inner treasure and surrender himself to meditation. When the seal is removed, the red ink becomes visible. Though the letter has not yet been read, the roles of the guest and host are already decided. Though I am not capable of understanding the teaching, I must give myself to the work that submerges me in essential being. Ejo is the seal, I am the sealed letter. I must remove the seal in order to find myself and know that this self is the same as that of Ejo, and the Buddha.

What is the meaning of the second maxim? The monk remains a prisoner of his search for ideal truth, for a personal self. Why should the work be inferior to the ideal? Without feeding words to the ravenous intellect, sit calmly, concentrate, and observe the unfolding of life until you are yourself the truth: this is the way.

What is the meaning of the third maxim? There is no distinction between first, second, and third truth. There are no degrees. Unity acts bluntly, like a hammer blow that breaks open our head. When the puppet dances on the stage, the movement comes from the hand of the actor hidden in its clothes. In the beginning, the master is the puppeteer and the student is the puppet. Finally, the student understands that the master is a force inside him, a force that does not belong to him.

If you understand the first maxim, you will become the Buddha's master. If you understand the second maxim, you will become a master of men and gods. But if you understand the third maxim, you will not even be able to save yourself. The reality that appears to us as something different in different situations is what it is, neither more nor less. In reciting these maxims, you can imagine yourself as a master greater than the Buddha. Like a blind man's dog, you think you are leading essence. You set up differences between men and gods, you have the impression that awakening has two faces, you make judgments about right and wrong so that finally you cannot even find yourself.

Sometimes you remove the man without removing the surroundings. This is an attitude of the mind in which the object dominates the subject. You abstract the man (subject), but not the surroundings (object). Sometimes you remove the surroundings without removing the man. Here, the mind fixes on the subjective pole, but it denies the objective. Sometimes you remove both surroundings and man. This is a state of emptiness in which the distinction between self and other is eliminated. Sometimes you remove neither the surroundings nor the man. In complete unity with yourself, like a child, you act spontaneously, thus returning to the ordinary world. Subject and object are recognized "as they are."

Ejo sat in meditation before me, indifferent as a mountain, but I knew that in some way, he was waiting for me. The situation was so important that my mind lost track of time. In a few seconds, I was able to complete thoughts that would have taken hours in other circumstances. The concepts of guest and host occupied my attention. Which of us was which? At first, I saw Ejo as the host, the one who was offering consciousness, and myself as the guest who is asking for consciousness. Yet this relation of master and disciple, subject and object, confused me. One of us represented the world of circumstances. Was it me? Then was Ejo the other, the one who produced them? He was the only totally honest man I had ever known in my life. I loved him with the love of an orphan looking for a father. He knew everything, I knew nothing. . . . Stop it, Alejandro! Enough of that sentimental self-indulgence! Was I seeking truth or a loving father figure to heal my sad, abandoned child?

Now my mind took another leap. Master and disciple are in reality symbols of an inner process: essential being and ego. Hence the host is the first and the guest the second. But I am not the owner of the house, nor am I the house itself. My reason is a simple guest, an ephemeral phantom in eternal consciousness. Before meeting Ejo, I considered my intellect to be reality. Anything that could not be put into words was untrustworthy. Thus the guest was usurping the place of the host. Having little or nothing to offer, this false host could only strut in front of himself, deaf and blind to the other. When I first sought out Ejo, I did so as a beggar, with the feeling that he was the generous guest and I was merely a thirsty, bottomless well. My demand was without limit, infinite. With mouth wide open like a baby, I wanted him to feed me without limit, for I wanted to devour the entire universe. The illusory guest of an absolute host, I lived like the seeker in the Sufi story who weeps constantly, thinking of his absolute need for God without ever imagining that God might also need him. When I had understood that the mind can never grasp itself, I realized that instead of emptying it, I should simply let it go, allowing thoughts and impressions to come and go without identifying with them. Ejo and I both were master and disciple. My ego created essential being and essential being created the ego. Finally, I realized that I was now with Ejo not because I needed to obtain something from him, but for the pleasure of being with him, vibrating at the same level of consciousness, him with his ego, me with mine, like two blind men who have learned to see but keep their guide dog—not because they need him, but out of affection for him.

A fresh wind blew away the gray fog. It shook the leaves of the trees, making a pleasant sound. From the whole forest a music arose like the vibrations of the surface of a lake agitated by shoals of fish. The birds began to sing. Even the noise of the traffic was in harmony with the whole. The world had transformed itself into an orchestra of angels. I ceased to see Ejo either as upon a heavenly summit or in the depths of the earth. He was a man like me, a clown like me, a Buddha like me.

"Ejo, it was my anguished ego that first brought me to your teaching. It is thanks to you, essential being and host, that on this day, the guest is finally a good disciple who has learned to be a mirror. He does not take anything for himself. He receives what is given without attempting to keep it. He sinks his feet in the mud but leaves no footprints."

Happy, and grinning so that I could see the metal caps on his teeth, Ejo said: "So! And what have you decided about the kyosaku?"

"I accept it, Master. But I will not keep it. I have no desire to give blows to sleepy monks. When Bodhidharma* sat in silent meditation before the wall of a cave for nine years, he needed no one to strike his shoulder blades. Neither did Eka,† a man who was capable of cutting off his arm to convince Bodhidharma to accept him as a disciple. Nor did Sosan,‡ the leprous disciple of Eka who died in meditation, standing under a tree."

At first I thought that Ejo was angry and was about to let out a roar that would frighten me and the hundreds of birds around us. He closed his eyes and began to sway back and forth, fanning himself. Suddenly, he snapped shut his fan, opened his eyes, and exclaimed:

"You're right! From Doshin§ on, the wandering life came to an end. Zen became a government-sponsored religion and monasteries began to take in children. From that time on, an iron discipline was instituted. They began to strike the young ones who fell asleep meditating—but is it really that important that individuals not fall asleep during meditation? There is nothing to lose, nothing to achieve. Arriving or leaving, essential being is always there. When you eat, you eat. When you meditate, you meditate. When you sleep, you sleep. The blows of the stick offer nothing except discipline for a childish mind.

---

*Bodhidharma, or Putidamo in Chinese and Bodaidaruma or Daruma in Japanese (ca. 470–543 CE), was probably the son of an Indian king. He was the twenty-eighth patriarch in the Mahayana Indian lineage since Shakayamuni Buddha. In the Chinese Ch'an lineage, he was the first patriarch. It is said that he traveled by boat from India to Canton in 520 CE and that the emperor himself questioned him to ascertain the merits of this man and of the Dharma he taught. But the emperor could not understand his answers, and Bodhidharma left for Luoyang, where he practiced zazen constantly in the monastery of Shaolin.
†Eka, or Huike in Chinese (487–593 CE), was the second patriarch of Ch'an. He had several disciples but had to flee, because his eloquence had caused jealousy and hostility among several rival teachers.
‡Sosa, or Sengcan in Chinese (d. ca. 606 CE), was the third patriarch of Ch'an and Eka's disciple.
§Doshin, or Daoxin in Chinese (580–651 CE), was the fourth Ch'an patriarch and a disciple of Sengcan from a very young age. He was one of the most ardent practitioners of meditation.

"In the Sierra Tarahumara I became ill with an inflammation of the heart muscle. My Indian disciples brought me back to the city. It seems I have to have an operation, but the real wound is to my child's heart, and it is the real sufferer. When I was nine years old and the doors of the monastery closed upon me, the first thing I did was cry out: 'I don't want to stay here! Let me out!' They put me in a dormitory where I was the youngest boy. When I failed to hear the bell ring at dawn, they kicked me awake. I had to scrub the floor while the other boys meditated. I didn't do a very good job, and I was kicked for it. At my first breakfast of rice soup, the cook hit me with the ladle because I made noise drinking it. He also made me chew in total silence, without wasting a single grain of rice, but I couldn't help spilling a few drops of the soup—more blows for that. Then they told me to use a hatchet to chop large pieces of wood into smaller ones. When I got splinters in my hand, they only made fun of me, calling me clumsy. At bedtime that evening, a twenty-year-old monk, the head of our group, asked me to massage him. The other boys started to giggle but stifled the sound quickly by covering their heads with the blankets. The monk told me that I was to spend the night in bed with him. 'You will learn our customs. From now on, your job will be to soothe and relax me.' Under the covers, he took one of my hands and placed it on his erect penis. 'Imagine you are cleaning a carrot. Go on, do it with all your strength!' For a whole year, I had to satisfy his whims. What could I do about it? Among monks, just as among prisoners or sailors, peoples' sexual problems are worked out by abusing the weakest. When a new boy arrived, my torture finally came to an end. Afterward, others followed him.

"I never thought of becoming enlightened. All I wanted was to play. And I was never allowed to."

"Ejo, I want to propose something. Let us bury this stick among the trees here, as if it were a plant. Let us imagine that someday it will sprout and produce branches, even fruit . . ."

After we finished burying it, my friend gave a huge sigh. It was as if he had shed an immense burden. He burst out laughing, then he took his monk's robe out of the net sack. "It was my master, Momon Yamanda, who gave me this *kesa*.* He wove into it parts of the funeral shrouds of his father and his mother. Do you understand? We often speak of the transmission of the light, but the real master transmits the shrouds of the dead. We must see life—both our own and that of the cosmos—as an agony. This is the teaching of the Buddha Shakyamuni. After his satori, he went to the place where they incinerate corpses, and he gathered pieces of cloth left there, washed them, dyed them, and sewed them together painstakingly and slowly, giving his total attention to every stitch. That kesa was transmitted from patriarch to patriarch through the ages. Everyone who wore it while meditating was burning in body and in soul. To reach the marrow of the soul, everything superfluous must be burned to ashes. By wearing the garments of so many dead people, Buddha taught that liberation is to be obtained for them as well. When a flower opens, it is springtime for the whole land. The Buddha is like the brilliant prow of a vessel that leads it and its blind passengers to the port of salvation. I know that my way is not the same as yours, for you are more attracted to artistic creation than to meditation. But you know—there is really no difference between us. Compassion inhabits us both. Just this once, please give me the pleasure of seeing you dressed in my kesa."

It was still so early in the morning that we were alone in the woods. I undressed slowly. Sensing an abyss before me and another behind me, I inhaled every breath of air deeply and exhaled each time as if it were my last breath. Then, feeling like a fugitive so weary of fleeing that he finally surrenders to his pursuers, I entered into the folds of the robe.

---

*A cloth that is the symbol of the transmission from master to disciple. According to Taisen Deshimaru (*Questions à un maître zen* [Paris: Albin Michel, 1984]): "In order to sew the first *kesas,* they collected pieces of funeral shrouds, clothes from women giving birth, and various other ornaments . . . [T]hey used material that was considered polluted, undesirable, and destined for the rubbish heap. They washed all the pieces carefully and made them into the noblest form of vestment, a monk's robe. Thus the most filthy garment became the purest garment, for everyone respected the monk's kesa."

Although its color was a uniform ochre, that of dry earth, it was composed of many pieces of cloth of different sizes, each connected to others with large stitches that dissolved into the form of the garment. It clung to my skin readily. I absorbed the years of meditation of Ejo, his master, and those of other masters and patriarchs all the way back to Shakyamuni Buddha himself. The sensation of my body changed, and I finally understood what it was to feel like a mountain. There was no more space or time. The voice of the first awakener resounded unceasingly: "Never pretend anything that is not certain. There is no substantial ego, no object that is not impermanent. Perceptions, feelings, and visions are processes empty of real substance. Life is suffering. Birth, illness, old age, and death are suffering. To be separated from those we love is suffering. To be forced to be with those we do not love is suffering. To be unable to satisfy our desires is suffering."

Yet Ejo's kesa seemed to be saying to me: "Do not dwell at the surface of things. Beyond the Buddha's words, in the deepest depths, in the highest heights, lives an exalted passion. Listen to cosmic consciousness, the phoenix surging forth from the mind in flames, for it is telling you: Life is pure happiness. Birth, illness, old age, and death are four gifts as marvelous as the cycle of the four seasons. You can never be separated from those you love, for they live in you forever. You cannot be forced to be with those you do not love, for you have let go of aversion. Your light, like that of the sun, is for everyone, and you love even those who appear odious. To be unable to satisfy your desires is not suffering—the important thing is the prodigious gift of desire itself, satisfied or not, which gives you your sense of being alive.

"Go beyond this litany of *The cause of suffering is attachment to desires and things,* because when attachment to desires and things is free from all possessiveness, it is sublime goodness. All that appears to be impermanent is engraved in the memory of God. Every second is eternity.

"Go beyond the litany of *Put an end to all attachments and end all suffering.* No—we cannot end these attachments. If all is one, then how can one detach itself from itself? Attachment through love is the way of realization. Eternal being is attached to you with an infinite tenderness.

"Go beyond even the litany of the Buddha's Eightfold Path of ending suffering by right seeing, right thinking, right speech, right action, right livelihood, right effort, right attention, and right concentration. Free yourself from all conceptual chains; trust in the wisdom of Creation. You are not merely a part of Creation, you are Creation. To live in full happiness, walk in the infinite, pathless land. Let your eyes see what they invite you to see; do not put blinders on them. Let your thought wander in all dimensions, let your every word be rooted in your heart, act like a beloved child of beloved parents, see a thousand lives in one life. Make no effort; instead, allow things to happen through you, for every natural act is a gift. Right attention and right concentration are the offspring of a passionate love. Think, feel, desire, and live with pleasure. A cat makes no effort to concentrate when it sees a mouse.

"Go beyond the litany of *Everything arises from ignorance. Why must we be born? Why must we die?* Unity is total knowledge. When you become one with it, there is no ignorance. When the sun appears, darkness dissipates. We must die in order to be born. Existence venerates death; it does not deny it. There is no will to exist, for we already exist eternally. Anxiety to live is born of a lack of generous contact with the world, which is neither inner or outer, because there is no separation. To look is to bless; to hear, touch, feel, taste is to bless. The body, soul, spirit, and mental functions are one and the same. Ignorance is the desire to separate ourselves from them.

"Go beyond the litany of *Everything changes ceaselessly. Everything passes. Everything is impermanent. Nothing is permanent.* In God, nothing changes ceaselessly. Everything is permanent, eternal, infinite. Nothing passes away.

"Go beyond the litany of *All is emptiness, ku, zero point.* Nothing is ku; emptiness is an illusion. All is filled with God."

At one crucial moment, as the rough cloth adhered to me, pressing upon me as if glued to my skin and bones, immobilizing me in a centuries-old posture while my thoughts flooded like a torrent in all directions, transforming legends, presuppositions, and written ideals into a mummified skin, Ejo Takata spoke to me in a voice full of kindness: "You are constructing everything that you think around the word *God*. If I took this word away from you, you'd have nothing left. Tell me: What is God for you?"

The first thing that came to mind was the definition that had fascinated poets and philosophers through the ages, from Hermes Trismegistus all the way to Jorge Luis Borges, including Parmenides, Alain de Lille, Meister Eckhart, Giordano Bruno, Copernicus, Rabelais, Pascal, and so many others. So I replied: "God is an infinite sphere whose center is everywhere and whose circumference is nowhere."

Then, to head off any possible critique from Ejo about my intellect needing to die, I shouted: "Kwatzu!"

But then I had to confess, in a grumbling voice, that this definition was unacceptable even to me, because as soon as it was formulated in my mind, it became just one more prison. There are thinkers who are seduced by the sublime, geometric beauty of it, the sphere being the most perfect of all forms for them, but for a lover of organic beauty, a tree, a leaf, or an insect could be a better incarnation of perfection. Defining God as an infinite sphere is as absurd as defining God as an infinite fly. In any case, the infinite is beyond form by its very nature. Besides, because the center is everywhere and the circumference nowhere, there can be no parts. If all is center, what does center mean? A center requires something other than itself. It is absurd to speak of a center while affirming that this center is the only thing that exists. It is the same as saying: "God is an infinite human whose navel is everywhere and whose skin is nowhere."

This provoked Ejo to a fit of uproarious laughter. Then he became serious again. "You still haven't answered my question. All you've done is quote someone else's definition, and then criticize it. Consult your *hara** and then reply."

"Ejo, my reason is always seeking distinctions and limits. It can neither define nor explain nor understand a reality in which absolutely everything is united and forms one unique truth, but if we grant that no concept is reality, that it is only a limited sketch, I can learn to use words not as definitions of the world, but as symbols of it. A symbol allows for a vast number of meanings, as many as there are individuals to perceive it.

"For me, the 'personal' God, the prime actor of every sacred work, cannot have a geometrical, mineral, animal, vegetable, human sexual, racial, or other form. He cannot even have a name and cannot be the special property of any religion. Any quality or category that I might give him would amount to only a superstitious approximation. He is impossible to define with words or images and inaccessible to search for. It is absurd to say anything about God. The only possibility that remains: to receive him. But how? How can I receive what is inconceivable, ungraspable? I can do so only through the changes and mutations that it works in my life in the form of clarity of mind, happy love, creative capacity, and a joy in living that remains in spite of the worst suffering. If I imagine God as eternal, infinite, and omnipotent, it is only by contrast with what I believe myself to be: finite, ephemeral, and impotent in the face of the transformation known as death. Yet if everything is God and God does not die, then nothing dies. If everything is God and God is infinite, then nothing has limits. If everything is God and God is eternal, then nothing has a beginning or end. If everything is God and God is omnipotent, then nothing is impossible. Though I cannot name that or believe in that, I can still intuitively sense it in my deepest being. I can accept its will, a will that creates the universe and its laws. And I can imagine it as allied to me, whatever happens.

*The *hara* is an energy center in the lower belly. In Zen as well as in the martial arts, it is considered to be the center of the human body. It is from this center that the shout "Kwatzu!" (or "Kiai!" in karate) originates.

"It's true that I need not say all this. Words are not the direct way—they point, but they do not go there. I accept that I belong to this unfathomable mystery, an entity without being, nonbeing, or dimension. I accept to surrender to its designs, to trust that my existence is neither an accident nor an illusion nor a cruel game, but an inexplicable necessity of its work. I know that this permanent impermanence is part of what my mind calls the cosmic plan. I believe that even if I am an infinitesimal cog in an infinite machine, I participate in its perfection, and that this destruction of my body is the portal I must cross to submerge myself in what my heart feels as total love, what my sexual center feels as infinite orgasm, what my intellect calls radiant emptiness, and what my body considers its mysterious home. If we are one with the universe, then it is our temple. We are renters beholden to a landlord who feeds us and supports and sustains us in life for the lot of time according to his will. This house is our certain refuge, but we can make it into either a Garden of Eden or a garbage dump. It can be a place of flourishing creativity or a dark, stinking realm where bad taste reigns. Between these impenetrable walls we can either thrive or commit suicide. The house of God does not behave in a certain way—it is simply there. Its quality depends on the use we make of it."

Ejo Takata smiled. Mimicking my last phrase and way of talking, he said: "The mind does not behave in a certain way—it is simply there. Its quality depends on the use we make of it.

"I would like to remind you of a koan from the secret book. The disciple Hokoji* was agitated and came to ask his master Baso: 'What transcends existence?' Baso answered: 'I will tell you when you have drunk the entire Western River in a single gulp.' Hokoji suddenly

---

*Hokoji, or Pangyun in Chinese (740–810 CE), studied the Confucian classics and realized that mere literary study was not enough. Accompanied by his daughter, he traveled in China, seeking the greatest Ch'an masters in order to learn from them. He became the most celebrated layman in Ch'an. He was a disciple of Sekito Kisen and of Baso Doitsu, or Mazu Daoyi in Chinese (709–788 CE). The latter made a major contribution to the reform of Chinese Zen, thanks to his character and his teaching methods.

became calm, bowed respectfully, took a cup of tea, and drank it down in a single gulp."

"I know, I know, Ejo. It is impossible to give a true reply to such questions. How can we define the indefinable, describe the indescribable, or think the unthinkable? Instead of giving a solution, Baso demanded the impossible of his student: to swallow a river. Hokoji realized that there is nothing beyond existence. By drinking a gulp of tea, he sided with the natural against the metaphysical. Yes, I know, but I am not a monk. I am a poet. And the poet's ideal—even though he knows the project is doomed to failure—is to express the eternal silence in words."

"Alejandro, neither of us is a monk or a poet. We are beings beyond definitions. When I asked you to define God, I was hoping that instead of elaborating on your 'artistic' theories, you would say something like: 'I will tell you when you drink an entire river and eat a herd of elephants, bones and all.' Now, how about leaving here and having a nice cup of tea or some tacos?"

I had the sensation of lightning striking my tongue, and I felt like biting it off. Of course I understood that words such as *God, spirit,* and *infinite circle* are interchangeable, but I was still enraged. I felt an immense rage that had been accumulating for years. By what right could this Japanese make fun of me when he himself was caught like a fly in the web of Buddhism? I began to spit out words in anger. I knew that much of what I was saying was foolish, but I could not restrain myself, because I still had an arrogant desire to shake that granite self-assurance I had always perceived in him.

"Ejo, you are fond of repeating that maxim of 'If you meet the Buddha on the road, cut off his head.' Yet you yourself continue to meditate in the same position as the first patriarchs. You have continued to wear your kesa, which imitates the Buddha's renunciation of the world, and you repeat like a parrot or a fanatic the sutras of his words. You fill your days with useless ceremonies that you learned as a child. You live in a past that is not even your own. Among millions of poor

Indians, Shakyamuni was the son of royalty and wealth. His father, the king, gave him everything: a palace surrounded by fabulous gardens, exquisite food, the most elegant dress, the most beautiful of women, hundreds of servants. Living in this luxurious prison, he did not know the misery of the lives of his numberless servants. Suddenly, because a small, dead bird fell upon his head, the future Buddha had a crisis like that of a hysterical woman. Reality was not what he thought it was! So he reacted as spoiled children the world over react, and instead of learning to accept life as it is, he began to hate it. 'Life is suffering!' he proclaimed. 'It is a horror of old age, illness, and death! This is all a result of being born! To be free, I must reject matter, reject incarnation, never create a new body by mating with a woman, never enjoy the pleasures of the senses. Flee, flee, flee this existence!' He was capable of leaving his entire family and exchanging his palace for the shade of a tree. He was able to deny himself. Ashamed of his earlier life of wealth and privilege, he became the poorest of the poor, wearing a robe made of funeral shrouds that he scrounged at the burning ghats. But this is still essentially the reaction of a spoiled child!

"We, on the other hand, have not been raised in the luxury of an artificial paradise; we have always known the misery and conflicts of the world. We grew up knowing that even if we had a roof over our heads, there were many others in this world who didn't and that every time we had food to eat, there were millions of children going hungry. We were raised among egoists, old people, sick people, dying people— yet we were still able to celebrate the dawning of every new day! Would we have agreed to don the garments of corpses? Never! This kesa of yours is not for us, because we do not want to escape life! Even if we see life as an endless cycle of reincarnation, why should we want to free ourselves from this sacred cycle? We shall return again and again. Little by little, we will make the world a bit better, we will alter the cruel laws of the cosmos, because we are the consciousness, the best aspect of the Creator. We must develop this consciousness from life to life by communicating it and multiplying it. Ejo, we are here in this life with an immense responsibility: We cannot cease to exist as long as we have not perfected this universe, as long as beings still kill and destroy each other. We must return again and again until everything is joy and the love of light is in perfect harmony with the love of darkness . . ."

At this point, I broke into tears and had to stop speaking. Ejo held me gently in his arms until my sobbing ceased. Delicately, he helped me out of the robe. He stretched out the kesa on the ground, folded it elaborately, like an origami design, as he had learned in the monastery, until it was reduced to a rectangle. Then he told me, calmly:

"My friend, it is easy for you to say that traditional sutras and teachings are lies, because they are only words. Yet these words propose experiences that can plunge us into a deeper reality. The foundational myths are necessary, because we cannot construct a society without them. It would be dangerous to try to destroy them, for such destruction would undermine the foundations on which human relationships are based and replace them with nothing. On the other hand, it is very useful to reinterpret them in a way that is in accord with what we both value. If you feel this interpretation, you will experience it.

"As for this kesa, it is now like an old, worn-out skin. Thanks to many generous hands, it has acquired its current form and served as a recipient for consciousness. It is like a caterpillar's cocoon, and now the butterfly is ready to spread its wings. It would be stupid to continue to live in the boat that has served to help you cross the river to the other shore.

"The reason I revere the memory of Shakyamuni is because of what his figure has given the world—unlike you, I don't bother about whether he was historically this or that or whether his deeds were mythic or real.

"Yet your poet's point of view has shown me something that my monk's imagination was unable to see: The patriarch gathered a bunch of funeral rags, sewed them together with care and respect, and made himself a robe. This amounts to an artistic creation, but for centuries, we have been merely imitating this creative act. Hence this kesa is not a creation of my own soul; it is ultimately an imitation of the work of Shakyamuni. It actually belongs to him, not to me. Times have changed, and we are not living in India or Tibet. Still less are we practicing the original Chinese Ch'an Buddhism. Zen must adapt itself to each country according to the customs of its people. Otherwise, it will become a form of religious imperialism. It is not Mexico that needs Japanese Zen, it is Japanese Zen that needs Mexico. The Tarahumaras weave a type of pure, simple, white linen cloth. It is a bit of luxury in their misery, symbolizing the desire for a cleaner and better life. I shall weave my own kesa with that cloth."

Ejo arose, gathered some dry branches, and lit a fire. Upon it he placed his carefully folded old robe. With great tenderness, he watched it burn; he wore the kind of expression of loving farewell to a friend who will never return. His eyes full of tears, he turned his back and took the path that led out of the woods and back to the city.

Very soon, I returned to France without seeing him again.

Five years passed. This time, I returned to Mexico wearing the hat of a therapist promoting my new book. As usual, the publishers had arranged a lecture at the Julio Castillo Theater.

It had been two weeks since my son Teo died, and I was broken by this terrible loss. When the accident happened, I was in the midst of a flurry of obligations, courses, conferences, interviews, therapy sessions, and preparations for this trip to Mexico. Nothing made sense to me any more, but I forced myself to respect my obligations, knowing that if I abandoned them now, I would never take them up again. When I arrived in Mexico City, I felt as though a secret weight was pressing me down into the earth. I had to call upon all my experience as an actor to put on a good face before the eager audience of readers and students and somehow transmit my message of the joy of life—but in the middle of my presentation, it was as if a spring snapped inside my throat. I lost my voice. A desperate sob was down there, trying to open up a passage.

I gritted my teeth and hid my face, pretending to use my handkerchief. I felt as though I could not continue.

At that exact instant, Ejo Takata came up onto the stage. He unfolded a Mexican version of a tatami mat and sat down to meditate. Instead of a kesa, he wore white linen pants and a simple shirt of the same material, like the Indians of the Sierra.

Here was my master, indeed—authentic as ever, solid as a mountain, his knees grounded in the earth and his head pushing against the heavens, at the very center of eternal time and space. His presence gave me the strength to continue. At the end, as on the last such occasion, he took advantage of the applause to disappear. I ran out, looking for him, but this time I could not find him at all. I needed his consolation, but I no longer had his address. I felt very sad. Jacqueline, a beautiful dwarf, came up to me and said, with great warmth: "I am a disciple of Ejo. He knows you need to see him. He told me to take you to where he is living, outside the city."

After two hours in a beat-up old taxi, we arrived in a poor suburb where Takata lived like an Indian, teaching his Tarahumara disciples to meditate. Discreetly, Jacqueline waited for me in the old car. As I related at the beginning of this book, the master consoled me with a single word: *duele,* "it hurts."

This was the last time I was ever to see him. I gave Jacqueline some money to buy flowers for his wife and adopted daughter.

"The wife and daughter could not bear the harshness of Ejo's life between the city and the Sierra," Jacqueline told me. "Tomiko married in the United States. She lives in Texas with her husband and three children. Michiko lives with them."

Two years later, Jacqueline called me in Paris. In tears, she announced the death of Ejo Takata. I tried to console her. "Yes, Jacqueline, it hurts. It really hurts terribly—but life continues. When a branch is cut from the tree, it never comes back and the scar always remains on the trunk. The tree covers it over with new cells, and then new sprouts appear from it. The wound underneath the bark becomes a haven for mushrooms that fall from the tree and nourish the soil in which it grows."

I received a fax from the Tarahumara disciple who now directed Ejo's group and had taken the title of Roshi Silencio. He asked me for a thousand dollars to build a *stupa*, a Buddhist monument that would contain the master's ashes and, later, those of his disciples. Instead of sending him a contribution for such a project, I sent a poem:

> *A pound of ashes,*
> *a thousand pounds of ashes,*
> *what is the difference?*
> *The Master's ashes*
> *are my ashes.*
> *When the wind carries away my remains,*
> *the Master's remains are dispersed with me.*
> *A stupa does not give peace*
> *when it is a stupa of death*
> *seen without a master.*
> *May his tomb*
> *not be the tomb*
> *of those who are afraid to traverse alone*
> *the dissolution of their consciousness.*

A Collection of Anecdotes

◥◤◢◣

"I never surrendered, because the more you struggle, the more possibilities you have of winning and receiving help. It has always been in the last minutes, when everything seemed lost that someone came to help me go beyond my limits."

SILVER KANE, *DISPARA, DISPARA, DISPARA*
(SHOOT, SHOOT, SHOOT)

Some readers may wonder what practical purpose koans serve. Granted, they express deep metaphysical questions—but what use are they in everyday life? Can a correct response to "What is the sound of one hand clapping?" ever help us find our place in contemporary society? I would answer yes. These seemingly insoluble enigmas that I spent countless hours struggling against and working with under Ejo Takata's guidance have gradually forged my character. Years later, I was able to apply them to many occasions in life, especially when I was confronted with a crucial choice. Reality repeatedly put me in situations where

I was faced with seemingly insoluble problems. I was forced to allow myself to be guided by some kind of incomprehensible intelligence so that I became like a famished hunter on the alert for game: a solution that would emerge suddenly from the depths of my being. There have been countless such occasions. Here are a few examples.

In 1967, in a Paris café, I met my friend Jorge Edwards. He was with Pablo Neruda, a genius poet, yet also a devoted worshipper of his own ego. Jorge later wrote this about our encounter in his book *Adios, Poeta:*

> Once, in the Coupole Café in Montparnasse, around midnight, we were having a bite to eat and some wine. Sitting nearby was Alejandro Jodorowsky, one of the most interesting figures of my generation of Chileans. He had emigrated early and never returned. . . . I invited him to our table, and introduced him to Neruda.
>
> "I've heard a lot about you," Neruda said, with the best of intentions.
>
> "And I've also heard a lot about you," replied Alejandro.
>
> This terse exchange was utterly cold. As you might expect, the conversation never got off the ground.

As Ejo Takata had told me: "If you meet a Buddha on the road, cut off his head."

As I was finishing the shooting of *El Topo* and beginning the editing process, I discovered that an essential scene had a serious flaw: a yellow scratch ran through the image from top to bottom. Federico Landeros, the editor, exclaimed: "It's a disaster—we can't use this shot." But I had neither the time nor the money to do it over. What could I do? Edit it out? Instead, I answered him: "If what I am saying in this scene is really important, no one will notice this scratch. Let's pretend it doesn't exist and keep the take." Which we did.

Thirty years have passed, and no one has ever noticed this terrible flaw.

At the premiere of *El Topo* in England, I was summoned to the department of film censorship. It was a hypocritical office, and people were barely aware that it even existed. Some very polite bureaucrats informed me: "In this country, there are many depraved people. We cannot allow the scene where you wipe your bloody hands on the naked breasts of the actress. We need your authorization to cut it, and also your promise to keep this cut a secret. If you refuse, *El Topo* will not be shown in England."

I wondered if I should I accept this mutilation, which violated all my principles. But then I exclaimed to myself: "The Venus de Milo had her arms cut off, but she is still a great work of art!" So I agreed, but only on condition that I be allowed to make the cut myself so that it would be properly done. This was granted, and they lent me a moviola editing machine.

When George Harrison learned that his company, Apple, was going to produce my film *The Holy Mountain* on John Lennon's recommendation, he asked to read the script. Then he expressed a desire to play the lead role, that of the thief. Dressed completely in white, he received me in his elegant suite at the Plaza Hotel in New York. He offered me some melon juice with cinnamon and congratulated me on the script. He said that he was prepared to play the role on condition that we cut one scene, which he read aloud: "At an octagonal sink, next to a veritable hippopotamus, the alchemist bathes the thief, turns him over on his back, his buttocks facing the camera, and rubs soap over his anus."

With an amiable grin, he said, "It's quite out of the question for me to expose my anus in public."

I felt as if the sky had fallen in. In those days, for me, a film was not a commercial or merely a work of art. I wanted this film to be the record of a sacred experience capable of enlightening an audience. For this, I needed actors—but only those who were prepared to put aside their egos. If Harrison played the lead role, it was important that he provide an example of total humility, exposing himself with the innocence of a child. This shot lasted only ten seconds, but it was vital to the work. It was obvious that if George Harrison played the role, the film would be assured of worldwide success, making millions—but this success would weaken the film, catering to the squeamishness of a famous musician. What a difficult koan!

Abruptly, and in total defiance of my own rationality, I rejected Harrison and hired a modest, young Mexican comedian to play the role of the thief. It was a choice between self-honesty and money and fame.

In the early days of the filming of *The Holy Mountain*, a young American named Robert Taicher approached me, expressed admiration for my previous film, and offered to work for free as my assistant. It turned out that I needed someone to run errands, bring me an occasional sandwich or drink, and help me learn English, a language that I spoke poorly but was obliged to use for economic reasons. He proved to be an exemplary assistant—modest, intelligent, dependable, hardworking, friendly, and understanding. He followed me like my shadow, immensely lightening the heavy work of shooting. When I insisted on paying him a salary, he refused. He said that because he was himself an aspiring filmmaker, this was the best school he could have hoped to find.

Suddenly, without any indication, my executive producer, Roberto Viskin, fled with his family to Israel, taking with him three hundred thousand dollars of our money. This theft paralyzed us. It was impossible to continue shooting, and the actors waited idly at the hotel, the costs continuing to mount.

"What are you going to do now?" Robert Taicher asked me.

"Nothing," I answered. "Miracles happen. In order to find his successor in China, Bodhidharma sat in front of a wall for years, waiting for the disciple to come to him. I shall do the same—I'm going to stay at home and wait for someone to come and bring me three hundred thousand dollars in cash wrapped up in a newspaper."

My assistant stared at me with such wide eyes that they seemed like two shining wheels. "Robert, your expression suggests that you think I'm mad—but in my view, real madness is to refuse to believe in miracles."

And I did as I said. I did not lift a finger in an attempt to obtain this money—and, in any case, my financial situation was such that no bank would agree to lend it to me. A week passed, during which Taicher disappeared. I learned that he had flown to Miami. Then he reappeared, knocking at my door. Happy to see him, I welcomed him in. In his hands, he held a newspaper, which he handed to me. Opening it, I found three hundred thousand dollars in cash! It turned out that Robert's father was extremely rich—the largest shoe manufacturer in the United States. Robert had asked for an advance on his inheritance. From unpaid assistant he had become my executive producer!

When my son Brontis was eight years old, I enrolled him in a modern private school in Mexico City called La Ferrie. All seemed to be going well until one day, when Brontis came home earlier than usual.

"They've suspended me for three days."

"Did you do something bad?"

"Well, the toilets were recently painted white, and I found a can of black paint in there. I wet my hand in it and made my handprint on the wall. The principal called me to his office, told me I was a bad boy, and sent me home. He says you will have to pay the costs of repainting."

I sat right down and wrote a letter to the principal.

Toilets are less important than the mind of a child. If toilets are damaged, they can be repaired easily, but when the mind of a child is hurt, the damage is not repaired so easily. When you told Brontis he was "bad" because he put his handprint on the wall, you committed an error. What do you mean by a "bad" child? When we label others in this way, it is because we are afraid to look reality in the face. No child is "bad." A child may have problems, may lack vitamins, may dislike their study material, or may be trying to test the limits of an outdated form of education. Perhaps Brontis was attempting to express himself artistically. I can well understand how tiresome it is for children always to have to relieve themselves surrounded by pure white walls. (If you have ever read the works of Jung on the creative significance of defecation in children, you can agree that children's rest room walls should instead be covered with colors and designs.) A hand wet with paint and used to imprint a wall or a cloth is an expression of one of the purest and most ancient forms of the pictorial instinct. We find such handprints in many prehistoric cave paintings as well as in paintings by artists of the stature of Miro, Picasso, and many others.

Frankly, I admire such an impulse in a child, whatever the color of the handprint or the wall. The black color of the print no doubt unconsciously suggests "filth," which places it in a system of mental associations that make it seem worse than it is: white = cleanliness, milk, virginity, a bride, and so forth, and black = stain, filth, poverty, sickness, and death. For Taoists—who accept death as something beautiful rather than horrible—a bit of black upon a vast white expanse represents a manifestation of life.

In summary, I propose a solution. If you accept my solution, I will not withdraw my son from your school: Instead of paying for a new coat of paint, I will instead purchase for your school an entire collection of cans of paint of different colors. Then you can have your children use this material to cover the walls of the toilet with handprints in all sorts of beautiful colors.

As might be expected, I had to find a different school for Brontis.

How I loved Teo, my departed son! Perhaps because I had a premonition of his early death, I did everything possible to offer him a happy childhood. On his seventh birthday, he asked to go alone with me to a Chinese restaurant, which we did. His mouth watered when he saw that the menu contained twelve different kinds of soup. All of them sounded delicious to him, and he became distressed when faced with having to choose only one. He asked me to decide for him, but I sensed that no matter what I chose, he would feel frustrated. Then I remembered an old joke.

A family sits down in a restaurant, the waitress arrives, writes down the orders of the adults, and then asks the little boy what he would like. Looking timidly at his parents, he says: "A hamburger."

But the mother protests: "Out of the question! Bring him a steak with mashed potatoes and carrots."

The waitress, however, seems not to have heard: "How would you like your hamburger? With ketchup or mustard?" she asks the boy.

"With ketchup."

"I'll bring your order right away!" the waitress answers, leaving before the mother can say anything else.

There is a stunned silence around the table. Finally, the little boy looks at everyone and says: "Wow! The waitress thinks I'm a real person."

This joke gave me the solution to the koan: I was there to satisfy my son's desires, not my own. I called the waiter and ordered all twelve soups at once. When Teo saw the table covered with these bowls filled with exotic soups, he was in ecstasy. He ate only a few spoonfuls of each, but he was happy.

While I was working on *The Holy Mountain,* I had just finished shooting at the revered Our Lady of Guadalupe Church. Some groups of fanatic Catholics had spread the rumor that I had performed a black Mass inside the sacred place, and suddenly I was greeted by a parade of a thousand believers whipped into a frenzy by right-wing extremists. They shouted insults, comparing me to the murderer Charles Manson and demanding I be expelled from the country. This whole business was so baseless and absurd that I didn't worry about it, thinking that the rumor would soon die down of its own accord. But it only grew worse. Newspapers seized on the situation to create a scandal, writing articles in which I appeared as the Antichrist.

One morning, there was a loud knock at my door. Three huge detectives, looking like professional killers, said roughly: "Come with us!" Without even allowing me to get my coat, they dragged me in my shirtsleeves into a black car and shoved me into the backseat, crushed between two of them.

They refused to say where we were going. After an anxious half hour of biting my lips, the car stopped in front of the Ministry of the Interior. Just as I feared, I was about to be deported from Mexico. I was led through numberless offices and waiting rooms full of solicitors, secretaries, bureaucrats, and policemen until I arrived finally before an imposing door. It opened.

Smiling broadly, Mario Moy Palencia received me. He offered me an armchair and then began (with no excuse or explanation for the violent nature of my summons).

"Jodorowsky—our president, the most honorable Luis Etcheverría, knows your work well and is one of your admirers. For example, this very year in his presidential report, he quoted one of your Panic Movement fables—the one in which the archer who has decided to hunt the moon shoots hundreds of arrows at it and is ridiculed by everyone. He never hits the moon, but he does become the best archer in the world.

"Do you see my point? The government is your friend—a very useful friend—but it can also become a dangerous enemy."

As he said this, I felt a tremor, remembering the brutal assassination—with the complicity of the Mexican government—of a crowd of young students by paramilitary Falcon troops on June 10, 1971. The government claimed that only twenty-five were killed, but the people counted two thousand of their dead.

"Now listen carefully. A large number of complaints have been lodged against you. You cannot get away with attacking our institutions or our religion or army. If you don't want something unpleasant to happen to you or to your family, then you must remove every religious image and every military or other official uniform from your film. I don't want to see even a fireman's uniform in that film! Now you may leave."

I had to walk all the way home, because I had left without a penny in my pocket. That night, we were treated to raucous shouts at our windows: "We're going to kill you!"

It was a very serious koan. If I obeyed and mutilated my film, I would kill it. If I disobeyed, I was risking my family's lives as well as my own. I spent a sleepless night.

Very early the next morning, I took all the negatives, representing thirty-six hours of filming, and sent them secretly to the United States in an express truck via Tijuana. In two days, I withdrew all funds from my bank accounts, settled my rental contracts and telephone bills, sent a ton of boxes of books out of the country, and generally pulled up stakes. On the third day, I flew to New York with my wife, children, and our cat, Mandrake. This was before Roberto Viskin had decided to abscond to Israel, and he proved to be a good friend. I was able to finish the montage and editing of my film without censoring any scenes.

As I was preparing the casting for my film *Dune* (based on the science-fiction novel by Frank Herbert—a project that was never to see the light of day), Salvador Dali put me through a moment of trial. I wanted the famous painter to play the role of the mad galactic emperor, and the idea appealed to him. In order to take the measure of this young upstart talent who presumed to be capable of directing the great Dali, he invited me to dine in a luxurious restaurant in Paris. I found myself seated directly across the table from him, surrounded by a dozen of his hangers-on.

With no preamble, he asked me: "When Picasso and I were young, we would go to the beach together. Every time, we would find a watch there simply by pushing the sand around with our feet. Have you ever found a watch at the beach?"

The artist's groupies watched me with contemptuous smirks. I had only a few seconds to reply. If I claimed to have found a watch at the beach, I'd pass for a liar. If I confessed I'd never found one, I'd be labeled as mediocre. But I didn't even have to think about my answer; it came to me by itself:

"I've never found a watch in my life, but I've lost a great many!"

Dali coughed, paid no more attention to me, and began to occupy himself with his retinue—but at the end of the meal, he said to me: "Very well. I'll sign the contract." And then he added: "But I want to be the best-paid actor in the world: a hundred thousand dollars per hour."

I changed the script so that the emperor possesses a wax-faced robot that looks like him, then I engaged Dali for only one hour. He appeared only in the scene where he was pushing the buttons on his robot in the laboratory.

For the role of the baron Harkonnen, a vulgar, cruel giant, I thought of Orson Welles. I knew he was in France but that he had become embittered at the lack of producers interested in his own work, and it was said that he wanted nothing more to do with film. Where could I find him? No one seemed to know. I had heard that the master had a passion for gourmet food and drink. I got an assistant to telephone all the best restaurants in Paris and find out if Orson Welles was a customer.

After countless calls, a small restaurant, Chez le Loup, told us that he came there once a week, though not on any specific day. I decided to dine there every night beginning on Monday. It was a discreetly elegant place with a fine menu and a superb wine selection. The owner himself took orders. Almost all the walls were decorated with Renoir reproductions. The one exception was a wall with a window. In front of it there was a broken chair. When I asked the owner about it, he said: "We are very proud of that piece of litter. One evening, Orson Welles sat in that chair and he ate so much that it broke."

I returned every night. Finally, on Friday, the great man arrived, wrapped in an enormous black cape. I watched him with the same fascination as a child at the zoo. His appetite and his thirst were stupendous. I saw him devour nine different dishes and drink six bottles of wine. For dessert, I sent him a bottle of cognac that the owner had assured me was his favorite brand. When it came, he looked around and amiably invited me to his table. For a half hour, I listened to his monologue before daring to speak of the role. No sooner did I bring up the subject than he answered: "Acting doesn't interest me. I detest contemporary cinema. It's not an art; it's a nauseating industry, a vast mirage born of prostitution." My disappointment was immense, and I swallowed with difficulty. How could I inspire enthusiasm in him so that he would agree to work with me?

I was tense and seemingly at a total loss for words when suddenly I heard myself say: "Mr. Welles, during the entire month that the filming of your role will require, I promise you to hire the head cook of this very restaurant. Every evening, he will prepare all the dishes you desire accompanied by any wines and liquors that please you."

With a big smile, he agreed to sign the contract.

For the combat scenes in *Dune,* I hired the karate master Jean-Pierre Vigneau, a huge man with muscles of steel. He was teaching martial arts to my son Brontis, who had the lead role of the young Paul Atreides. One day, in front of my son and other students, he decided to challenge me.

"You are an artist, which is an admirable profession. But I wonder—would that wonderful intellect of yours that you rely on so much be of the slightest use to you in surviving a direct attack by a dangerous enemy?" And then he stepped up to me and assumed a position of attack.

To me, this man was invincible. I had watched him demolish several karate champions. I decided to accept the playful duel, knowing that I was bound to lose. Suddenly, I leaped into the air and hung upon him, holding on to him like a baby holding on to its mother's breast.

I let him shake me violently, offering no resistance. Then he set me down and used all his weight and strength to put me in a stranglehold. Impulsively, having no idea why I was doing it, I made a delicate movement with my hand and inserted my little finger into his ear. Immediately, Jean-Pierre slapped the floor in the classic signal of surrender!

He arose and announced to everyone: "That's the first time I've lost a fight. I'm sure my adversary didn't realize it, but he found a fatal point with his finger. By shoving your little finger with enough force into an enemy's ear, you can pierce through the eardrum and kill him."

After two years of intense work in Paris, just when it seemed that *Dune* was finally about to be completed, the producer abruptly aborted the project. It was a dreadful blow to all of us. Dan O'Bannon, the future special effects director, returned to Los Angeles so stressed he had to spend two years being treated in a psychiatric clinic. Giger, the painter hired to design the sets, raged angrily at me about this "failure." I refused to let myself be brought down by this assault of reality.

As I told my friend, the artist Moebius who had worked on costume designs and also designed the three thousand images used in the film: "Failure does not exist. It is a concept of the mind. Instead, let us call this a *change of path.*"

And then, because we could no longer express our visions in cinematic form, I proposed we work together on graphic novels. Thus was born the success of *The Incal.*

Shortly after his twelfth birthday, my son Cristobal told me he didn't want to return to his school at St. Mandé. I asked him whether he was bored with the studies or with the teachers.

"No, it's not that. It's that I've been humiliated."

Then, between two sobs, he told me the story. The biggest and strongest kid in the school, Albert, was jealous because a girl he liked preferred the company of my son. This Albert had pasted photocopies of a sort of poster on the walls of the school and courtyard: it displayed Cristobal's photo and the words DWARF, JEW, and THIEF. Now the other students were laughing at him.

"This is a koan," I told him. "Don't run away from the situation; instead, solve it. You must find a way to punish your enemy and restore your dignity with the other students."

"But how? He's a lot stronger than I am. If I fight him, he'll smash my face in. It's just the excuse he's looking for."

"Cristobal, not all fights are equal. That's why strategy is important. You must strike him at a time and in such a way that he can't defend himself."

I helped him work out a plan. The next day, Cristobal returned to school. He waited until Albert, who was in a more advanced class, had entered a classroom with his fellow students. When he knew they were all seated, he opened the door without permission, ignored the teacher, walked straight over to where Albert was sitting, and began to administer a flurry of violent slaps to his face. The sheer surprise of this paralyzed Albert. By the time he started to react, the scandal already had the class in an uproar. He and Cristobal were held immobile by the other boys, and the teacher, who was both very angry and intrigued, led both boys to the principal's office.

Cristobal showed the principal a copy of the poster and complained of being publicly humiliated and racially slandered. He stated that he had slapped Albert in order to regain his self-esteem. The principal reacted by summoning Albert's parents and threatening to expel him from the school. Still following our strategy, Cristobal said that he would be willing to forgive Albert on condition that the boy apologize in public. Albert offered his apology before an assembly of the student body in the courtyard.

At the Cannes Film Festival, the producer Claudio Argento organized a press conference for me to present the project of my next film, *Santa Sangre*. More than ten years had passed since *The Holy Mountain*. The journalists there regarded me as a has-been filmmaker. One of them opened the discussion with a nasty remark:

"Do you think you can still shoot a film? After all, you're a little rusty."

"A rusty knife has a double power," I replied. "At the same time it cuts, it poisons."

I was shooting *Santa Sangre* right in the middle of Garibaldi Plaza in Mexico City when the idea came to me to have a blind choir sing a religious hymn in the scene we were going to film the next day inside the church. My casting director told me it was impossible to find a blind choir on such short notice. At the end of the day's work, I decided to walk back to my hotel. A blind man carrying a guitar walked toward me, and his cane tapped against my leg. He excused himself and went on. Suddenly, I realized that this was an example of what I have always believed: accidents are miracles in disguise. I ran after the man, stopped him, and asked him if he knew any religious songs.

"Of course I do," he answered. "I've even composed one. I belong to a choir of blind musicians. There are thirty of us, and we are all Protestants. Right now, I'm going to a rehearsal."

I went with him. The thirty blind people, each playing a guitar, sang a hymn that began, "The end of the world is almost here . . ." The next day, my casting director was flabbergasted to see them arrive at the church for the filming.

When *Santa Sangre* premiered in Rome, some journalists asked me which film director had most influenced me.

"Fellini," I answered without hesitation. When I was very young, it was his film *La Strada* that first made me feel I wanted to be a film director someday.

This homage appeared in the press, and one of the master's secretaries telephoned me to say Fellini would like to meet me. I was invited to come that very evening to watch the shooting of a scene from *La voce della luna.* A car arrived to pick me up and take me to a huge vacant lot outside the city. Very shyly, I walked toward a group of technicians working in the shadows and getting ready to plug in the projectors. Then a shadow that seemed huge headed toward me with open arms. I recognized Fellini.

"Jodorowsky!" he exclaimed, with a great smile.

On the verge of tears, I answered, "Papa!" and we embraced.

At that instant, a torrential rain began to fall. Amid the great disorder and consternation of this, we both ran for shelter along with all the actors and technicians. I lost sight of him and never saw him again, but that brief exchange of two words is one of my most treasured memories.

In the year 2000, the Chilean film and TV actor Bastian Bodenholfer was appointed as cultural attaché at the Chilean embassy in Paris. Full of enthusiasm, he was determined to teach the French about the culture of his own country, but he ran up against the barrier of insufficient funding. He was being asked to engage in many activities without spending a penny. He had heard about my Cabaret Mystique, conferences that I held every Wednesday in a very uncomfortable karate dojo with a large audience that had no problem with sitting on a hard wooden floor. He offered me instead a comfortable room at the Chilean embassy.

Wanting to collaborate with my amiable compatriot, I accepted his suggestion that I give a free conference there every two weeks. We set up a meeting to have a look at the auditorium. It was very comfortable and could hold at least five hundred people, the usual size of my audience. Then he told me, with an embarrassed look, that the wife of the ambassador wanted to meet me right away, and he asked if I would mind.

"Of course not, Bastian, let's go."

He led me into a smaller reception room. Now I understood his look of embarrassment. With foreboding and resignation I submitted to a tedious process of being interrogated by this woman who saw herself as a representative of Chilean "aristocracy." She treated me as though I were some indigent asking for a favor rather than offering one. Summoning all my patience, I recited a curriculum vitae, but this did not stop her from wanting to know full details about the content of my conferences and warning me: "As you know, this embassy cannot allow people to take whatever liberties they please." My attaché friend was red with shame and anger. I took a deep breath. Then Bastian arose and, inventing a pretext that we were late for an important meeting, took leave of her, thus extracting me from her claws.

As we walked toward a nearby café, he apologized profusely for her behavior. "That woman is always meddling in things that are none of her business. She is not the cultural attaché—I am! I never thought it would be like this. I can well understand if you're having second thoughts about running your conferences here . . ."

"You're right, Bastian. With that woman on my back, it would be impossible."

My friend was now so angry that his hands were shaking as he drank his coffee. "How can I hope to get any decent work done in such conditions?"

He was so distressed that I offered to give him a tarot reading. He accepted gladly, but as I shuffled the cards, taking my time, I had the intuition that I should take advantage of his distracted state of mind and try to speak directly to his unconscious. Still shuffling the cards, I asked, in a very soft, calm, casual voice: "When a turtle is swimming deep under the sea and needs to breathe, what does it do?"

Still distracted, he answered without thinking: "I don't know—what does it do?"

In the same soft tone of voice, but speaking very slowly, I told him: "It returns to land."

He forgot this hypnotic conversation immediately. I gave him a tarot reading, but it was only superficial. I felt the real work had already been done, and we said good-bye.

A week later, he resigned his post and returned to Chile to resume what he should never have interrupted: his real career as an artist. The turtle had resolved the koan.

For obscure reasons, the graphic novel editor of Casterman Publications got into a quarrel with my friend, the artist François Boucq. We were working on a series called *Face de lune,* and it was suspended because of the quarrel. François could not forgive the editor for having made a public threat: "I'll have Boucq's skin!" Now a lawsuit was being threatened in return.

I took it as a koan, and went to see this director. I brought him a tanned goatskin.* When he received me, I spread out the skin on his desk and said: "You wanted the skin of a goat? Here it is!"

He burst out laughing. I suggested he send a bottle of champagne to my friend, which he did. The koan was resolved, and we completed the series.

In 1997, I had just had my sixty-seventh birthday. Divorced for the past fifteen years, I lived in a large apartment with my son Adan. I had mistresses stay there with me from time to time, but never for more than a week. Most of the time, the atmosphere was one of emotional peace and solitude. I was giving a tarot course to twenty students in the library when Marianne Costa arrived, slightly late.

Absorbed in my explanations, I didn't even look at her. On the other hand, my large, reddish cat Moiche was so fascinated by her that for the entire hour and a half that the lesson lasted, he pawed unceasingly inside her purse. Perhaps my unconscious was influenced by the sensuality of this feline assault. At the end of the lesson, as was my custom, I embraced my students good-bye, French style. When Marianne's turn came, I somehow placed my hand on her waist, something I would

---

*[There is a play on words here. In French, the word for goat is *bouc,* pronounced the same as the artist's name. —*Trans.*]

never permit myself to do normally. An electric shock coursed through my entire body, from head to foot. Suddenly, I felt the beauty of her nudity and the intensity of her soul. She murmured: "It must be wonderful to be a cat in your house."

Giving her a kiss on the cheek and heedless of the risk involved (with a thirty-seven year age difference between us), I replied: "Then I adopt you!"

Thus began a strange, marvelous, and difficult couple relationship. If I had followed my reason instead of my intuition, I never would have dared to take such a step and would have missed the most beautiful experience of my life.

"Between doing and not doing, always choose doing."

The monstrous egotism of movie stars is disgusting to me—but unfortunately, if you want a producer to invest the millions that are necessary to realize a work in this industrial art, you have to present a cast with at least two or three stars. Because of this disgust, for years I lost all desire to turn my stories into films. One evening, tired of reading too much, I turned on the TV and zapped rapidly through the channels, protecting my soul from many of them instinctively, not unlike the way I avoid instinctively all dog excrement on the sidewalks of Paris.

Suddenly, in the midst of this stinking wasteland, a perfumed ego manifested itself. I had stumbled on an interview with the rock star Marilyn Manson. His whitened face, reddened lips, Goth style, and sincere statements followed no script or rules, and I found myself fascinated by him. I sensed genius and exclaimed to myself: "With actors like him, I'd find stories to film again!" I made inquiries in the music and film worlds as to how to get in touch with him. I was told it was impossible. He received tons of fan mail and thousands of pleas for professional meetings, but he never answered any. I gave up.

Two weeks later, I was awakened at three in the morning by a phone call.

"Mr. Jodorowsky? I'm Marilyn Manson."

I could not believe my ears. At first I thought someone was play-ing a bad joke on me, but it was really him—I did not have to go the mountain; it had come to me! He had called to tell me that my films, especially *The Holy Mountain,* had inspired him so much that he had made a clip in which he paid homage to it by imitating the scene in which the thief wakes up amid cardboard Christs modeled in his image. He had even been inspired by the title to write a script for a film called *Holy Wood,* and he wanted me to direct him in it. I told him to send me the script by express mail. Two days later, I read it—a monumental, scathing attack on Hollywood. I calculated that he would need about twenty-five million dollars to realize it. It was clear to me that he had no hope of getting this money from Hollywood producers, because they would never accept the ferocity of such criticism of their world. When I told Manson this, he understood. Instead, he offered to work on one of my projects. He had heard that I wanted to make *The Children of El Topo.* I told him that it would be an honor and a joy to direct him in the lead role—but a legal obstacle prevented me from doing this film.

On the enthusiastic recommendation of John Lennon, *El Topo* was bought and distributed in the United States and the rest of the world by Allen Klein, the president of a company called Apple, which distrib-uted records by the Beatles and the Rolling Stones. Also on the rec-ommendation of John Lennon, Klein wrote me a check for a million dollars for me to make any film I wished. This allowed me to film *The Holy Mountain.* The success of these two films pleased the producer but also excited his greed. He made me a big offer: the filming of *The Story of O,* a bestselling novel of sadomasochistic pornography, depict-ing beautiful women being humiliated in numerous ways. Klein had already secured some notable English investors who were excited about the project and was confident it would be a record blockbuster. The temptation was enormous. I accepted the invitation to go to London with him. In a tube-shaped hotel that looked like some sort of tower, the English producers were waiting to sign the contract. Before he went to meet with them, Klein promised me that he would emerge with a contract ready for me to sign. As soon as I did, I would receive immediately two hundred thousand dollars as an advance on my salary as director.

My heart was pounding. On one side of the balance: wealth and fame. On the other side: my artistic honor. After a half hour of anxious vacillation, I resolved the koan. I left the hotel at a run, took a plane back to New York, and called Michel Seydoux in France. He was a multimillionaire who had previously offered to produce a film of mine. I proposed *Dune,* and he accepted. In a few hours, my wife and I packed our bags and left with our children for Paris, without even leaving an address where Klein could contact me. His reaction was one of uncontrollable rage. A friend who was one of his employees told me that he had said, "Who does this traitor think he is? His artist's vanity has caused me to lose millions of dollars. I'm going to lock the negatives of his films in a safe as of now, and until the day he dies, no one will ever see them."

And this is exactly what he did—he called in all copies of my films from distributors around the world. Every time some film festival managed to get hold of a copy of *El Topo* or *The Holy Mountain* from a collector, Klein dispatched his lawyers and prevented the screening.

I was also consumed with hatred. I saw Klein as a cultural murderer, an accursed gangster, and a repugnant vulture who hoped for my death so that he could enrich himself with posthumous screenings. I was able to defend myself somewhat, because I had some video copies of my films. I gave them away for free to pirates in every country I visited. Although of poor quality, they managed to sell in Italy, Chile, Japan, Switzerland, Russia, and other countries for about thirty years. When the Internet came along, Klein used it to find the address of one of these pirates and threaten him with a lawsuit. Frightened, this man called me. I decided to assume responsibility for the "piracy" and defend myself legally. The trial began in France, and I was lucky to be accepted as a client by Maître Bitoun, a great lawyer who specializes in difficulties related to author's rights. I felt like David challenging Goliath: Klein had already waged lawsuits against the Beatles, the Rolling Stones, and Phil Spector, and he won them all. Now he was suing me for millions of dollars in damages. If I lost, it would spell financial ruin for the rest of my life. I was shaking with fear when the trial began, but I reminded myself that feeling fear was normal; it didn't mean I had to be a coward.

The discussions between my lawyer (a man afflicted with a muscular disorder that gave him a crippled walk and made it difficult for him to speak easily) and Klein's top-notch English lawyers went on and on and on. Two years passed, and the battle was far from over. It was around this time, when it seemed it would drag on forever, that I received Marilyn Manson's call about *The Children of El Topo*. Klein held all rights to this and any other prequels or sequels of *El Topo*. It was at this point that I realized that if I kept on fighting Klein, the project would never see the light of day. What could I do? Another koan. I picked up the telephone and called Klein's son Jordi in New York.

"Our quarrel could drag on for ten years or more. Your family is wealthy, but your lawyers are costing you a fortune. They have an interest in dragging it out as long as possible. As for me, I'm not spending a penny, because my lawyer has agreed to work on a percentage. Wouldn't it be better if we found a way to settle this out of court?"

"You're right," he answered. "Also, the younger generation is eager to see your films. Right now, I'm handling the DVD sector of our business. It would be great if we could make DVDs of your films available to a large public as soon as possible."

"Then why don't we try to meet and find a way out of this conflict?" I said.

"I agree—in fact, next week would be especially good, because my father and I will be in London, not far from you."

The three hours on the Eurostar train from Paris to London seemed to last for centuries. I could not be sure of what might happen, nor could I imagine what it would be like to meet this monstrous enemy of mine. Thirty years of mutual hatred! Would we fall into insulting each other or even come to blows?

A taxi dropped me off at a centrally located hotel. Jordi came down to the lobby to meet me. He was a robust, calm gentleman with intelligence in his eyes. In silence, he led me to his father's suite. When Allen Klein opened the door, I saw a man of my age, not at all fat, with a sensitive face and a noble forehead crowned with white hair. He could have been my brother. He looked at me for a few seconds, then exclaimed in great surprise:

"Incredible. I never imagined you as handsome!"

"And I would never have imagined you as looking like a spiritual sage," I answered.

We embraced. The hatred fell away from my body like a tattered old overcoat.

Then we sat down, had tea, and looked at each other. Jordi had vanished discreetly. With great enthusiasm, Klein showed me photos of his two beautiful grandchildren, a boy and a girl. I described my family. After chatting for an hour as if we were old friends, we approached the subject of the lawsuit. In five minutes, we came to an agreement.

As we hugged again, saying good-bye, I told him: "If you and I can make peace, then I feel that even the Israelis and Palestinians can do it."

The next day, in Paris, going against their grain, the lawyers drew up an agreement with two winners, instead of a winner and a loser.

I realized that one of the great joys that life offers is the experience of the transformation of enmity into friendship. I also understood the extent to which I had unconsciously obeyed a neurotic need of my own in my construction of a despicable enemy. No doubt Klein—like me, the offspring of persecuted Jewish emigrants—had also transformed me into odious scum. Each of us had projected upon the other a monster that had been implanted in our souls over centuries of persecution and pogroms. Our reconciliation was a blessing to our families, to our audiences, and to the world.

The Works of
Alejandro Jodorowsky

Films

La Cravate (1957) also known as *The Severed Heads*
Fando y Lis (1968) also known as *Fando and Lis*
El Topo (1970)
The Holy Mountain (1973)
Tusk (1980)
Santa sangre (1989)
The Rainbow Thief (1990)

Books

Cuentos Pánicos (1963)
Teatro Pánico (1965)
Juegos Pánicos (1965)
El Topo, fábula pánica con imágines (1970) screenplay from the film
  El Topo
Fábulas Pánicas (1977)
Las ansias carnívores de la nada (1991)
Donde mejor canta un pájaro (1994)
Psychomagie/Approches d'une thérapie panique (1995)

Griffes D'Ange (1996)

Antología Pánica (1996)

Los Evangelios para sanar (1997)

La Sagesse des blagues; Le doigt et la lune; Les histoires de Mulla Nasrudin (1997)

El nino del jueves negro (1999)

Albina y los hombres-perro (2000)

La Trampa Sagrada (2000)

No basta decir (2000)

La danza de la realidad (2001) Jodorowsky's autobiography

El loro de las siete lenguas (2001)

El Paso del ganso (2001)

Ópera Panique, ou l'éloge de la quotidenneté (2001)

El tesoro de la sombra (2003)

Fábulas Pánicas (2003)

El dedo y la luna (2004)

Piedras del camino (2004)

La voie du Tarot (2004)

Yo, el tarot (2004)

Index

suffering, 45, 46, 208–9
Suzuki, D.T., 132

Taicher, Robert, 222–23
Tantra, 129n
Tarahumaras, 158, 206, 216, 217
tarot, 235–36
Teo, son of AJ, 216, 224–25
the Tigress, 56–78
  business proposition with AJ, 68–69
  creating her body, 60
  described, 55, 58–59
  devil-possessed mannequin and, 65–66
  erotico-musical (AJ's) and, 71–72
  first meeting with AJ, 58–64
  gold ring given to AJ, 78, 79–80, 81, 83, 93
  imitation castle of, 61–62
  as legend, 64
  lesson AJ learn through, 81
  in *Lucretia Borgia* (play), 77–78
  in *Nana* (play), 57–58
  ocelot pet of, 62–63
  scandals and lies of, 68–71, 74–77
  as witch, 64–65, 72–73

Tokusan Senkan, 84–86
Tomiko, adopted daughter of Michiko, 125, 217

Ummon Bunen, 101
unity, 172, 209
University of Mexico, 194–97

Valerie, wife of AJ, 69–71
victim, living like, 117
Vigneau, Jean-Pierre, 229–30
viscera/organs, 115
Viskin, Roberto, 222, 227

Welles, Orson, 228–29
Wumen Huikai, 130n

Yosai, 2, 157

Zarathustra (play), 14–15
Zen Buddhism
  Ejo Takata on, 205, 216
  founder of, 18
  as heroic undertaking, 4
  need to adapt, 216
Zhi Ming, 86

BOOKS OF RELATED INTEREST

Psychomagic
The Transformative Power of Shamanic Psychotherapy
by Alejandro Jodorowsky

Metagenealogy
Self-Discovery through Psychomagic and the Family Tree
by Alejandro Jodorowsky and Marianne Costa

The Way of Tarot
The Spiritual Teacher in the Cards
by Alejandro Jodorowsky and Marianne Costa

The Shamanic Path to Quantum Consciousness
The Eight Circuits of Creative Power
by Laurent Huguelit

Black Smoke
Healing and Ayahuasca Shamanism in the Amazon
by Margaret De Wys

Peyote Dreams
Journeys in the Land of Illumination
by Charles Duits

DMT: The Spirit Molecule
A Doctor's Revolutionary Research into the
Biology of Near-Death and Mystical Experiences
by Rick Strassman, M.D.

Inner Paths to Outer Space
Journeys to Alien Worlds through
Psychedelics and Other Spiritual Technologies
*by Rick Strassman, M.D., Slawek Wojtowicz, M.D.,
Luis Eduardo Luna, Ph.D., and Ede Frecska, M.D.*

Inner Traditions • Bear & Company
P.O. Box 388
Rochester, VT 05767
1-800-246-8648
www.InnerTraditions.com

Or contact your local bookseller

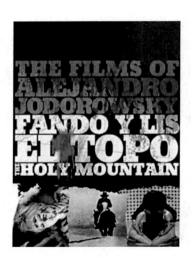

Films of Alejandro Jodorowsky
now available on DVD

Alejandro Jodorowsky's films have been restored and remastered for widescreen video. Released by Anchor Bay Entertainment in 2007, the 6-disc DVD box set includes *El Topo, The Holy Mountain,* and *Fando y Lis.* Also included are Jodorowsky's previously unreleased first film, *La Cravate,* and two music soundtrack CDs from *El Topo* and *The Holy Mountain.* In addition to the audio commentary by Jodorowsky, the DVD set also includes original theatrical trailers, a 2006 on-camera interview with Jodorowsky, original script excerpts, deleted scenes, *The Tarot* short with commentary, a restoration process short, and a photo gallery. Subtitles are available in English, French, Spanish, and Brazilian Portuguese. *El Topo* and *The Holy Mountain* DVDs are also available separately.

Available at major retail outlets and online:
www.anchorbayentertainment.com